DISTRESSED INVESTMENT BANKING

DISTRESSED INVESTMENT BANKING:

TO THE ABYSS AND BACK

Second Edition

HENRY F. OWSLEY AND
PETER S. KAUFMAN

Beard Books
Washington, D.C.

Printed in the United States of America
ISBN 1-58798-304-4

CONTENTS

PREFACE

When asked what we do for a living, we answer that we address complex financial challenges, usually for companies in distress. At Gordian Group, our practice in distressed investment banking consistently presents issues that are at the cutting edge of finance, at once the most difficult and the most interesting. Ours is a world where investment bankers perform a high-wire act without benefit of a net. Further missteps can bring ruination to these companies' constituencies.

Seldom is a silver bullet solution found that makes everyone wealthy and happy and whole. Instead, ours is a world where the relative merits of potential solutions must be evaluated, considered and selected, knowing that there are likely going to be unattractive qualities about all such solutions. In distressed investment banking, creativity, ingenuity and cleverness rule the day. It is not the venue for on-the-job training – the tasks are too difficult, and the stakes are too high. The challenges require investment bankers. We are not accountants. We are not consultants.

Within the larger universe of investment banking, working with distressed companies is a remote corner where a blend of art, science and black magic reign. No cookie-cutter could turn out the types of problems our clients face. Nothing is standard about the design and implementation of the potential solutions we explore. Not for us the far easier world of plain vanilla investment banking. In our business there is no such thing as "let's mark up the last deal."

How did we wind up on the dark side? Lucky accidents of fate. Henry Owsley was a member of Goldman Sachs' technology group early in his career. As he fixed the broken companies that ensued in the 1980s, he morphed into a restructuring expert. Peter Kaufman began with a legal career that encompassed restructurings and bankruptcies and segued into the world of distressed investments at First Boston in the mid-1980s.

Gordian Group was founded in 1988, our name derived from mythology. We seek not merely to unravel thorny financial "knots," but, like Alexander the Great, we seek to slice through them. Our firm began with a premise still true today: that conflicts of interest are intolerable, and that large investment banks cannot help but have conflicts of interest when working in the distressed patch. In a mid-course strategic correction in the early 1990s, we ceased representation on the bondholder side, a decision we'll discuss more fully in subsequent chapters. We also believe the work is too complicated and the judgments too difficult in this sector to be delegated to junior professionals, and that was another reason for founding Gordian Group. We take our clients' challenges personally, and we pursue success for them with enthusiasm and zeal.

To be sure, fraudulent behavior and scoundrels abound in our world. We regularly meet characters such as the executive about whom it was said, "He long ago mastered the art of selling horses with bowed legs in tall grass." We are never bored.

It is impossible to convey adequately the adrenaline rush we feel when we sit in a boardroom with a group of directors who are beginning to realize that their enterprise is at risk of failure and that their own liability may hang in the balance.

One Christmas Day, we were in the Pacific Northwest, having called an emergency meeting of a client's board of directors to advise them that we had uncovered that their CEO and Controller had been falsifying representations to their bank in order to keep loans flowing. We told them they needed to advise the bank immediately.

The tension in the room was palpable, and one director looked at us and said, "But if we do that before arranging for other financing, the company will be out of money and will hit the wall." We looked at each other, took a deep breath and said, "Then we're out of money – and all of us in this room will have to figure how to deal with it."

The board took our advice, and we were able to convince the bank (through overnight analyses and persuasive arguments that it was in the bank's economic best interest to play ball with us) to keep lending – in return for which our client fired the CEO and Controller, installed a crisis manager and agreed to commence an immediate sale process. That night, we switched to another hotel – just in case the CEO was desperate enough to try to eliminate the spokesmen for truth, justice and disclosure.

The situation ended with a sale of the company, with tremendously positive results for all of the company's constituencies, given the circumstances we inherited and the likely prospect of a liquidation that Christmas Day.

Among the many companies and agencies with which we have worked are Alamo/National Car Rental; Alert Centre; Allied Digital Technologies; Ambac; AmeriServe; AMR; Anker Coal; Bayou Steel; Ben & Jerry's;

Chiquita Brands; CJC Holdings; Colfor/Colmach; Enron; Farmland Industries; the Federal Communications Commission; Hooked on Phonics; Hostess; Intelogic Trace; Interfaith Medical Center; Liberty House; London Fog; LTV Steel; Martin Color Fi; MBIA; Merisel; MiniScribe; Mississippi Chemical; Montreal, Maine and Atlantic Railway; Morrison-Knudsen; Nationwise Automotive; the Office of Thrift Supervision; Ogden; Olympia & York; Pentacon; Petsec Energy; Phar-Mor; Pinnacle Towers; RailWorks; Refco; Riedel Environmental; Safeguard; Safety-Kleen; Silicon Gaming; Spansion; Spiegel; the State of Vermont's involvement with electric utilities issues; Stereotaxis; Sudbury; Thortec; Tracor; Tri-Union; Vlasic; the Walter Karl Companies; Waste Systems; and Zale.

Because we face a broad array of issues within our narrow field of distressed investment banking, the tools of our trade comprise a working expertise and conversance with finance, valuation, law, taxes, capital markets and the trading of securities, as well as old-fashioned horse-trading sense. Precisely because all of these skills are needed, there is no substitute for experience and seasoned judgment in our field.

To be effective, we must be able to:

- impose order onto chaos;
- gain the confidence of boards of directors;
- advise on courses of action, in the midst of great uncertainty;
- understand valuation as precisely as possible;
- design and implement effective financial strategies, with the legal and tax implications of each in mind;
- negotiate effectively with creditors and financing sources;
- run competitive merger processes in the face of incredible adversity; and
- convince a trier of fact and law of the rightness of our views when clarity is at a premium

We must be able to assist our clients in recognizing and articulating their goals, and we must figure out how to reach those goals. Lewis Carroll laid out the relationship between goals and strategy neatly, in Alice's encounter with the Cheshire Cat:

"Would you tell me, please, which way I ought to go from here?"
"That depends a good deal on where you want to get to," said the Cat.

"I don't much care where –" said Alice.
"Then it doesn't matter which way you go," said the Cat.
"– so long as I get somewhere," Alice added as an explanation.
"Oh, you're sure to do that," said the Cat, "if you only walk long enough."

In some cases, a board knows precisely where it wants to go, and even if the destination is unusual, we can be there to help.

Consider Ben & Jerry's, for example. Its ice cream is one of the best-known consumer brands in the U.S., but despite the brand-name cachet, the Company faced significant strategic issues – particularly with respect to distribution. Consolidation within the food industry also made competition increasingly difficult for such middle-market companies as Ben & Jerry's.

New management was brought in to improve profitability and refocus its strategy, and Gordian Group was retained to assist in evaluating the company's strategic and financial options in order to enhance shareholder value. At the time, the stock traded in the mid-teens.

The prism through which Ben & Jerry's evaluated its options was most unusual in American corporate governance – an eclectic weighing of value, a desire for independence and a strong sense of social mission. Without satisfying each of these often-conflicting criteria, it was unlikely that any solution would meet the board's approval. Yet, given the competitive and distribution dynamics the company faced, it needed to find a solution.

Over several years, Gordian analyzed and pursued a variety of transactions, including sale of the company, investments in the company, distribution joint ventures and additions to the company's product lines.

Initial indications of interest from would-be acquirers valued Ben & Jerry's shares in the $20s. But these proposals failed to address the board's goals of independence and social mission. Through a negotiating process stretching over months, Gordian was eventually able to craft a viable solution that:

- resulted in Unilever buying the company in a deal that valued the shares at $43.60 each (almost double the original indications), or about $360 million;
- kept the existing board in place to monitor the social mission and product quality; and
- provided significant additional sums to the Ben & Jerry's trust.

Gordian was honored for its work on this transaction by *Mergers & Acquisitions* magazine with an award for the Middle-Market Deal of the Year.

Almost no one is ever glad to have to interview us for a potential engagement, or to have to hire us. The legendary football coach Bear Bryant was once asked if there were any common characteristics among his six head coaching jobs. He responded, "If they are hiring me, at my price, they ain't been having much success." Similarly, we inherit difficult situations where parties usually have already been deeply disappointed – and they look to us to help them make the best of a bad set of circumstances. We believe in having a client prepare for war, in order to "encourage" an acceptable peace to break out.

Like Bear Bryant's clients, those who engage us "ain't been having much success," and accept that they will have to pay reasonable fees for our services. Such fees are usually a combination of a periodic (*e.g.*, monthly) fee and a "success fee" (*i.e.*, a percentage of monies raised or value achieved) basis. Investment bankers also receive expense reimbursement and wide-ranging indemnification.

If our work were not challenging enough, in bankruptcy court havoc often erupts over fees. Judges and U.S. Trustees often express outrage at the magnitude of the fees and try to convert the periodic and success fees into a per-hour basis, in order to evaluate the fees for "reasonableness." They also express outrage when investment bankers seek indemnification for their services. "Lawyers do not get indemnification," these parties say. "Why should you?"

These attitudes, while understandable on their face, are at odds with an essential tenet of the bankruptcy code: The system was intended to ensure that bankruptcy cases attract top professionals, and to do so the compensation for any given type of professional advice is supposed to be on a par with what is paid outside of Chapter 11 to any given genre of professional. If the bankruptcy courts seek to impose on investment bankers different, and less financially attractive, fees and protection arrangements than what is customary outside Chapter 11, the skilled investment bankers will gravitate away from restructurings and toward the more financially remunerative areas of investment banking. The public interest requires that the best financial advisors be available for bankruptcy matters.

When we were asked to write this book, we paused to contemplate how we could find time in our practice to get it done. But we have long been aware that the financial literature is bereft of thoughtful reflection and insights on distressed investment banking. And because we love what we do for a living, we determined that we would try to fill that void. We hope the lessons we have drawn from our years of practice shine some light on the dark world of distressed companies and provide illumination for those who, by choice or of necessity, journey into these parts.

We are very grateful to Beard Publications for the opportunity to share most (but not all) of what we have learned. We would like to thank Josh Mills for his deft touch and insight in editing our work. We are also deeply appreciative of our colleagues for their assistance in commenting on certain parts of the book, particularly David Herman, Dennis McGilligan and Leslie Glassman.

We dedicate this book to our families – Lexi and Theresa, and Camille, Cory, Maddie Kate and Rubie Lee – without whom none of this would be possible, or meaningful.

Henry F. Owsley and Peter S. Kaufman
New York, New York
Fall 2014

Henry F. Owsley is a founding partner and Chief Executive Officer of the New York-based investment bank Gordian Group, LLC. He has over 35 years' experience in the business of solving complex financial challenges as an investment banker. He is the co-author, with Peter Kaufman,of "The Role of the Investment Banker in Distressed M&A," *Bankruptcy Business Acquisitions*, LexMed Publishing, 1998.Hehas consistently beennamed one of the ten leading investment bankers involved in bankruptcies and financial restructurings by *The Deal.* Mr. Owsley graduated summa cum laude from Princeton University and has a Master of Science degree from Massachusetts Institute of Technology, Sloan School of Management. He may be reached at hfo@gordiangroup.com.

Peter S. Kaufman is President and Head of Restructuring and Distressed M&A practice at the New York-based investment bank of Gordian Group, LLC. He has over 35 years' experience in the business of solving complex financial challenges as an investment banker and, formerly, as an attorney. Mr. Kaufman is the founding Co-Chairman of the Committee on Investment Banking of the American Bankruptcy Institute (ABI). He istheco-author, with Henry Owsley, of "The Role of the Investment Banker in Distressed M&A," *Bankruptcy Business Acquisitions*, LexMed Publishing, 1998,and "Trading in the Distressed Market," *Investing in Bankruptcies and Turnarounds*, Harper Collins Publishers, 1991. He has consistently been named one of the ten leadingnational investment bankers in financial restructurings by *The Deal.* Mr. Kaufman graduated with honors from Yale College and received a J.D. degree from the University of Virginia School of Law. He may be reached at psk@gordiangroup.com.

CHAPTER 1—CROSSING THE STYX: THE LAND OF THE DISTRESSED

Companies do not set out to become financially distressed. Yet, every year, many significant public and private companies default on their indebtedness. Almost invariably, the company loses value as a result of the ensuing damage: shareholder value erodes, competitors encroach as they perceive financial weakness, key employees leave, management is distracted by financial crises, and boards of directors are faced with new challenges, duties and potential liabilities.

Once this vicious cycle starts, it is critical to stop the erosion of value. In well-managed restructurings, the company may be able to restore positive cash flow to the point where an internal restructuring is possible. In other cases, distressed companies ultimately resort to a sale of all or substantially all of their operations (*i.e.*, an external restructuring transaction). In new and more stable hands – those of either a strategic buyer or a well heeled financial buyer – the company may be able to restore confidence and arrest the fall.

But regardless of how it ends, many of the company's constituencies will be sorely disappointed. Trade and financial creditors may experience losses, which could be of significant magnitude. Shareholders may be wiped out. Many employees may lose their jobs. Current and former employees may lose their pensions or life savings. Directors will wish they had never taken a board seat.

On the other hand, various parties see opportunities in such a distressed situation. "Vulture capitalists" and others may seek to buy debt securities at advantageous prices. Competitors and other potential buyers may try to buy assets at "fire sale" prices. Lawyers, turnaround managers and investment bankers will see opportunities to offer their services, both to the company and to its creditors.

For all these "victims" and "opportunists," early problem recognition can provide a significant advantage. The warning signs are there for those who know where to look as the company moves toward the "Zone of Insolvency," whether in a slow drift or on a rush tide.

Solvency and Liquidity

Just as an army travels on its stomach, a company travels on its cash. A serious disruption in cash adequacy may easily lead to the vicious cycle of distress. So a conservative board may choose to husband its cash. But failing to spend money is also a potential path to business failure. Competitors will spend to become larger and more efficient, thereby marginalizing their "too conservative" rivals over the long term.

Moreover, business conditions are never static. Industry-specific fortunes rise, fall, and rise again. Credit conditions change, and banks' willingness to lend waxes and wanes. Conditions in the capital markets change as well, with investors' appetite to finance companies through debt and equity offerings ebbing and flowing.

If only one of these underpinnings is removed, the company may remain stable. If the company experienced operating losses, for example, but the equity markets were strong and willing to believe that the company's problems were temporary, the company might be able to obtain external funding to keep it afloat. Cash losses could be financed by repeated trips to the capital markets, at least for a while. Many technology and biotechnology firms have had this experience.

Conversely, many companies have sufficient cash reserves or profitability to last many years. Yet junk bond conditions may be such that the company's unsecured debt trades at "distressed" prices. Assuming the company can maintain stable operations, then these junk bonds may be real bargains for the opportunistic vulture or even the company itself, if it elects to repurchase the bonds.

The "perfect storm" that overwhelms a company comes when it both bleeds cash operationally and experiences a loss in investor confidence, in the form of mandatory debt repayments and a curtailment of financing availability. Companies in this position are most likely to become severely financially distressed – and to lose enterprise value. Advance knowledge of these companies' situations may be of enormous importance to employees, unions, existing creditors and bankruptcy professionals.

The key to understanding the difference between the merely bruised and the severely ill is through a concept called "solvency." In lay terms, a company becomes insolvent when it runs out, or is about to run out, of cash or the financial wherewithal to support its debt burden.

From one perspective, a company is solvent if the market value of its assets exceeds its liabilities. Given enough time, such a company should be able to monetize its businesses in order to repay its debts in full. This ability to sell or finance businesses in an orderly fashion is critical to obtaining full value. But distressed sellers, forced to dispose of assets quickly, may be unable to obtain full value from the sale. By the same token, a company with positive net asset value – and sufficient time – should be able to raise equity or long-term debt from the capital markets in order to meet near-term debt service obligations.

Yet even if such a positive value relationship currently exists, there is no guarantee that it will last indefinitely. Companies can incur huge cash losses. They can make large capital expenditure commitments on assets, and then see those assets lose value. In the late 1990s, for example, telecommunications companies poured billions of dollars into infrastructure investments, including fiber-optic cable and switch-gear. The industry's need for such capacity never materialized, and the capital investments swiftly became saleable only at pennies on the dollar. In other cases, value can be derived from passing investor enthusiasm, only to decline dramatically later (*e.g.*, Internet startups).

A similar thing happened during the financial meltdown in 2007 and 2008. Real estate prices, together with a panoply of financial assets built upon real estate (Mortgage Backed Securities; Collateralized Debt Obligations; CDOs of CDOs, known as CDO^2) had been "pumped up" through low interest rates and easy credit. When the residential real estate bubble burst, the whole house of cards came down. Many financial institutions did not have adequate capital to weather the storm and faced insolvency or government-led bailouts. Part of our role was to straighten out the mess through restructurings, as well as providing expert witness services in connection with litigation against those that pushed the envelope way too far. Had these institutions been more diversified or had greater liquidity, they could have withstood the crisis – and even perhaps taken advantage of it by acquiring assets on the cheap.

A company that loses sight of its short-term liquidity needs can trigger its own valuation demise. Decreasing liquidity can create problems with suppliers and with customers. It can cause precipitous declines in prices of public securities and, in turn, in a company's ability to finance. Then the timing pressures of an emergency debt paydown may preclude a company from getting full value for an asset it must sell.

The relationship between such business values and a company's debt or classes of debt must be studied. If a company's business values significantly exceed its liabilities and it is presumably solvent, its creditors and other constituencies will tend to treat the company accordingly. As the gap between values and liabilities shrinks, or liquidity becomes a crisis, attitudes and actions begin to change. Under these circumstances, a company with excessive liabilities enters the Zone of Insolvency. Once the insolvency is generally recognized, the vicious cycle becomes even more severe, as the liquidity situation worsens. For example, trade vendors can cease providing trade credit to the company. The stock price frequently declines toward relatively low, speculative values. Unsecured claims, including public bonds, tend to decrease in price to levels that reflect the increased risk associated with such claims. Depending upon the severity of the value erosion, even secured claims can experience downward price movement. These factors inhibit a company's access to capital.

Quite often, the liquidity crisis leads to the need for a financial transaction to address the problems – either in or out of bankruptcy. Once in the Zone of Insolvency, corporate governance issues and board and management responsibilities may shift from a shareholder-oriented focus to one that incorporates creditors as well.

Almost invariably, companies do not leap abruptly from solvency into insolvency. As they begin their slide, warning lights begin to flash. While there is no standard cookie-cutter set of causes (or solutions), certain early-warning indicators are available to experienced eyes.

Operational Issues

Downturns in operational performance frequently presage a company's insolvency. These operational issues vary widely, and they can be manifested in downturns in sales or in operating margins. Such declines may significantly reduce operating cash flow. Depending upon the size of the company and its capitalization, the time between the onset of such problems and an ultimate insolvency can be years. Larger companies may have more flexibility to weather a storm for longer periods of time, because they tend to have multiple sources of capital, as well as non-core businesses that can be divested relatively quickly. Better-capitalized, less-leveraged companies can also ride out a downturn for a longer period.

Companies often get into difficulty by aggressively expanding their balance sheets. Even a company showing positive income-statement trends can experience severe cash problems through rapid growth in working-capital items. Beware rapid growth in such financial ratios as days receivable or a severe decline in inventory turns. If such asset growth later results in "bad" receivables or inventories the company must write down, the working capital investments may never be recouped. Nevertheless, any debt incurred in connection with the working capital buildup must still be repaid.

Similarly, a company that embarks on an aggressive capital expenditure program will spend significant sums of cash. The outlays may be predictable, and the returns anything but. This type of asset growth, if unsuccessful, can be measured by dramatic declines in such ratios as asset turnover or return on assets.

Another large potential use of capital is acquisitions. Many acquisitions do not work out as planned. To the extent that problems arise, they may show up in one or more of the financial ratios mentioned above. Even if difficulties do not immediately arise, experience suggests the financial analyst should be skeptical for several quarters after a deal's consummation.

In most situations, then, insolvencies are rarely a total surprise. They are preceded by measurable deterioration on the income statement, the balance sheet, or both. And they are associated with periods of significant cash usage – financed with external debt or equity capital, or with internal cash. Whether such problems grow into insolvencies depends upon the duration of the difficulty and several other factors.

Of course, some insolvencies occur because of a single lawsuit that results unexpectedly in a massive liability (*e.g.*, Pennzoil v. Texaco). Other litigation-related insolvencies occur from more anticipated causes, such as asbestos and other tort claims.

Stock Prices

A public company's stock price is both one of the most important indicators of its solvency and one of the most unreliable. In addition to its role as a signal containing information about a company's health, the stock price can be seen as a measure of a company's ability to repay its debt.

A company with a stock price of $20 and 50 million shares outstanding, for example, has an equity market capitalization of $1 billion. Even if the company had debt of $250 million and its operations were losing money, the CFO could argue that insolvency was no danger, because she could tap the equity markets to repay the debt. In other words, a large equity market capitalization in relation to debt is a strong indicator of solvency, at least in the near term.

A high stock price generally signals Wall Street's approval of the company and the execution of its business plan. To the extent that this view is based on strong financial performance, a high stock price can be a strong indicator of the company's solvency. Conversely, a low stock price can signal investor disappointment or fears that the operating performance or financial position is precarious.

Yet we all know that a great many factors are incorporated into a stock price. It reflects the company's historical performance (the past) and anticipated prospects (the future). It reflects overall market conditions (*i.e.*, "where is the Dow?"), investor sentiment regarding particular industry sectors (some being in favor and others out of favor), company size (are "mid-caps" in vogue or not?), the extent of research analyst coverage, and the degree of financial leverage in light of current market realities (debt incurred in years past may not be refinanceable today). Prices also reflect expectations about interest rates and credit spreads over the risk-free note (see below).

And this seemingly rational analysis begs the question of whether a company's financial statements are "correct." We have witnessed numerous examples in recent years of companies that have reported misleading, misstated, or outright fraudulent financial statements. Any stock price predicated upon such erroneous financial information is obviously suspect. Stir it all together, and share prices can be extremely volatile.

Even if a company appears to be solvent based on the ratio of its equity value to debt outstanding, that strength can vanish virtually overnight. Consider the decreases of more than 90% in the value of many internet and real estate stocks in the periods after their respective market peaks. Refer back to that money-losing company with the $1 billion market capitalization. If its stock price declined by 95%, its market capitalization would shrink to $50 million. Equity offerings from such an aggregate equity value would not make much of a dent in $250 million in debt.

But stock prices do not tell the whole story. Not only can they be very wrong, especially in the short term, but they reflect fickle investor sentiment. And, of course, many significant, leveraged companies have no publicly traded stock.

Bond Prices

In our experience, bond prices tend to be a more reliable indicator of a company's financial health than the stock price, because they are less susceptible to the euphoria that sometimes engulfs stock prices and because they are so sensitive to concerns about credit quality and solvency. Yet these useful warning signals are available only if companies have publicly traded bonds, and many do not.

Most bonds trade at "yields to maturity" based on their relative credit quality. Frequently, these yields are compared with yields on comparable maturities of United States Treasuries. This "spread over Treasuries" is measured in basis points (hundredths of a percentage point). If the Treasury of comparable maturity yields 3%, and the bond trades at an 8% yield, the spread over Treasuries is 500 basis points.

In general, the riskier the bond, the greater the spread over Treasuries. All investment grade bonds should trade at smaller (often referred to as "narrower") spreads than junk bonds, and the higher-rated "Single A" bonds should trade at narrower spreads than "BBB" bonds. Within junk bonds, "BB" spreads tend to be narrower than "B" spreads. (Most investors refer to ratings classifications published by the Standard & Poor's and Moody's rating agencies, although other such agencies also publish ratings.) The best credit instruments receive "investment grade" ratings, which range from AAA (S&P's highest rating) to BBB-. The lower-rated instruments are considered "below investment grade" – also called high-yield or "junk" bonds. These range from BB+ down through the CCC's, CC's, C's and defaulted bonds.

Within any given ratings category, individual bonds will frequently trade at spreads significantly different from the average, because investors find distinctions among industry segments or bond-specific quirks, or they hold expectations regarding credit changes not yet addressed by the rating agencies. Overall, though, we believe the average BB and B yields (published regularly by brokerage houses) provide a good indication of where the market is for junk credits.

When a bond trades at a yield level materially greater than the average "B" yield, that can be an important signal of impending financial distress. The trading level indicates that some investors are demanding a significantly higher expected return in order to compensate them for the risk that they perceive to be in the credit. These investors might expect the bond to continue interest and principal payments (although with some uncertainty of payment), or they might expect the issuer to halt payments, in which case the bond price represents the present value of the future "restructured" value of the bond.

For example, a 10% bond due in three years might be trading at 50 cents on the dollar. The yield to maturity would be 40%, a very high (*e.g.*, distressed) yield and a very high spread over Treasuries. In such case, traders could be pricing the bond based upon an imminent default and an ultimate recovery in, say, two years. (The assumptions of a two-year horizon, a 25% required return and a future 78-cent recovery on the bond would produce the 50-cent price.)

In this case, the junk-bond market would clearly have a pessimistic view of the solvency of the company. Although such an indicator is not definitive, we believe that junk yields are an important measure of financial health.

Credit Availability

A company's relationship with its ongoing senior lenders is highly important. Typically banks, these lenders are supposed to be knowledgeable about all aspects of a company's business and its prospects. If the banks are supportive of a company and willing to provide additional liquidity, that is a strong signal to others that the company remains in reasonable financial condition – even if it is experiencing losses.

Companies that make regular filings with the Securities and Exchange Commission must disclose key factors regarding their relationships with their lenders. Such disclosures can provide significant insight into the implications for future availability of liquidity.

In filing the annual 10-K and the quarterly 10-Q statements, companies complete a Liquidity section within Management's Discussion and Analysis of Results. At a bare minimum, this section should indicate whether the company has additional liquidity available from banks or other sources, whether it is in default on any agreements and whether it has recently amended its loan agreements. The filing should also provide intelligible commentary on the company's ability to manage its liquidity needs for the balance of the fiscal year or longer.

In theory, this section (and a detailed study of the related financial statements) should give a careful reader a good sense of the company's solvency. Unfortunately, companies often paint too rosy a picture. In some cases, management may be in denial, or even ignorant of the financial warning signs at its company. Or it may be trying to paint a "balanced" picture to avoid frightening key constituencies (*e.g.*, the trade and its shareholders). In other cases, of course, management may be willfully misleading investors. In all these instances, the disclosure provided may not allow a reader to appreciate fully the gravity of underlying financial problems.

For analysts willing to dig deeper, additional documents are available. In most cases, companies need to file their main credit agreements with the SEC, and these contain key terms – particularly the financial covenants. If a company is frequently amending its credit agreement to restate the financial covenants because of weak performance, that company may have material financial problems. A review of the covenants in all such agreements and amendments, compared with the actual financial performance, can be highly informative.

If the lenders have simultaneously curtailed credit availability in the face of covenant amendments, that is a worrisome sign. If the curtailment is coupled with the granting of additional collateral by the company to the bank group, that is downright alarming, because the company may be putting itself completely at the mercy of its banks with such a grant. And of course, knowing whether the company is going to be operating on a cash positive or negative basis is key.

This type of analysis is likely to be more meaningful when the analyst has a sense of the behavior of the particular financial institutions involved (based on experience with such institutions in other credits) and understands the underlying values of the company in relation to the bank debt. For asset-based credit facilities, the most important relationship is usually between the outstanding loans and the collateral formula (*i.e.*, percentages of receivables and inventories). For other loans, it may be critical to understand whether specific businesses have sufficient value, if sold, to repay all or a portion of the bank debt. Even if such a step is ultimately unnecessary, the banks are certain to be taking such factors into consideration in their continuing evaluation of the credit.

Depending upon how all these dynamics work in relation to one another, a particular company might expect to enjoy a bit more time with one group of lenders – or to face a hard line from another such group.

Security Buybacks

Management's inside view of a company does not necessarily mean that it has a clear picture of a company's future. For example, companies have undertaken large share-repurchase programs in the quarters immediately preceding a bankruptcy filing – buying back common shares (subsequently deemed to be valueless) and using tens of millions of dollars of much-needed cash. In general, boards approve such repurchases because of their perception that such buyback prices represent a "bargain" compared with the company's historical performance. If the company were subsequently to rebound, they would look like geniuses.

In many such cases, however, management and the board are blinded by "all trees must grow to the sky" forecasts and by misguided optimism. Often, the buyback exacerbates the problems.

Indeed, we regard major stock buyback programs at distressed prices as a potential red flag of pending insolvency.

Lawsuits

Companies experiencing financial distress are frequently encumbered with a variety of litigation claims, including shareholder suits alleging inadequate disclosure. Other companies are in financial distress precisely because of significant litigation claims (*i.e.*, asbestos and other tort liabilities). To the extent that such litigation claims have merit, they can materially and adversely affect a company's ability to finance at the equity and unsecured debt levels. Investors coming in at such levels in the capital structures would be severely harmed if these contingent claims were to come home to roost. Accordingly, these lawsuits have a chilling effect on investor appetite and upon the company's ability to access additional liquidity.

Fraud and Accounting Irregularities

Companies that announce the need to correct materially misleading historical financial statements frequently experience distress. Lenders and investors may avoid advancing new capital until they have a clearer picture of actual operations. Mistrust of management may be such that nothing short of a complete "regime change" will do – and even that sometimes will not suffice.

Such financial statement problems are almost invariably accompanied by further investor lawsuits (curtailing additional liquidity). Add in customer and vendor disaffection, and there is a recipe for disaster. Unsurprisingly, many companies that experience these financial statement problems end up in bankruptcy.

A Company's Self-Awareness

Just as a person with a serious medical problem will go through various emotional phases, so will a company with a serious financial health problem. In both cases, the first phase is often denial.

During denial, the company is unlikely to seek the specialized help it needs. At best, it might consult its existing legal and financial advisors, who might offer some useful insights but who are probably without insolvency expertise. Often, these advisors are unlikely to be able to recognize the gravity of the situation – and thereby feed into management's denial. Moreover, such advisors, if inexperienced in insolvency issues, will be unprepared to deal with the onset of insolvency and its attendant issues and demands.

Compounding the difficulty of relying on existing advisors are the potential conflicts of interest, particularly among investment bankers. In many cases, the existing investment banker will have placed, as agent or underwriter, the company's debt and equity securities with many of its investor clients. In such cases, the banker may have incentives to protect itself and the interests of its continuing brokerage clients rather than those of the distressed company – a client that has a potentially dim future.

In fact, the existing investment banker can be placed in a situation where the conflict can actually harm junior constituencies, such as equity. Assume that a company has $90 million of asset value and $100 million of liabilities. Viewed from one perspective, the equity is 10% "under water."

Now assume that the existing investment banker advises the company to sell assets. This has the superficial appeal of raising money to appease a pack of hounding creditors. If the company sells assets (even at full value) for $50 million and uses the funds to pay off debt at par, it will have $40 million of asset value and $50 million of liabilities.

When the dust settles, what has happened? The investment banker has received significant M&A fees. Certain creditors (many of which may have relationships with the investment banker) have been repaid at par. But the equity holders will now be deeper in the hole – 20% "under water," rather than 10%.

Hence, one of our key tenets is: when enterprise value is less than the face amount of debt, selling assets to pay down debt at par is deleterious to equity value.

First Contact with the Company – the Professional's Perspective

While the company remains in denial, management is unlikely to reach out to professionals with the requisite specialized expertise. So the burden to initiate contact is often with any legal, operational or financial professionals wanting to assist the company.

After determining that the company has potential advisory needs – from public sources or word of mouth – professionals must determine the best way into the situation, keeping in mind that they may know only part of the story and might not understand the insiders' mindset. Not surprisingly, we have found that contact with management through a board member or existing professional advisor is far better than a "cold call."

As in so many things, timing is critical. If the professionals approach the company too early, they risk being thrown out of the boardroom for offering the heretical view that the Company has problems. If the professionals compound the sin of being premature with that of being overly aggressive in the pursuit of the business, they run the risk of alienating management and causing personal embarrassment to whoever facilitated the meeting.

The professional can be too late, as well. After a certain point, reality tends to catch up with financially distressed companies, and they will hire a team of outside advisors. Once that decision is made, it is extremely difficult to dislodge an incumbent restructuring professional.

So, much as in *Goldilocks*, the search is for the "just right." A fairly narrow window opens during which the company will recognize its problems and the need for professional help. The restructuring professional can be clued into the right timing by a good relationship with an incumbent officer, director or ordinary course professional (particularly if the incumbent professional knows his own firm is over its head). But just as often, great timing can be purely fortuitous.

The Hiring Process

Sometimes, a company will meet with a single legal, financial or operational advisor and hire that firm. That generally happens only when the company selects the restructuring group of its existing investment banking or law firm or when it has let the crisis become so acute that it must make a decision immediately, without "shopping around."

More often, if it has the luxury of time, the company will meet with a range of advisory firms and select the one with which it is most comfortable.

By shopping around, the company may feel it has the best chance of finding a good fit of talent, approach, personality and cost. At its most awkward, this process is a "beauty contest" in which company representatives meet sequentially with different would-be advisers in one location, with the professional competitors seeing each other come and go.

A client may perceive that there are advantages in using large firms. Or small firms. Or firms with industry-specific knowledge. Or those that specialize in "mega-cases." Or with middle-market companies. It depends on what the company's needs are, what the various firms have to offer and to a large extent how comfortable the individuals involved feel about working together.

However, several factors should be very important in every hiring situation. One is experience; another is creativity. The company requires advice from professionals who have "been there before" and have a track record of creatively solving financial problems. Accordingly, the mix of senior to junior personnel on the assignment is critical, as is the commitment that senior people will handle the key meetings and calls.

Another, and critical, factor in the selection of advisors should be lack of conflicts of interest. This is dealt with more comprehensively in Chapter 2, but bears summary mention here. The company's historical advisors may have obvious conflicts of interest from previously consummated deals. They may seek to cover their own rear ends or to protect the investors to whom they sold the company's bonds. In fact, the Bankruptcy Code expressly acknowledges this conflict, and many courts prohibit conflicted investment banks from being retained. This reality gives rise to still another conflict – the company's historical financial advisor has a blatant economic incentive in seeing its client avoid Chapter 11, even when it might be in the company's interest to seek bankruptcy protection.

Perhaps most significantly, financial advisory firms that regularly represent (or trade with) creditor groups may pose a threat, when hired by a company, to boards and management teams seeking to preserve value for management and old equity constituencies. Such firms that work "both sides of the street" may very well seek to advance the interests of their repeat-business bondholder clients at the expense of a company that is unlikely to survive independently. These firms epitomize the old saying about many investment bankers: "If there ain't no conflicts, we got no interest."

These entire beauty contest processes can be messy and, at times, raucous, so it seems fitting to end this chapter with some wisdom from the film *Animal House*. The motto of Faber College is "Knowledge Is Good" – something to remember when working with distressed companies. A company considering a hiring decision should know an advisory firm's strengths, experience, track record and conflicts of interest. Advisors seeking business should be as well prepared as possible. At the very least, the advisory firm should make every effort to analyze the company and its problems, and to suggest various approaches to solutions, as part of its pitch – rather than just showing up and saying, "We're great, hire us."

CHAPTER 2—DRAMATIS PERSONAE

A distressed company and its advisors must coordinate and lead a multi-ring circus, comprised of many constituencies with competing agendas and goals, all potentially advised by professionals highly experienced in the game, its tactics and its strategies. It is a daunting task. Instead of managing and overseeing for growth and profitability, management and the board of directors find themselves in a far different position than they had ever anticipated. Now, they are managing for cash and presiding over a financial crisis that threatens the viability of the franchise and the value of the company's equity.

Much to the frustration of boards and management, at a time when they most need to focus on operational issues, their attention is taken up with financial restructuring and communications issues with various constituencies. What is good for the bondholders may not be good for secured lenders, trade creditors or shareholders. The trade may wish to see a more deleveraged company than an aggressive bondholder group wants to own. Shareholders may have legitimate and significant option value that will be eviscerated inappropriately if management and boards simply do the bondholders' bidding. To protect themselves legally, management and boards must take into consideration the disparate agendas around the table, receive unconflicted advice and do what they think is right and appropriate under the circumstances.

As they go forward, boards and management will find that in an insolvency, the twin coins of the realm are liquidity and credibility with key constituencies. To keep their focus, boards and management need to differentiate quickly between the key financial restructuring issues and much less important issues. Failure to do so makes it likely that they will waste time and energy, and possibly drown, in irrelevant exercises.

The sooner the board and management face up to the fact that the company's capital structure may not be appropriate to the capabilities of its operations, the more options they will find and the more equity value that can be maintained. Conversely, the longer they delay in meeting their financial challenges, the fewer the options that will remain available.

Let us consider the perspectives of the various players in this complex circus:

The Board of Directors

While they are partners in distress, management and the board of directors have very different issues. The directors may still, rightly and understandably, want to maximize recoveries for shareholders. But once a company has reached the Zone of Insolvency, the board will find that its fiduciary obligations now may extend more broadly. Various laws enacted in recent years have increased the pressure on, and accountability of, boards. In turn, this pressure will create the need for boards of insolvent companies to receive unconflicted advice from their financial and legal advisors.

Of course, this means that boards are likely to need to spend even more time as stewards of the company. The tasks they must now oversee may not be appealing, but they may well be judged, in hindsight, on how they evaluate and decide on possible courses of action.

The directors will also be concerned about their individual liability to creditors and shareholders, particularly when they operate outside of Chapter 11. The directors' individual net worths may be at stake as the board makes such tough decisions as whether to restructure financially or sell the business, file for Chapter 11 or not and engage a crisis manager or not.

With all that in mind, we reiterate that one of the board's essential steps and best defenses is to engage credible legal and financial professionals, receive their advice, create a record and then make decisions based on that advice. The business judgment rule is a broad and effective shield against suits from disgruntled shareholders, bondholders, and the like. A board, if properly advised, may even embark on high-risk (to creditors) strategies designed to benefit old equity if it has a good-faith belief (again, based upon advice rendered by advisors and management) that those strategies will benefit the entire franchise and improve value for all constituencies.

Having said that, we note that as they shepherd a company through insolvency, the directors may be strongly focused on their own liability – as individuals. This very understandable concern can actually accelerate a company's move into Chapter 11, because any good-faith board decisions made after a Chapter 11 filing are largely immune from subsequent scrutiny. And it is possible to include provisions for director releases and indemnity for post-bankruptcy actions in connection with successful Chapter 11 reorganizations.

Management

Management has similar fiduciary duties to the board, but it also has its own distinct issues. Because management usually has significant equity option incentives that are likely to be well "under water" if the bonds are trading at distressed levels, one truism of financial restructurings is that management and equity are functionally working for the benefit of the unsecured creditors. So long as the capital structure is over-leveraged and the prices of the bonds are highly distressed, operational improvements will largely strengthen initially the value and price of the bonds, rather than old equity. So not only are the stockholders functionally disenfranchised, but management's equity incentives will have been rendered virtually valueless by the decline in enterprise value.

Very often in these situations, one goal of managers is to remain with the company, and management will perceive that the new, *de facto* equity owners will be the existing creditors. Thus, while the board may be focused on overall solutions, including how they affect old equity, management may be almost myopically focused on its own economics. And it may perceive that its remuneration can be enhanced through bargaining with the creditors and making "friends" of them. (Conversely, the board may believe – correctly, in certain circumstances – that any deleveraging or financial restructuring may be exactly the worst thing for old equity).

Management needs to understand that however appealing the idea of embracing the unsecured creditors, this approach can be shortsighted indeed. By ceding control to a large creditor group (such as bondholders), management may be opening the door to unintended consequences, including a sale of the company at sub-optimal prices (more on this below), excessive leverage or disappointingly low option grants for management – or even the termination of current management.

Stewards of an enterprise cannot abdicate their fiduciary responsibilities and must act to protect all constituencies – whose respective financial perspectives, as we shall see, may be very different from those of a single (albeit large) group such as the bondholders.

One chairman and CEO of a large Southern textile company, as he told us that he was hiring another firm – one with close ties to bondholders – said, "I really like you fellas, but I realized I don't give a hoot about what happens to old equity. I just want to turn the keys over to the bondholders and keep my job." His short-sightedness and naïveté bore just rewards. A year later, that company was liquidated instead of being restructured.

The Court

In the bankruptcy context, various administrative entities may have extremely significant roles. First and foremost, there is the judge. Bankruptcy judges have a great deal of discretion in making their rulings, so the outcome of a case may very easily be determined by which Circuit the case is filed in and who the judge is. It is important to recognize that Chapter 11 can lead to outcomes that are as much "results driven" as they are "legally driven." Some judges have a reputation of being "debtor-friendly"; others may perceive their role is to "do the right thing"; others still may be known for postponing making rulings, while encouraging the parties to settle the matter in the hallway. Professionals and their clients need to be keenly tuned in to the proclivities of the court in which they find themselves, and act accordingly.

The variance experienced across legal jurisdictions has created an interesting dynamic in the bankruptcy business over time. In part due to a desire to have more predictable outcomes, attorneys have concentrated their case filings in the venues of the Southern District of New York and in Delaware. The bankruptcy judges in these jurisdictions are highly experienced, and true "surprises" from the bench are relatively rare. An interesting ploy is frequently used by attorneys to direct the case toward one of these two venues. If a debtor has a subsidiary or other operation in the general geographic neighborhood, they pull the entire enterprise into New York or Delaware court based simply on that nexus. In the case of Delaware, the nexus may be simply that the company incorporated in Delaware. As a practical matter, as long as no one objects strenuously, the venue choice sticks.

But New York and Delaware are not the only bankruptcy venues, and many companies opt for other ones for good reasons. Some attorneys believe that courts located where the debtor has its primary operations can give the debtor a "home field" advantage. Whether or not this is true, having the court nearby certainly saves wear and tear on a company's executives. Further, we have found that the variance of outcomes across jurisdictions has diminished over time. Bankruptcy judges today are serious, well-versed and dedicated. Organizations such as the National Conference of Bankruptcy Judges have done a lot to promote this state of affairs.

But regardless of whether the case is in New York or in Podunk, bankruptcy judges are people, and as with any court, judges will gravitate toward arguments made by people they find to be credible. And most will react poorly if they determine that one side or the other has been trying to pull the wool over their eyes.

Another government professional playing an important role is the U.S. Trustee. This is a court officer whose role is to maintain the integrity of the bankruptcy system and to look out, at least in part, for unsecured creditors. In a Chapter 11 case, the U.S. Trustee appoints the unsecured creditors committee, which typically has a vital role in the proceedings (many judges may view their primary obligation in cases as making sure the unsecureds get a fair shake). The U.S. Trustee also acts as a "traffic cop" with professionals to make sure that they are disinterested, and that they don't take advantage of the debtor through excessive fees and expenses.

The court also may appoint other professionals to deal with problems or specific issues in the case. If there is appearance of impropriety or another serious allegation, the court may appoint an Examiner to investigate and report back. If the situation turns out to be so conflicted (or worse, in the case of fraud) that the existing management and board regime is incapable of acting in the best interests of the debtor, the court may go to the extreme measure of appointing a Chapter 11 Trustee (which is not the same thing as the U.S. Trustee) to take over the operations of the enterprise and the management of the case itself.

GORDIAN KNOTS/Montreal, Maine and Atlantic Railway (MMA)

With the discovery of significant quantities of shale oil in North Dakota and other locations where pipelines did not exist, North American railroads reinvented the late 1800s concept of the "rolling pipeline." Unfortunately, neither the petroleum nor rail industries were prepared for what followed. The particular crude coming out of the ground was far more volatile and explosive than conventional crude. When one of

MMA's trains carrying this crude derailed in Quebec, an entire town was decimated in an explosion and 47 lives were lost. Faced with a gargantuan amount of environmental, property and personal injury claims, MMA filed for bankruptcy protection in both the U.S. and Canada.

Amid perceptions of potential management culpability in the tragedy, as well as Canadian ire with respect to how management handled the crisis, the U.S. court removed the old CEO and appointed a Trustee to assume control of the case and the company's operations. The Trustee moved swiftly to administratively consolidate the U.S. and Canadian cases, to operate the company as cross-border system, and to sell the business as soon as was practical. The Trustee on behalf of the U.S. court, together with the Canadian authorities, engaged Gordian Group to run the sale process.

Until the shale oil boom, MMA had been operating as an unprofitable cross-border carrier. After the crude started flowing, MMA started earning significant profits. The ultimate sale valuation, therefore, would be predicated in large part on the continuation of the oil transportation business. In the months following the Quebec derailment, other railroads experienced similar (but not fatal) accidents in both the U.S. and Canada, and the governments started calling for more regulation. Actual or threatened regulation that would have significantly curtailed the oil business could have rendered MMA virtually worthless.

Gordian orchestrated a competitive sale process utilizing a bid strategy that took advantage of the strategic sections of track MMA controlled in each country. After an extensive M&A effort, Gordian reached an agreement with Fortress to be the stalking horse bidder for all of the company's assets in a Section 363 bankruptcy auction sale. Fortress was ultimately the successful bidder at the hearing.

The court may also insert a Chief Restructuring Officer (CRO) – a professional with significant powers, although somewhat short of those of a Trustee. In recent years, such appointments have occurred with increasing frequency in situations where the parties in interest may be at loggerheads and distrustful of one another. Typically the CRO will be responsible for the restructuring discussions among the various constituencies, and may be the ultimate architect of the bankruptcy plan. In certain cases, the CRO may also have cash monitoring and other operating responsibilities.

Secured Lenders

By the terms of their credit agreements, the secured lenders generally have access to fresh and continuing non-public financial information from the borrower, so they usually have the earliest view of impending financial and operational bumps in the road – in contrast to other outside constituencies.

When it comes to restructuring dynamics, the composition of the secured lender group has become a pivotal issue in recent years. Once upon a time, secured lenders were almost exclusively banking or other lending institutions of one stripe or another. The composition of this group would generally stay the same through the conclusion of the restructuring, and the debtor would be able to take some comfort in the predictability of this group, its goals and its approach.

More recently, "vulture investors" have become increasingly active in this tranche of debt. No longer is there any assurance that bank debt will stay in the hands of the original lenders. When the quoted prices of secured debt get to low enough levels (in a range of 50 to 80 cents on the dollar), the secured debt often migrates from traditional banking institutions to the vultures.

While traditional secured lenders generally seek to receive 100 cents on the dollar (more or less) and to maintain their reputations as constructive lenders, vulture investors are essentially focused on internal rate of return (IRR) considerations and, by and large, unconcerned about maintaining a "regal" reputation. The IRR is a function of the price paid, the recovery and how long it takes to effect the recovery. If a vulture purchases a piece of secured debt (paying 5% per annum interest on its face amount) at 70 cents on the dollar and can realize a 90-cent recovery in a 12-month time frame, it will have achieved an IRR of more than 35%. For a vulture with a 25% target return, such an investment would be viewed as a success.

But should the vulture try to hang on to get 100 cents? Assume that the passage of another year would bring a par recovery. The IRR for the second year would be 17%, well below the 25% target. In the absence of other considerations, the vulture should not wait around for par.

The implications for the debtor and its other constituencies are profound. Because the motivations and goals of the two types of secured holders are so different, together they make an unwieldy constituency. The difficulty of achieving consensus – and success – ratchets up when a vulture investor becomes involved. Particularly when the debtor is seeking additional liquidity or waivers, or asking for patience from its secured lenders, the disparity in the secured lenders' motivations will require creativity and dexterity from the debtor and its investment banker.

When a company nears or is in the Zone of Insolvency, its loan usually moves from the lending officer at the bank to the workout group at the institution. This frequently comes as a shock to the borrower, which may have enjoyed a good relationship with the lending officer for years. Yet this is not wholly bad news. At least the workout team from the lender should be experienced with insolvencies and can be more predictable and decisive.

Another complicating factor can be the secured lenders' relative impatience level. The impatience can be a function of collateral or value coverage, actions of other creditors, the company's cash flow and the credibility of its management. Everything else being equal, a high degree of impatience can lead to quick asset sales to repay the secured lenders – unless the company has other liquidity options. And quick sales can have dire consequences for more junior constituencies if such sales occur at disadvantageous prices.

Now, companies are not always wholly at the mercy of bank groups. There are a variety of ways to deal with banks. When a company engages insolvency counsel and an investment bank experienced in such matters, one of the advisors' first tasks is to examine the documentation underpinning the secured loans. Issues that will be immediately scrutinized include whether the secured lenders adequately documented the loans and if the loans can be re-characterized as "fraudulent conveyances" to the benefit of the company and its other constituencies (see Chapter 7). The purpose of such analyses is, simply, to determine whether the company will find the ammunition to challenge the security interests of the secured lenders. This would enhance the company's negotiating position.

In the absence of such a "silver bullet," the company must develop a plan that provides adequate liquidity for operations – while maintaining a level of collateral protection acceptable to the secured lenders (or at least to the bankruptcy court if and when the company files for Chapter 11 protection). If the banks are supportive, they may voluntarily extend additional credit or allow the company to retain its cash flow. Alternatively, the company may need to manage for cash or divest certain operations. Or the company can seek to refinance the bank group (typically with aggressive lenders or vultures). Or it can attempt to use the bankruptcy process to litigate use of cash collateral with the secured lenders (generally a bloody process).

Failure to accomplish at least one of the foregoing may result in a sale of all or part of the business, usually for the benefit of the secured lenders.

Most secured lenders have a relatively predictable reaction when a borrower stumbles and falls way out of compliance with covenants: they scramble to understand exactly to whom they have loaned money, exactly what the business is, and what the value of their collateral might be under various scenarios. To do this, they usually engage outside professionals.

The focus of these professional analyses is to determine if there is a serious accounting problem (such as fraud or a meltdown in management information systems, (MIS) at a borrower, what the value of the collateral will be under various liquidation scenarios, the M&A value of the business, and what the borrower's true liquidity needs are under various scenarios. Typical tasks include:

- determining whether, and to what extent, a new money decision (*e.g.*, new funds extended to a borrower) must be made;
- determining whether the lender may be able to improve its position in the credit;
- encouraging the borrower to engage suitable professionals to effect an expeditious financial transaction (presumably a transaction attractive to the secured lenders, such as a refinancing of the secured debt or sale of all or part the company);
- perhaps entering into debtor-in-possession (DIP) discussions with the borrower, so as to be prepared for a "soft landing" if the borrower elects to or needs to file for Chapter 11;
- determining whether any prior acts by the lenders could give rise to claims of lender liability; and
- most importantly, keeping the borrower on a short leash through a series of waivers or amendments that enables the secured lenders to maintain or gain, as the case may be, a seat at the decision-making table.

Secured lenders who find themselves to be a reluctant source of credit to a bankrupt borrower can, through adroit moves, find a way to improve their economic lot in life.

GORDIAN KNOTS/Alamo/National

Like many rental-car companies, the Alamo/National Rental Corporation suffered mightily from the markedly reduced travel after the September 11, 2001 terrorist attacks. As rental volume dropped, ANC found itself with an oversized fleet and an unsustainable capital structure. ANC filed Chapter 11 in November 2001 with more than $5 billion in liabilities.

The MBIA Insurance Corporation insured certain of ANC's financings and was at risk for $3.6 billion of ANC's car fleet financing at the time of the filing. MBIA retained Gordian Group to assist in working out its exposure to ANC. After analyzing ANC's strategic and financial situation, Gordian developed strategies to reduce MBIA's exposure and assisted MBIA in its negotiations with the debtor, other constituencies and prospective acquirers of ANC. A successful sale of ANC ensued.

Through a combined strategy of creative and tough negotiating and active participation in ANC's operational and financial restructuring efforts, MBIA reduced its exposure by more than two-thirds, while the fees it earned from ANC quadrupled, including an enormous amount of fees in excess of the original arrangement. Overall, it was a wildly successful result for MBIA.

Bondholders

Bondholders are usually the linchpin of major financial restructurings – assuming that the senior secured lenders are "money good" from a valuation perspective.

Bondholders often consist of two different groups: par holders that purchased the originally issued bonds and vulture investors that have roughly the same economic goals as the secured-lender vultures discussed above. Here, too, the dynamics of these two groups make for complexities and difficulties in the restructuring process.

Speaking broadly, par holders may be willing to endure a longer restructuring period than vultures, for the reasons cited above under Secured Lenders. Vultures may be willing to accept a wider array of restructuring consideration than par holders, who may prefer to retain a restructured bond. On the other hand, vultures generally need a liquidity event on the heels of a restructuring in order to capture their gains and move on to the next deal.

But, by and large, bondholders are purely financial players who care solely about maximizing their value. Interestingly, while the bondholders often become the most important players in getting a restructuring deal done, they are not necessarily the first constituency with whom a company in financial distress needs to deal. The reason is simple. Bondholders have already put their money into the company – and have very limited ability to get it back quickly.

In terms of triage and damage control, we believe that the priority creditors early on should be the providers of ongoing liquidity – the secured lenders and the trade. Without the support of these "priority" constituencies, the company's liquidity would be jeopardized, the customer base would have increased concerns, and the company's reorganization alternatives would be severely limited. In addition, as set forth below, unions may also merit up-front focus.

We note that bondholders may argue that reaching a prompt accord with them is in the company's best interest, because the world will not have to fear the effects of a potential (or even current) financial default with the bondholders. Moreover, such an accord would forestall any involuntary Chapter 11 filing by a bondholder group in default. These arguments are truisms that miss the point. An early accord with the bondholders can be tantamount to simply giving such creditors the keys to the company. We do not generally see this as a proper exercise of business judgment by the stewards of the enterprise. Bondholders are entitled to a slice of the value of the enterprise. But before the value is established, the company needs to stabilize. And that requires liquidity – and the support of the secured lenders, the trade and key employee constituencies. Any different order can ensure materially worse results for a board, the company and its non-bondholder constituents.

So if bondholders are very important, but not key to the stabilizing and value-building process, what does a company do with them in the interim? As in so many things, it depends.

Typically, the "right" (and certainly, the conventional) answer is to communicate continuously with the bondholders. Most of the time, the bondholders will insist on obtaining far greater detail than normally is contained in SEC filings. And most of the time, companies will resist including such additional information in public filings. This is generally resolved through the formation of an informal (out-of-court) or official (in Chapter 11) committee. Members of such a committee will enter into confidentiality agreements with the company that restrict disclosure and trading on inside information.

Organization of such a committee can be an arduous effort, at least in an out-of-court context. Parenthetically, it is sometimes difficult to obtain the bondholders' attention unless the company has already missed an interest payment. If a company is supportive of its bondholders' organization, it will want a majority in face amount of bond claims to participate as a negotiating committee. Without such a majority, the company can be negotiating with an insufficient number of claimants to actually do a deal – which will assuredly result in a worse deal for the company when the rest of the bondholders eventually come to the table and seek to "re-trade" what has already been negotiated. The bondholders must select counsel and a financial advisor. The fees of such advisors are generally borne outside of court (and always in Chapter 11 as part of the unsecured creditor committee process) by the company as a cost of the communication and negotiation process with bondholders. And one of the first tasks of these professionals can be to negotiate a confidentiality agreement with the company.

This confidentiality agreement is a thorny issue that can take many weeks to negotiate. These days, many bondholders typically demand that confidentiality agreements contain "sunset" provisions that provide for a debtor to make public all non-public and material information given to the bondholder negotiating committee if an agreement on a restructuring is not reached within a certain number of days (potentially 45 to 120). Such public disclosure would then allow bondholders to trade with the public once again. Borrowers then have to weigh carefully the pros and cons of giving certain information to negotiating committees.

We would like to emphasize a word of caution for companies at this point. Bondholders are repeat customers for almost all investment banks that provide distressed financial advisory services. Most investment banks work "both sides of the street." Frequently, this means advising borrowers on occasion and bondholder groups on a regular basis. Most investment banks also sell and trade securities with bondholders. Certain investment banks first try to get engaged by the borrower, and if that fails, seek to be engaged by the bondholders.

As we have noted previously, borrowers need to think very carefully about the inherent conflicts of interest presented by hiring such advisors. Precisely because value is a finite – and never a big enough – pie in restructurings, boards, management teams and old equity require advisors that will zealously pursue value for non-bondholder constituencies – all consistent with whatever responsibilities an advisor has to all constituencies in an insolvent situation.

Investment banks that have bondholders as regular trading partners or that solicit bondholder financial advisory business are very vulnerable to pressure from bondholders, which do not want the advisors to take aggressive or creative positions that might reduce the value received by the bondholders.

When pitching bondholder groups, investment banks will stress their ability to value the enterprise, to monitor borrower-side advisors in an M&A process, to take an active role in seeking to push the borrower into the arms of an acquirer if that is the bondholder strategy, and generally to negotiate on behalf of the bondholders with the other professionals in the case to effect a restructuring or M&A transaction.

Bondholder financial advisors may receive a success fee, in addition to monthly fees of $100,000 to $250,000 (paid by the borrower). The success fee is often pegged to the value received by the bondholders in a restructuring and is sometimes paid "in kind." This can create an incentive for an advisor to push the case toward an M&A transaction that will pay cash to the bondholders, as opposed to a reorganization that provides securities.

Bondholder strategies are generally broader than those of the secured lenders. They range from wanting a fast sale (although this may be relatively rare unless a liquidity crisis exists and no fresh capital can be found), to conducting a methodical sale or refinancing once the company is stabilized, to investing new capital themselves in conjunction with a global recapitalization of the borrower, to negotiating for a dominant interest in the new equity of a restructured borrower through an equity-for-debt-exchange – with a variety of offshoots to all these strategies.

But most of these dialogues start similarly: a borrower is, or prospectively is, in major default with its bondholders, and at the outset of communications the bondholders inform management and the board that the bondholders "own the company." There is no better spectacle in this business than the vulture investor who buys a claim for 20% of face value and then shows up and pounds the table, piously demanding that the company make good on the entire 100% amount of the claim.

In addition to pounding the table, bondholder groups can take a number of effective steps to try to force the company's hand, including, but not limited to:

- threatening litigation if the debtor does not adhere to their demands and fails to run the company and the restructuring process to the bondholders' own advantage (see Chapter 7):
- seeking to limit the amount of any new financing that may impair bondholders' future recoveries (and potentially offering new bondholder-sponsored money instead);
- demanding that the bondholders' favored crisis manager be hired to assume control of the company;
- threatening to file an involuntary Chapter 11; and
- soliciting outside M&A interest in the debtor.

In short, the bondholders may seek to wrest control of the process from the company and the board, and will generally use all available tactics to achieve such ends.

As noted above, managements and boards that respond by handing the keys of the company to the bondholders typically find that the bargain was a poor one. The trade can receive worse results, old equity will be wiped out, management can be short-changed or terminated, and boards do not receive the protections they might otherwise have if they had acted in a more stalwart and independent manner.

Conversely, if a company does act deliberately, all sorts of good things can happen.

GORDIAN KNOTS/Sudbury, Inc.

Sudbury, a former Fortune 500 holding company, had 23 operating subsidiaries that manufactured a broad range of industrial products. Approximately 70 percent of its revenues was derived from the domestic automotive industry, and after a downdraft in the automotive cycle, Sudbury found it difficult to service approximately $170 million of bank and subordinated debt. The bondholders were making all of the usual noises and threats.

Gordian Group was engaged to advise Sudbury, and it assisted management in evaluating and restructuring Sudbury's business and financial operations. The situation was, to say the least, roiled – we served five CEOs in a 12-month period.

Despite the bondholder pressure, the Board was unwilling to sell the company quickly in the merger market at prices it thought were depressed. For their part, the bondholders were unwilling to support any plan that contemplated the continuation of current management.

The Board then broke the logjam through a compromise suggested by Gordian Group. Sudbury would pursue a measured plan of recapitalization – shedding non-core assets in the merger market over time to pay down the secured banks, and reorganizing around the remaining assets. Gordian Group designed a comprehensive plan to restructure Sudbury's balance sheet, which was confirmed in bankruptcy court.

The reorganization structure permitted all classes of creditors and stockholders to benefit from the subsequent significant appreciation in Sudbury's operations, and included "hard" forms of consideration, as well as contingent securities designed to accommodate the differing needs and demands of the parties.

This outcome was a classic example of what we call "stabilize, monetize, reorganize." And the Board got what it wanted – a significant recovery for old equity through stock warrants and repayment of the trade in full. The Board also obtained releases, backstopped by an escrow funded by a cash contribution from the estate and indemnification.

If the Sudbury Board had simply rolled over for the bondholders, this outcome would never have happened.

In addition to advising Sudbury in implementing its plan of reorganization, Gordian Group assisted it in divesting certain assets as contemplated by the plan. The recovery of Sudbury's shareholders was one of the largest recoveries in restructuring history, relative to what the bondholders achieved. A true home-run result.

Thus far, we have discussed a consensual commercial and negotiating approach with the bondholders. As we alluded to earlier, other alternatives are available.

Depending upon circumstances, the company may find it advantageous to avoid a negotiating dynamic with bondholders that begins with "we own your company." If the company has sufficient liquidity, it may be possible to effect buybacks of the bonds at a discount through open market purchases or tenders (more on this later). Or, the company could launch an exchange offer in which it gives bondholders a lower face amount of a more senior bond. In such cases, it may be tactically unwise to encourage (and pay for) the bondholders to organize.

Trade Creditors

In certain respects, the trade is the most important creditor constituency. Without the trade's support, the borrower is going to have severe liquidity problems.

Generally, the trade is concerned about both maximizing its recovery and maintaining its customer's viability as a going concern. The trade typically wants its recovery in cash, not in stock. While the trade has a claim of 100 cents on the dollar, its cost of that claim may be somewhere between 50 and 90 cents on the dollar. The rest is markup and profit, and thus, the trade can take a "haircut" on the face amount of its claim and still not "lose" anything more than anticipated profits.

The trade's credit managers have become increasingly sophisticated about monitoring the credit quality of customers through analysis of public information and word of mouth, and determining which participants in their industry have liquidity problems. When a borrower must make public disclosure of certain liquidity-related issues, the most important audience may not be shareholders or bondholders, but the trade (along with the company's own customers). Thus, the news release that discusses the status of liquidity and discussions or negotiations with secured lenders should be carefully crafted and shaped with the trade in mind, consistent with all applicable securities laws. What happens to the pre-restructuring stock price on the heels of any such announcement is interesting but may not be particularly relevant to the success of the overall restructuring (or even to how old equity will fare). It is the trade's response to such a news release that is extremely important to overall success – or failure.

While little good (and lots of bad) can come from the CFO and CEO spending a lot of time on the phone with disgruntled bondholders, these officers must be responsive to the trade. Early on, the company must take a leadership role in dealing with trade inquiries and in developing an overall trade creditor strategy. What is pivotal is the trade's confidence that sufficient liquidity backs the borrower's purchases to ensure payment in accordance with terms. The trade's underlying fear is that it will be left holding a large empty bag of unsecured claims if it supplies product and the borrower then files for Chapter 11 shortly thereafter.

If the trade as a whole becomes so uncomfortable with the company's credit profile that trade credit is shut off or severely curtailed, then the result will be a "run on the bank." The liquidity crisis such an event can create can force a company into bankruptcy, or worse.

A management team can make several serious mistakes in dealing with its trade. The first is to say, "We're on 30-day terms, and we can get millions of dollars of additional trade credit with each day we extend, so let's push out the trade days to 40 or 45 days." Sophisticated trade creditors can react badly to this tactic, and cease providing any terms – thereby placing the company on COD, or even CIA, cash in advance. Accordingly, any trade "stretch-out" needs to be evaluated very, very carefully – because in the blink of an eye the company may see its aggregate amount of trade credit shrink rather than expand.

Another potentially serious mistake is to take product on credit terms when a company knows it does not have the wherewithal to pay for the goods and will need to file for Chapter 11 after receipt of the goods. This tactic leaves corporate directors vulnerable to charges of not doing business in good faith.

Interestingly, many executives of distressed companies seem to misunderstand how the trade may react to a bankruptcy. Many times we have heard, "You don't understand. If we file for Chapter 11, our trade creditors will not supply us with any more product." This is generally an ill-informed view, however heartfelt the belief may be.

Martin Color-Fi (MCF), for example, was a public company that was in the business of converting recycled plastic materials, such as processed film and bottles, into polyester fibers and yarn for automobile fabrics, carpet, apparel and other products. For 20 years, MCF was highly successful, but it was eventually overcome by a combination of over-leverage, excess inventory, foreign price-pressure and its inability to integrate recent acquisitions successfully.

Success in restructuring textile companies has historically been uneven, and an imminent liquidation of MCF seemed likely, which would have resulted in about a 10 percent recovery for its senior secured creditors.

MCF engaged Gordian Group, which embarked upon a three-pronged program: stabilize, monetize and reorganize. Working closely with senior management, Gordian Group assisted the company in taking dominion over its cash management, and assisted in achieving a smooth transition into Chapter 11 (something demanded by its senior secured constituency) – notwithstanding management's protestations that a Chapter 11 filing would result in the loss of all trade and customer support. Gordian Group assisted in stabilizing MCF operationally and in directing the monetization of non-core assets, and it then embarked upon a comprehensive search for new financing. A key part of the program was the active support of the trade during MCF's bankruptcy.

These efforts culminated in a new package of debt and equity provided by GE Capital and Dimeling, Schreiber & Park, and these funds were infused in connection with a consensual and successful plan of reorganization of MCF. Senior creditors received about a 60 percent recovery, and even junior creditors achieved a recovery – a tremendous result given the inherited circumstances of this situation.

Outside of Chapter 11, an unsecured trade creditor is vulnerable to significant losses on its exposure to the company. But inside Chapter 11, it is a very different story. Trade claims generated after the bankruptcy petition (*i.e.*, "post-petition") enjoy what is called an "administrative priority." This means that post-petition trade claims are senior to all pre-petition unsecured claims, and are generally only behind the DIP financing and secured loans.

The implications of such administrative priority status are significant. Congress wrote the Bankruptcy Code in this way to encourage trade creditors to do business with a company that has filed for Chapter 11. We have found that the trade is very willing to provide such post–petition support as long as the company has adequate operating liquidity (through DIP financing or otherwise). Well, asks the puzzled CFO, how can that be? Are not these people going to be angry because we owe them pre-petition money and now that we have filed Chapter 11, they are not likely to receive 100% on the dollar for their pre-petition claims?

The answer, as one of our favorite CEOs put it, is that the trade creditors are likely to balk at post-petition credit only if they are "mad at money." Because they enjoy administrative status for post-petition credit, the trade's prospects for recovery of these monies is relatively strong. It can simply make good business sense for the trade to continue shipping to the company.

Providing post-petition credit can also enhance the prospects for a better recovery on pre-petition exposure. A company with greater post-petition liquidity provided by the trade is more likely to be able to reorganize than one without such trade credit. And a reorganized enterprise can provide substantially more value to its pre-petition creditors than one that is forced to liquidate. By helping the bankrupt company, the trade is helping itself (along with all the other unsecured creditors). Moreover, in certain bankruptcies, trade creditors extending new credit are allowed to receive payment in full during the case on amounts owed pre-petition. These are all powerful incentives to support the company.

GORDIAN KNOTS/Nationwise Automotive, Inc.

A 300-store chain selling automotive after-market parts, Nationwise Automotive faced a severe financial crisis brought on by increased competition and other factors. Gordian Group was engaged by Nationwise's board to devise a strategy that would maximize value for all constituencies. At the time Gordian was engaged, Nationwise was on the verge of liquidation, and it had lost the support of its senior lender and the confidence of its trade vendors.

Gordian Group immediately implemented a communications program with all creditors and evaluated the few options remaining to Nationwise. The board elected to pursue a sale.

Gordian Group called an emergency meeting of the 50 largest trade creditors and told them that the debtor wanted them to continue to supply product on modest terms outside of Chapter 11, and that the debtor would not pay down anyone's existing outstanding payables during the proposed fast-track sale process. Gordian also outlined the alternative, which was not pretty – a likely liquidation. None of the trade was enthusiastic, but the combination of economic reality and faith in the process prevailed. Gordian Group was successful in inducing considerable support and cooperation from both the senior lender and the trade during the sale process.

Gordian Group actively assisted management in reducing Nationwise's cash "burn" and stabilizing operations. Gordian also participated in the strategic evaluation of Nationwise to determine whether all or a portion of the operations could be reorganized as a "stand-alone" business.

Gordian Group concomitantly conducted a sale program, grabbing hold of the first legitimate bidder that it could find, Autozone, and entering quickly into a stalking-horse contract (and we negotiated a contract without a breakup fee). The sale process resulted in the disposition of a substantial portion of Nationwise's assets through a subsequent bankruptcy auction process, as Gordian used the 363 auction as the forum to shop the company. This process featured a vigorous bidding war that we engineered between two of the country's largest automotive after-market parts retailers, and Nationwise's secured creditors achieved a full recovery and its unsecured creditors received substantially more value than they had anticipated.

Through the competitive bidding process, Gordian Group was able to increase total consideration paid by approximately 146 percent over the initial offer and 30 percent over the next highest proposal. The largest and happiest beneficiary was the trade – and the deal could not have been reached without the trade's support. The bottom line, as with any creditor constituency, is that credibility is key to life and success with the trade. The trade does not have to like everything it is told. But it does have to believe it.

Unions

Labor unions have regularly been an important constituency in many industrial bankruptcies. And given the unions' relatively large presence in sectors we perceive as being the subject of significant future restructuring activities, including the municipal and health-care sectors, we anticipate even greater union involvement.

Union leadership frequently needs to wear many hats in a restructuring. Like the trade, unions may have antecedent unsecured claims and may wish to see a viable ongoing entity coming out the other side of a reorganization. And also like the trade, unions may be represented on the unsecured creditors committee. But unions also may need to take care of pension obligations for current employees, as well as pension and benefit payments for already-retired union members. Not to mention renegotiate current labor contracts for existing employees.

These goals can be difficult to achieve, and can actually conflict. For example, medical benefit payments for retirees can saddle a company with significant costs, which could otherwise go toward wages or other payments for active workers. On the other hand, if retiree pension obligations do not exceed government maximums, then a pension plan termination (coupled with the help of a "top off" from the U.S. Pension Benefit Guaranty Corporation) could be a good outcome for retirees – but not for current workers that may not yet have vested in their plans. High-benefit retirees (such as airline pilots) have yet other agendas vs. the other rank-and-file employees. The list of potential conflicts goes on.

GORDIAN KNOTS/AMR Corporation

AMR, the parent of American Airlines, was the last of the major air carriers to seek bankruptcy protection. Very few sectors have been as financially troubled as the airline business.

When AMR filed, Gordian Group was engaged by the Transport Workers Union of America (TWU), one of AMR's three major unions and an AFL-CIO affiliate. The TWU faced a number of significant challenges, including the tension between current workers and retirees. In addition, the internal union decision-making process was very decentralized, with "locals" having an important voice. Because AMR's proposed job cuts were not geographically uniform, the opinions of individual locals were disparate.

Gordian Group worked with the TWU to understand the values that would be available through both "internal" reorganizations as well as "external" ones such as the transaction that was ultimately consummated with US Airways, as well as to negotiate terms of a deal with the other constituencies. Valuation was an important consideration for the TWU because the debtor was proposing that the unions receive restructured equity value in the reorganized company in exchange for their give-ups. In connection with our engagement, Gordian Group testified in court as to the merits of pursuing the US Airways merger – over the strenuous objections of AMR – given our views as to the significantly increased value that the union's members could achieve. Pursuant to the request of the TWU, we also regularly appeared on national business media in order to convey the union's position as part of TWU's broader strategy of using an orchestrated communications program to enhance its negotiating position.

Understanding these competing challenges confronting the union is essential for the investment bankers involved in the restructuring. While maintaining a viable and motivated work force is generally of paramount importance, being oblivious to the other considerations may not be an optimal strategy – even if the debtor may legally be able to impose onerous conditions on retirees. Being "too tough" on behalf of active workers can result in adverse blowback, including with respect to retirees.

It is our experience that union leaderships are very experienced and adroit negotiators. And unions may play on a broader stage than simply the economic one that holds the attention of the banks and the bondholders. In addition to media outreach, we have seen union leadership effectively use community organization to achieve their objectives. On a relatively diffuse level, this can translate into a local, regional or even national boycott of goods and services. Even if such actions work only for a period of time, they can be effective in putting pressure on a debtor and its other constituencies.

We have also witnessed unions adopting even more effective tactics when issues of politics and public money come into play. For example, when a publicly-funded enterprise (such as a hospital or educational facility) becomes insolvent, unions can and do join forces with community activists opposed to any closure. The ensuing political pressure can be acute enough to cause a significant delay in any downsizing activities – which can at the very least continue union employment for the time being. And it's possible that the pressure can be so great that the government "bails out" the enterprise for the benefit of the union.

There is another issue worth mentioning. If a company is planning to close facilities and lay off significant numbers of workers, it needs to comply with the Worker Adjustment and Retraining Notification Act law. The WARN Act requires a 60-day notice period before effecting a layoff of more than 100 workers. If a debtor initiates a closure after entering Chapter 11, then the WARN Act liability becomes an administrative claim in bankruptcy, and must be satisfied. If the debtor's professionals fail to plan for this, it can create extremely large impediments to a successful reorganization.

Old Equity

Old equity's role can be much more passive than those of the other constituencies. Who will speak for old equity of public companies? Outside of Chapter 11, only the board of directors, and, unless conflicted by bondholders ties, the company's investment bankers. For private companies controlled by dominant shareholders, clearly old equity would have a voice directly on the board. However, public stockholders can indeed find themselves disenfranchised. One problem for public equity holders is one of cost. It can be uneconomic for one or two holders to absorb the expense of financial and legal professionals. And the problems associated with trying to assemble an equity committee to pick up the bill may be insurmountable. Nevertheless, such groups do form from time to time. Occasionally, an official equity committee is appointed in bankruptcy if the court believes that equity value may exist. Or a few large like-minded holders may have enough "skin in the game" to justify the expense, either in or out of court. But in most cases, old equity must rely on management and the board to look out for its interests.

Let us make a philosophical point here. A year ago, old equity might have been in the money, and in another year or two it might be again, but today old equity is under water. If this dynamic is not permanent, why should the bonds be able to crush old equity today? Why not cap the recovery to bondholders at some amount? Say at 100 cents recovery plus, perhaps, some additional rate of return? Alternatively, should not the equity holders receive at least a material chunk of warrants that kick in at or near the point where the bondholders reach the aforementioned targeted recovery?

As noted throughout this book, we are advocates of this philosophy. We believe that old equity possesses both option value and control value, and that *if advised by zealous, creative and unconflicted investment bankers*, a board may achieve superior results for old equity.

The CEO/entrepreneur who owns a material portion of the company's stock will have a very different incentive than the CEO who merely owns stock options. The former may have a financial incentive to do just about anything to play for time, hoping the markets will come back and his operations can grow back into the over-leveraged capital structure – because distressed equity value is a function, simply put, of time and volatility. At the very least equity should have option value. The CEO who only has stock options, of course, may be primarily motivated by maintaining his job rather than any equity value associated with way out-of-the-money options. The CEO may also reason that new owners may give him a new stock option package.

Old equity can achieve meaningful recoveries through various paths. One way is to demonstrate that the value of the enterprise is such that the equity has value in excess of the debt. Another is to reinvest proceeds in high risk/high return ventures that will generate rewards for old equity – if the ventures are successful and there is enough time to pull off such a strategy. Yet another is to defer dealing with the debt problems in the hopes that operations will turn around. Another is through the use of "coercive" offers for bonds. And there are numerous creative options, such as the following "ugly duckling" strategy.

If a company has component parts, for example, and it is deemed prudent to break up the components in order to maximize value, old equity might receive some combination of ability to reinvest (through a rights offering), an outright stock grant and warrants – and perhaps get relatively more "stuff" in the less-favored component parts (the "ugly ducklings").

GORDIAN KNOTS/Tracor

Nowhere have we used this approach to greater advantage than on behalf of Tracor, a company with about $1 billion in sales, most of which was defense-related. Shortly after its LBO, Tracor went bust, with more than $1 billion in debt.

The Tracor Board cared deeply about old equity recoveries and was willing to exercise its negotiating leverage relating to exclusivity and taxes (see Chapter 3). This negotiating leverage opened a window of opportunity in discussions with the bank and bondholder creditors. The key to success for old equity was that Gordian Group's valuation proved to be superior to the views of the other advisors. Gordian Group split Tracor into its component parts and gave what were perceived by others as the more "attractive" parts largely to these creditor groups. Gordian Group concentrated old equity's recovery into the "ugly" defense business through a package of common stock and warrants representing a 50% ownership in defense.

Ultimately, old equity's package grew to more than $300 million in value. It received this consideration through a bankruptcy plan that saw junior bondholders initially receiving less than a 10% recovery. Using "conventional" wisdom, old equity would have been wiped out. Instead, old equity hit a home run – and, incredibly, achieved a higher dollar recovery than the junior bondholders.

If a company is insolvent or in the Zone of Insolvency, bond prices will be trading at distressed levels, and the stock will likely be at an all-time low. It may not seem fair or appropriate to cut the legs out from under old equity at its most vulnerable time, but that is precisely the result of most financial restructurings. Old equity therefore needs to adjust its goals and ambitions – it needs to hope for as much of a recovery as is possible under the circumstances, as opposed to expecting the sun, moon and stars. While each situation is different, it is extremely difficult to get a recovery anywhere near the $300 million value realized in the Tracor restructuring.

But the bottom line is that old equity starts out behind the eight ball in an insolvency, and it will require fortitude and the right advisors to move out of that position.

CHAPTER 3—THE IMPORTANCE OF BEING STRATEGIC

As we have just seen, the successful resolution of a financially challenged situation requires a careful balancing of a host of competing objectives and interests. The steps taken to stabilize the business and obtain needed liquidity can have profound and limiting effects on the company's subsequent opportunities to pursue certain long-term financial alternatives. Selling a division at distressed prices in order to obtain needed cash, for example, can ease near-term problems but result in a long-term loss of value. And then, after the business is stabilized, value needs to be allocated in a zero-sum game. Almost invariably, insufficient value exists to make everyone whole – leading to spirited negotiations among the various constituencies.

Many of these issues are reasonably foreseeable at the outset. Understanding how such factors are likely to play out will enable a company to develop a strategy. Having a coherent strategy through the pendancy of a restructuring will give the company the ability to evaluate the appropriate next steps to achieve its reorganization objectives. Absent such a strategy, the company is left to lurch from pillar to post throughout the restructuring process. Such lurching invariably results in less-than-optimal outcomes, including the possible demise of the company. Sometimes, time frames are so short that second chances are not available.

An investment banker needs to guide the company as to the relative merits of its available strategic and financial alternatives. The investment banker is thus a key member of the overall restructuring team, which also includes attorneys, crisis managers, accountants, and perhaps others. In many cases, various alternatives will need to be explored simultaneously, in order to maximize the possibilities within a limited time frame. Understanding how these alternatives are likely to play out – and what their effect will be on the overall restructuring effort – is critical in being able to set the appropriate strategic course for the company. As the football coach Bear Bryant liked to say, "You've got to have a game-plan for all conceivable situations." Failure to be so prepared will assuredly result in a "cluster fuck," a Vietnam-era term referring to a hopelessly disorganized situation.

Goals and Objectives

One critical element of developing a strategy is determining the company's goals and objectives. Obviously, this analysis needs to focus on realistic possibilities. Preservation of the status quo is usually unrealistic (see Chapter 8). Changes in operations, management, capital structure and ownership are almost always necessary. The analysis also needs to weigh the importance of the company's different possible objectives.

Is maintenance of existing equity's ownership control critical? Or the maximization of value for one or more constituencies? Or allowing existing management the ability to rebuild business values? What of the tradeoffs between the risks and prospects of maximizing values through long-term growth, compared with the benefits of achieving a short-term resolution through a sale in the merger market? Will the company be able to implement its strategy through an out-of-court process? Or will it need to resort to Chapter 11?

These questions need to be answered in the contexts of both the realistic options available and the company's and the board's fiduciary duties to various constituencies. When a company enters the Zone of Insolvency, it may have a broader fiduciary duty than just to its stockholders. This creates divided loyalties.

If a company is not yet in default on its debt instruments, has a lot of cash and yet has bonds trading at distressed prices, what should it do? This conflict has arisen repeatedly with technology (both electronic and bio) and telecommunications companies. Their business plans may entail spending significant sums on risky R&D, capital expenditures or other areas, with the expectation that such bets will pay off down the road. If the bets do pay off, the stockholders and creditors all benefit. If they do not, then all of the players lose. In a potentially insolvent situation, however, the risks are borne disproportionately.

Assume that a company has $200 million of bonds, $150 million of cash and a $25 million per quarter net cash "burn rate." In other words, in 18 months the company will be out of cash. Assume that the company and its investment bankers believe that the business plan the company is pursuing has a 30% chance of succeeding, and if it succeeds, the present value of the enterprise will be worth $500 million. If it fails, it will be worth nothing.

Working through the arithmetic, the expected present value of the enterprise is $150 million (30% expectation × $500 million successful outcome). The expected present value of the equity is $90 million (30% × ($500 million – $200 million of bonds)). And the expected present value of the bonds is $60 million (30% × $200 million). The bonds are thus "worth" 30 cents on the dollar.

But note that the company today has $150 million in cash. So if it shut its doors today, it would be able to give all that money to the bondholders, giving them 75 cents on the dollar.

Therefore, the company can provide its constituencies with $150 million in value in two ways. Liquidate today in a relatively risk-free fashion and give it to the bondholders in hard currency (with perhaps a slice going to old equity to facilitate the transaction) or stay in business, whereby the stockholders have a speculative current value of $90 million.

Assume further that the bondholders are threatening to sue unless the company gives them the money back. Points of view vary on how the company should respond. Some people argue that unless a company is in actual or imminent default with debt holders, it has no duty to honor a request to return the cash. To do so, they say, would be a contravention of the indenture contract and would also deprive equity holders of their rightful value. Another point of view is that a company in this position may subject its board to significant liability should it pursue a risky operational strategy and fail.

What are a company and its board to do? We are reminded of a passage in Woody Allen's *Love and Death*: "One path leads to death and destruction. The other leads to ruin and despair. God must give us the wisdom to choose the right path." Or as another contemporary philosopher, Yogi Berra, once said, "When you get to the fork in the road, take it."

Resolving this type of vexing question is one of the most important issues in any restructuring. Generally, the use of internal resources to build business values is the best way to maximize the value of the enterprise – and to protect boards of directors. Achieving such value increases, however, generally benefits the junior constituencies more than the senior ones, which is why it is sometimes referred to as "playing with the senior creditors' money." Senior classes invariably complain that such a dynamic is unfair to them; classes that are more junior will aver that they are contractually and legally entitled to such benefits. Both arguments are right, each in its own way. In any event, this is one factor that gives junior classes their "option value" (see below).

Due Diligence

One of an investment banker's most critical tasks is to conduct an early assessment of the company's problems and develop views of its alternatives, in order to help the client develop a coherent strategy. Because of the press of time and crises, the due diligence underpinning such assessment must frequently be conducted quickly. Said differently, distressed investment bankers live in a world of imperfect timing and information. Because of those pressures, the financial advisor should revisit its analysis and conclusions from time to time, to ensure that they were not founded on incorrect and misleading information.

This difficult situation is compounded by the extent to which bad management information systems (MIS) are frequently present in financially distressed companies – which might be because bad MIS led to bad decisions and thus financial crises, or because poor management (which was responsible for other problems) did a poor job with MIS. Or both. Should the company also have accounting irregularities, sifting through the financial information is even more difficult. In other words, the financial advisor needs to help the company make decisions under great uncertainty, frequently using flawed information.

All this requires that the investment banker have broad, far-reaching goals for the due diligence process. Among the questions the investment banker must ask are:

- What near-term financial crises threaten the company? Are these resolvable through such financial mechanisms as refinancings, extensions or asset sales?
- To the extent knowable, how much time does the company have before it is "too late" from a liquidity perspective?
- What is the current bank debt availability vs. the company's collateral base?
- Does the company have a functioning cash-forecasting system? If not, can it be developed quickly? What does this cash forecast imply about generation or use of cash? And what effect does that change in cash have on the relationship between drawn bank lines and the collateral base down the road?

- What is the company's historical financial picture? Is the current problem an aberration or part of a longer-term trend?
- Are there accounting problems, irregularities or any indicators of fraud?
- Where does the company stand within its industry? Who are the critical players, and what is their financial condition?
- Who are the critical customers and vendors? How are they likely to react to the company's problems? Are any of them in financial distress themselves?
- What is the company's "steady-state" profit picture? Are there any non-recurring events that need to be adjusted in the historical financials to render them more meaningful?
- What are the company's long-term business plans? Do they make sense in the context of the current financial crisis, and can they be implemented? Or are they just wishful thinking by management?
- How do the company's financial forecasts compare to "steady-state" historical results? Does management have a track record of meeting forecasts, or does it consistently underperform "hockey stick" projections?
- Are the company's balance sheet projections consistent with historical relationships to the income statement? Are cash flows?
- Is the current management team capable of handling the financial and operating crises they are certain to face? Or capable of executing the long-term plan?
- What is the going concern value of the company or its component parts? Are there any hidden values? Is it greater in an M&A context than if the company retains the assets? Would the values dramatically increase through an operational turnaround? What would the risks be in undertaking such a turnaround?
- What is the likely liquidation value of the company or its component parts? Would those values change if the liquidation were conducted over time through a more orderly wind-down?
- Who are the logical buyers? Have any of these strategic or financial buyers expressed interest in the company?
- What is the capital structure of the company, and who are the holders of each instrument?

- How does the capital structure break down by legal entity? Are there any guarantees?
- How do the company's values correspond to its various legal entities? What entities are solvent? Which are insolvent?
- Are any of the insolvent entities in foreign jurisdictions outside of the reach of Chapter 11? Does Chapter 15 of the Bankruptcy Code help (see below)?
- Are there any weaknesses in the documentation of the bank agreements or indentures?
- Did the company consummate any transactions in the last several years that might give rise to litigation claims?
- What are the company's contingent liabilities? Are there any environmental or asbestos-type claims?
- What are the company's tax attributes, such as net operating losses, and how do they interrelate with various restructuring alternatives that might entail forgiveness of indebtedness? Has there been a "change of control"? Are there any potential tax refunds?
- Are there any high-cost leases or other onerous contracts the company would like to be relieved of?
- What are the company's unfunded pension liabilities? Unfunded retiree medical obligations?
- Is there any material litigation, including class-action suits? Conversely, does the company have litigation claims against others that could be considered to be an asset?
- What are the goals of the management? The board? The principal equity holders? The senior lenders? The bondholders? The trade? The unions?
- What would happen if the company did nothing?

The answers to these questions will form much of the basis for the investment banker's recommendations to the company. The investment banker must draw heavily on his or her experience in forming the recommendations and related strategies for implementing them. Indeed, the experience of the investment banker can prove to be one of the distressed company's most valuable, albeit intangible, assets.

The Business Plan

Out of the due diligence emerges the company's business plan. In some cases, the investment banker will construct most of the plan; in other cases, the investment banker acts as a sounding board to aid the company in developing a plan that is realistic. In either case, the plan will play a vital role in the determination of strategy.

The business plan (and variations on it) help determine the company's debt capacity, a process similar to evaluating solvency. The financial professionals need to perform a variety of analyses to assess the likelihood of the company meeting its obligations and having a feasible capital structure after the restructuring. The plan will also form the basis for valuation analyses. Such inputs, in turn, will drive views with respect to capital structure, as well as the form and amount of consideration available to each constituency.

The determination of a business plan is not a static analysis performed in a vacuum. Frequently, the investment banker and the client need to assess whether the restructuring plan (based on the business plan) results in an optimal outcome in terms of overall goals and objectives. If not, the team needs to consider changes to the business plan that could improve the effectiveness of the restructuring plan.

Short-Term Issues

In order for a company to implement its long-term restructuring strategy, it needs to survive the short-term challenges. Frequently, the most severe of these is meeting immediate liquidity needs. These near-term cash crises can be caused by a number of factors, including "maxing out" secured bank lines, demand for repayment of bank or other indebtedness, losing trade credit or experiencing an unexpected cash outflow, such as payments relating to litigation damages.

The investment banker to a company facing such a liquidity crisis needs to examine alternatives for generating sufficient cash to finance the company's activities. Expanding on some of the topics covered under "Due Diligence" above, certain issues must be examined:

- What are the company's needs, immediate and longer-term? What is the timing of these needs? Can any expenditures be postponed? If the cash crisis results from a lender demanding repayment, what are the prospects of having the lender forbear?

- What are the company's immediately available financial resources from existing relationships? Can existing bank lines be increased? Is there cash (or readily monetizable assets) that can be used?
- What are the company's near-term financial alternatives? Will it be able to access new bank facilities? Can it access sources in the private capital markets for either debt or equity? What is the relationship between collateral values and the amount of existing secured debt? Is the company currently operating on a cash-positive basis before debt service? Or is the company so far "under water" from a secured debt-and-liquidity standpoint that it may be forced to monetize assets for the benefit of the secured lenders?
- Does the company have any businesses that can be sold quickly? If so, how detrimental would quick sales be to long-term values?
- If the company can obtain new sources of financing or encourage buyer interest in a quick M&A sale, will it be able to consummate such transactions out of court or will it have to implement such transactions in Chapter 11?
- If loss of trade credit is a problem, would a Chapter 11 filing help the company restore such trade credit?

From these analyses, the investment banker should be able to develop a rough idea of how long the company has until it hits the cash wall, its likelihood of obtaining additional financing – in or out of court – and the Chapter 11 fallback positions it may have if existing creditors do not cooperate out of court.

With the investment banker's recommendations, the company should be in a position to explore its near-term liquidity alternatives and to develop a view on whether the liquidity fix is more likely to happen in Chapter 11 or outside of it. And the investment banker and the company must try to determine whether solving the near-term liquidity problem might have a material adverse impact on long-term values and objectives.

In most cases, financial distress does not have fatal long-term effects, but the extent of the damage varies widely. In a worst-case meltdown, the company is unable to obtain interim financing and closes its doors. Solving the near-term liquidity problem would head this off. However, the liquidity fix could itself cause serious value deterioration if the company were able to obtain financing only on terms that required it to monetize its assets at unfavorable prices in order to repay senior secured lenders. In such circumstances, the company's other constituencies would be deprived of the opportunity to obtain higher values through operational turnarounds.

Control and Publicity

When a company weighs the pros and cons of making a coupon payment to its bondholders, it tries to balance the control issue against the use of (likely) scarce financial wherewithal to make the coupon payment. A company retains relatively greater control over the process if it is not in default with its bondholders (*i.e.*, coupons are paid), thereby preventing bondholders from threatening to walk from the negotiating table at any juncture and file an involuntary Chapter 11. Conversely, if the bonds are not in default, it may be difficult for a company to get the bondholders to pay attention to a situation, which does not on its face constitute an emergency.

With respect to publicity, a company in Chapter 11 lives in a publicity fishbowl, and companies and boards generally wish to avoid that scenario. This is much less the case in out-of-court negotiations, as companies can usually proceed in a much more "quiet" fashion until it comes time to implement whatever has been negotiated among the parties.

Chapter 11 vs. Out of Court

We consider ourselves to be bankruptcy-agnostic. Bankruptcy is not a solution to a company's financial woes. Nor is it a particularly good place to look for such a solution; *companies that enter Chapter 11 with a solution in hand fare far better than companies that enter Chapter 11 in order to find one.* Bankruptcy is, in fact, a venue – another forum to implement or seek a financial transaction. The bankruptcy process can be used to buy time, in order to implement a solution efficiently – one that the company has, hopefully, identified before filing for bankruptcy protection.

Bankruptcy may also provide an attractive venue for companies that, as part of their reorganization, wish to restructure through the issuance of public securities. The Bankruptcy Code provides that a company may exempt certain securities from registration that would otherwise be required by the SEC. This can provide considerable flexibility and an enormous cost and time savings.

In essence, under the Bankruptcy Code, the company may issue new public debt or equity as part of a reorganization so long as the securities are issued or sold as part of a plan of reorganization and those securities are issued entirely in exchange for an existing claim against or interest in the debtor. A company could, for example, issue new public debentures in exchange for an existing privately held bank facility or could issue new warrants to its existing equity security holders pursuant to its plan of reorganization, without any need to file a registration statement with the SEC.

And, as set forth below, tax considerations play an important role in the choice of venue.

The analysis of bankruptcy alternatives is critical in shaping the overall strategy.

Exclusivity

One of a company's most important strategic assets in a bankruptcy restructuring is its exclusive right to file a plan of reorganization. By statute, this period is 120 days at the outset of a case – but the period is frequently extended by the bankruptcy court for a year or more. During this exclusive period, no other constituency has the right to file a plan of reorganization.

As a practical matter, this means the company controls the exit strategy – at least at the outset of a case. Creditors and other constituencies are therefore bound to the company's timetable and may not be able to force a quicker resolution. For creditors concerned about extensions of the restructuring time frame (for example, vulture investors that require a very high rate of return), exclusivity gives the company valuable negotiating leverage: "Take this deal now, or maybe get a better deal down the road" at a lower present value (due to the vulture's high discount rate).

But as powerful as exclusivity is, it is also a "wasting asset."; while extensions are available, if any time after the 120-day original exclusivity period the bankruptcy court perceives the case to be a rudderless ship, it may refuse to extend exclusivity. Once exclusivity is terminated, the company's control of the case is greatly diminished. Accordingly, it is important that the company take charge of the direction of the case from the outset. That, in turn, requires that it have a firm grasp of the strategy it wants to pursue.

The rules of bankruptcy are central to determining what types of restructuring will – or will not – be able to be consummated. The rules are also instrumental in determining the relative strengths of the various players (the banks, the bondholders, labor, old equity).

Relatedly, bankruptcy rules directly influence the outcome of non-bankruptcy restructurings, which generally are conducted along similar lines to a more formal bankruptcy process. This "mirror structure" occurs because virtually any major participant in an out-of-court process can cause the restructuring to take place in bankruptcy – if it feels there is too much of a deviation from what it would obtain in an actual bankruptcy. Not only does the company itself have the ability to file a "voluntary" bankruptcy petition, but creditors whose debt is in default frequently have the option to file a petition against the company, which may very well result in the company ending up in an "involuntary" bankruptcy proceeding.

DIP Financing

Many companies are driven into bankruptcy because they lack immediate liquidity. Fortunately, financial advisors have a number of powerful tools in bankruptcy to assist their clients in obtaining new financing.

Bankruptcy can provide incentives and assurances to existing lenders so that they may be willing to advance more monies than they would outside of bankruptcy. One common complaint from pre-petition bank groups is that additional bank advances go toward paying down unsecured trade credit or making interest payments on unsecured bonds. In bankruptcy, these pre-petition obligations are typically frozen, and new bank advances are to build business values rather than to repay antecedent debts.

Existing lenders may be encouraged to provide additional post-petition financing because of the potential risks should other lenders do so in their stead. Depending upon the relationship between collateral values and pre-petition secured debt levels, it may be possible for the bankruptcy court to "carve up" the pre-petition banks' collateral and give a senior slice to new lenders. This process, called priming, is unpalatable to the pre-petition banks, which would oppose such court action fiercely. The risk to their interests posed by priming may be a powerful incentive for the pre-petition banks to provide additional DIP financing themselves.

On the other hand, pre-petition secured creditors do have special rights in bankruptcy – whether or not they are being primed. Such secured creditors are entitled to "adequate protection" to prevent the value of their collateral from being dissipated in a bankruptcy. In the case of priming, the implication is that the bankruptcy court must find the pre-petition secured creditors to be fully covered by collateral both immediately after a senior slice of their collateral has been given to other lenders and on a continuing basis. Similarly, the bankruptcy court must take steps to ensure that pre-petition secured creditors (with mortgages and other such liens) are not losing material collateral value during the case.

GORDIAN KNOTS/AmeriServe

An $8 billion distributor serving the fast-food restaurant industry, AmeriServe had grown rapidly through acquisitions financed primarily with debt. Following an ill-advised secured financing, AmeriServe suffered a dramatic decline in trade support, which led to a liquidity crisis and a bankruptcy filing.

AmeriServe's largest customer was Yum! Brands, the nationwide franchiser of Pizza Hut, Kentucky Fried Chicken and Taco Bell restaurants. If AmeriServe had ceased operations because of illiquidity (which it seriously contemplated), many Yum! owned and franchised stores would have "gone dark" for weeks, perhaps longer. To avert this disaster scenario, Yum! agreed to provide a very significant debtor-in-possession financing facility to AmeriServe.

In addition to its DIP commitment, Yum! had a variety of other potential exposures in the case. Yum! engaged Gordian Group to assist in minimizing its AmeriServe-related losses and to expedite the bankruptcy restructuring process. Gordian Group used Yum!'s status as DIP lender to shape the process and outcome to Yum!'s advantage. Gordian Group also advised Yum! with respect to various restructuring options, assisted in the negotiations leading to a sale of AmeriServe to a subsidiary of Wal-Mart and assisted in the restructuring negotiations with the debtor and various creditor constituencies.

Particularly in respect to DIP hearings, some cases may be "won" or "lost" at the outset. In the Zale Corporation and Gordon Jewelry restructuring, we were able to prevent Gordon from being absorbed into Zale.

GORDIAN KNOTS/Zale and Gordon Jewelry

Zale Corporation purchased Gordon Jewelry in an acquisition financed largely with debt. Zale itself had earlier been taken private through a leveraged transaction. The combined companies' sales represented approximately 10 percent of the U.S. fine jewelry market.

Soon after the acquisition, operating results at Zale and Gordon had significantly deteriorated because of the adverse economic climate, and the companies were no longer able to meet their substantial debt-service requirements. Certain bondholders filed an involuntary bankruptcy petition, to which Zale subsequently acquiesced.

The Official Committee of Unsecured Creditors of Gordon Jewelry (one of the last bondholder-side engagements undertaken by Gordian) retained Gordian Group for assistance in:

- Preserving flexibility for Gordon Jewelry to reorganize independently from the other Zale entities. Through a difficult series of negotiations and court testimony, Gordian Group altered DIP financing arrangements that would otherwise have inextricably bound Gordon to Zale's reorganization
- Developing a controversial "stand-alone" plan
- Negotiating a consensual plan of reorganization
- Securing "exit" financing in the form of a receivables securitization, a gold loan and a working capital line of credit

Being absorbed into the Zale collective at the outset would have left Gordon burdened with the DIP-related obligations without any benefit. Directly because of our work, Gordon creditors were able to obtain a significantly higher recovery.

Chapter 11 Mechanics

"Chapter 11" is sometimes used as a generic shorthand for bankruptcy in the United States, though other sections in the U.S. Code deal with other aspects of bankruptcies (*e.g.*, municipalities, farms, corporate liquidations). Because Chapter 11 is the body of law that most commonly deals with large corporate reorganizations, it is the focus of this book.

We acknowledge that bankruptcy laws and restructurings differ dramatically from country to country. Those permutations are beyond the scope of this work. However, we do note that Chapter 15 of the Bankruptcy Code can be used (with varying degrees of success) to attempt to reconcile and coordinate a U.S. bankruptcy with affiliated proceedings abroad.

Chapter 11 reflects decades of refinements in legislative and case law designed to facilitate the rehabilitation of businesses and to preserve jobs. Among the more powerful aspects of Chapter 11 are:

Automatic stay: Creditors, litigants and other parties are immediately prohibited from foreclosing on assets, hounding the company or taking other actions without bankruptcy court permission. This is intended to give the company breathing room to reorganize.

Administrative priority: Unlike pre-petition liabilities (which are subject to compromise), post-petition claims are entitled to priority status. This rule is intended to encourage trade vendors, professionals and other key partners to continue to do business with the company. These post-petition claims must be repaid (or otherwise satisfied) before the company can emerge from Chapter 11 through a Plan of Reorganization.

New financing: The bankruptcy court has the ability to help the company obtain incremental liquidity through new bank loans – generally referred to as Debtor-in-Possession financing. Almost invariably, the court grants DIP financing lenders "super-priority" administrative claims, as well as an interest in the collateral. The bankruptcy court has far-reaching powers to grant rights to DIP financing lenders that violate the contractual rights of pre-petition lenders, including limitations on additional debt and the ranking of such old lenders' interest in collateral.

Ability to bind groups of creditors: In many out of court situations, a company cannot force a creditor to compromise its claim. Even if the vast majority of creditors is willing to engage in a restructuring, a small group of holdouts may refuse to go along. In bankruptcy, the court can bind all holders within an impaired class (two-thirds of the aggregate claims voting and half of the individual creditors voting are required to bind the class). Moreover, even objecting classes can be made to accept the terms of a restructuring through what are known as the "cram-down" provisions of the Bankruptcy Code. As long as at least one impaired class accepts a plan, that plan can be imposed on all other classes – provided that the class that objects gets more than it would in a liquidation, and is either made whole or that no class junior to the objecting class gets anything. The cram-down provisions provide companies and their advisors with powerful weapons. Frequently, creditor classes object to the form of their recovery (*i.e.*, "We don't want equity, we want debt"). But if the debtor can demonstrate that the securities being offered are worth 100 cents (perhaps after a valuation fight), then the recalcitrant class may be more amenable to compromise. In fact, this strategy can even be used to deal with senior classes, if one or more junior classes agrees to their own treatment. This latter tactic is sometimes referred to as a "cram-up."

Ability to reject leases and other contracts: The Bankruptcy Code allows companies to reject "executory" contracts. This encourages a company to examine its leases and other contracts, including labor contracts, to determine whether any are uneconomic. If so, the company has the ability to terminate the contract (for which the counter-party would derive an unsecured pre-petition claim against the company) or to renegotiate the contract on a basis that would produce a similar economic result.

Ability to void preferences: In the period leading up to bankruptcy, various constituencies may receive benefits from the company, such as pre-petition paydowns of debt or granting of collateral to backstop the debt. If these benefits occurred within 90 days before bankruptcy for third parties (or a year for insiders), the transactions would be subject to review by the bankruptcy court for possible return of the preferences to the estate. The transaction could be construed as being a preference if the recipient obtained more value than it would have in a hypothetical Chapter 7 liquidation.

Ability to effect "clean" sales: Sometimes financially distressed companies find it extremely difficult to consummate M&A and other transactions outside of bankruptcy because of concerns that the seller may subsequently fail. If the seller's creditors can show that the sale was for "inadequate value" and that the seller was insolvent at the time of the transaction, the buyer can be subject to substantial liabilities or other penalties. See the discussion of "fraudulent conveyance" in Chapter 7 of this book. Chapter 11 provides a venue in which companies may sell all or a significant portion of their assets, and, in such a sale, the court is able to give buyers essentially the cleanest title known to man – which is a powerful tool for the investment banker in restructuring a bankrupt company.

Taxes: When a company restructures its indebtedness, it frequently does so in a fashion in which the new consideration given by the company is worth materially less than the face amount of the original debt. This results in a tax gain to the company equal to the value differential, which can be offset by certain tax assets (such as net operating losses, or NOLs) in both in-court and out-of-court restructurings. NOLs simply represent prior losses that can be offset against future taxable income.

In connection with this "cancellation of indebtedness" (COD) issue, tax issues arise involving change of ownership. Section 382 of the Internal

Revenue Code sharply restricts a company's ability to use NOLs after a change of control. And a "change of control" means that large stockholders (owning more than 5% each) have traded more than 50% of the company's stock during the last three years. The interplay between Section 382 and COD can lead the company into several levels of purgatory. An analysis of examples is helpful.

Assume that the company has $100 million in NOLs and $100 million of COD income. If the company had no change of control before the transaction (either in or out of court) triggering the COD income, then the two amounts would offset, and hence the company would owe no tax.

However, if there had been a prior change of control, the use of the $100 million NOL would be curtailed. The annual usage of the NOL would equal the federal long-term tax-exempt rate, published monthly by the Internal Revenue Service, multiplied by the company's then-current equity market capitalization. For an insolvent company, the amount represented by this annual limitation, therefore, could be *de minimis*, due to the prior change of control occurring when the stock was depressed. In such case, the cash tax owed (at a 40% rate) would be almost $40 million in an out-of-court restructuring. Such a tax payment could be a deal killer.

This problem can be somewhat mitigated in Chapter 11. However, ultimately the piper (*i.e.*, Uncle Sam) must be paid, through reduction of tax basis in certain assets, or otherwise.

For those companies fortunate enough to have avoided a change of control, Chapter 11 can provide additional alternatives for companies whose NOLs exceed the COD income. After offsetting the COD income against the NOLs, there will be an excess. However, in most restructurings, there also will be a change of control as equity is given to debtholders – thereby triggering Section 382.

Outside of bankruptcy, annual utilization of the excess NOL can also be limited by the product of the federal tax-exempt rate and the pre-transaction equity value. In bankruptcy, the options are more varied. For example, it is possible in bankruptcy to preserve some of the NOL – without annual limitations. The downside of such election, though, is that if another change of control occurs within two years, the NOL is wiped out. And, also, there may be limits on the amount of claims that have traded during the restructuring process.

Sound complicated? Well, yes. And we have been deliberately imprecise here to spare the reader painful tax arcana. But, there are a few key take-aways. Monitor historical stock trading to see if Section 382 is at risk of being triggered. And if it can be prevented through a prohibition on insider sales, by all means try to stop it. And make sure a competent tax professional is on the case.

The failure to pay attention to these tax details can be fatal to restructuring the company. The premature triggering of Section 382 can cause a reorganization to be prohibitively expensive due to tax payments. The remedy may range from an extended stay in Chapter 11 to a piecemeal sale strategy designed to circumvent tax liabilities.

Debtors can use tax issues as weapons against unwanted suitors. Companies can petition bankruptcy courts to prevent claims trading and acquisition of claims by third parties under the guise of protecting tax attributes. Tax issues can even be used as negotiating "chips" in a restructuring.

GORDIAN KNOTS/Smithfield Foods

Smithfield Foods, Inc., the world's largest pork processor and hog producer and the fifth-largest beef supplier in the United States, engaged Gordian Group to advise it with respect to its interest in the pork assets of Farmland Industries. Farmland had filed for Chapter 11, and had rebuffed Smithfield's interest prior to the Chapter 11 filing.

Together with a bulge-bracket investment bank, Gordian Group advised the Smithfield executive committee on, among other things, potential distressed acquisition strategies, valuation and implementation mechanics.

Farmland was determined to block Smithfield from acquiring "back-door" control through a purchase of a controlling portion of Farmland's unsecured debt (one of several courses of action Gordian Group had considered). Accordingly, Farmland petitioned the bankruptcy judge to prohibit claims trading during the pendency of the bankruptcy proceedings, arguing that if sufficient claims traded, Farmland's tax options might be limited. The court complied with this request.

But with Gordian's advice, Smithfield was able to establish itself as a viable alternative to the standalone Plan of Reorganization that Farmland sought to implement. Ultimately, Smithfield's tactics limited Farmland's ability to effect a transaction without Smithfield being provided the opportunity to evaluate and price the assets. Smithfield became the stalking horse in a Section 363 auction in the bankruptcy court, and Gordian and its co-advisor advised Smithfield on the purchase price, transaction structure, the contents of the asset purchase agreement and bid procedures, and bid strategy.

Smithfield acquired the Farmland pork assets for a purchase price of $367 million, plus the assumption of $90 million in debt, and the acquisition has been a huge success for Smithfield.

These issues are complex and require a sophisticated and experienced tax counsel working with an investment banker to understand the options and decide how to approach these issues.

Just as Chapter 11 has its powerful benefits, it also has significant drawbacks. Bankruptcies can entail huge professional fees, rivaling the unsecured interest costs forgone in the case. The drain on management because of the time required to run the case is huge and can cause serious distractions that divert attention away from the business at critical times.

Evaluation of Litigation Values

There is a discernable trend that junior creditors are receiving recoveries lower than they have experienced in previous distressed cycles. Is this a result of bad economic and stock-market conditions? More leverage and, in particular, more senior leverage? More fraud? Whatever the cause, creditors are looking for alternate sources of recovery, and litigation has become an important tool.

The types of litigation pursued in restructuring situations vary widely. Among the possibilities are:

- Fraud or other malfeasance claims against management and the board, particularly when accounting problems surface. In general, these actions may be designed to achieve a recovery from the directors' and officers' insurance policy carrier, but in some circumstances, plaintiffs have been successful against other deep-pocketed defendants.
- Negligence and similar claims against professionals that failed to meet the levels of care required.

- Fraudulent conveyance actions against lenders and transaction counter-parties to recover monies paid out while the company was insolvent (this subject is discussed more fully in Chapter 7). An investment banker needs to work with litigation attorneys to assess the merits of such litigation and to assist in quantifying the extent of damages in these potential claims.

The Case for Old Equity and Management

Two schools of thought exist about how old equity and management should be treated in a restructuring. One school holds that restructurings should closely hew to the "absolute priority" system – no class of claims or interests gets any recovery until the more senior classes have been paid in full.

In short, the absolute priority rule of Section 1129 of the Bankruptcy Code provides that there is a cascading "waterfall" of value, starting at the top tier of creditor class. Unless the most senior creditor class receives a 100 percent recovery, no class of creditor or interest holder may receive any recovery. Continuing down the waterfall, if the top two creditor classes are paid in full and the third-highest ranking creditor class receives less than a 100% recovery, no creditor or equity holder ranked below can receive any recovery whatsoever.

The rule is clear, and it is the backdrop to most out-of-court negotiating scenarios. When the dialogue commences (almost invariably prior to a Chapter 11 filing) between a financially distressed company and its bondholders, the most pleasant sentiment the bondholders usually express to management is along the lines of "Hello, our bonds trade at significantly less than par, so we are the true economic owners of your company and you and old equity are now wiped out."

A minority school of thought – to which we adhere – advances the concept of an "equitable sharing of the pain," in which the many constituencies suffer varying degrees of compromise. In this view, old equity or management might be severely diluted but would still receive something meaningful. Old equity might, for example, receive a modest percentage of the equity outright, or it might receive a larger ownership position through a slug of warrants. Or it might be able to provide cash in connection with a restructuring plan that enabled it to buy back its ownership in the company. We note that, in a bankruptcy context, such a capital injection could come under close scrutiny.

The theoretical underpinnings of having old equity receive a material recovery stem from two fundamental economic issues. First, the old equity class can still have economic value, even if it is "out of the money" today. This reality springs from the concept of "option value." Such an option can indeed be worth a lot depending upon how far out of the money it is, the length of time before option expiration (*i.e.*, the consummation of the restructuring), and the degree of volatility in the underlying business.

The other issue is the concept of control. Old equity generally controls the board and the restructuring process, at least at the beginning. Even though the board and management owe fiduciary duties to a number of constituencies, we believe that – subject to the appropriate discharge of such duties – they still can, and should, negotiate on behalf of old equity. The control of the restructuring process gives them that ability.

This is no mere academic debate. Real money is at stake, and a lot of it. As we noted in our discussion of Tracor in Chapter 2, although old equity – pursuant to "conventional wisdom" – should have been wiped out, it was ultimately able to recover more than $300 million.

Imposing something other than absolute priority usually requires a consensual deal involving the debtor's key constituencies.

We have raised previously the issue of an investment banker's conflicts of interest, and this is perhaps the most important place where these may come into play. These conflicts are usually fatal for the interests of old equity and, often, for management. Where an investment banking firm (i) has a trading desk whose customers are bondholders of troubled companies and/or (ii) has as part of its financial advisory client base the same bondholders of troubled companies, that firm will have difficulty rendering unbiased advice that may siphon value away from bondholders in favor of old equity and management.

We believe the debtor's investment banker – if unconflicted (*i.e.,* derives no revenues from a company's bondholders), creative, clever and zealous in his pursuit of value for old equity (consistent with its fiduciary duties to the estate) – should be striving to allocate value in a manner inconsistent with the absolute priority rule. The investment banker should work with counsel to construct negotiating and other strategies that can encourage constituencies to reach agreement notwithstanding the absolute priority rule in order to enable recoveries for junior constituencies that would otherwise receive nothing.

These strategies might include creating classifications of voting interests that will advantage one constituency vs. another, developing "prisoner's dilemma" restructuring choices for creditors, and demonstrating that values may be far in excess of those perceived by other constituencies – thus potentially providing higher recoveries for lower-ranked classes. Clearly, old equity's recovery is incredibly sensitive not just to valuation ranges but to the company's ability to negotiate alternatives to the absolute priority rule.

CHAPTER 4—EQUITY AND ENTERPRISE VALUATION

Valuation of companies and their securities is integral to all aspects of investment banking and investments. In situations such as IPOs and mergers, the valuation exercise is the prelude to an actual transaction, and the valuation estimate is generally trumped by the subsequent reality of the marketplace. In restructurings, however, there may be no actual market test. Accordingly, in distressed situations, the valuation itself is frequently a key factor in how the size of the pie is eventually determined and then allocated. Our valuation work in the Tracor matter (discussed in Chapter 2) led directly to an unprecedented recovery for old equity.

The valuation of a company engaged in a restructuring may be determined through negotiations between two or more investment bankers representing competing constituencies. The stakes are high. Assume, for example, that a company has $100 million in debt. The debtholders' investment banker argues that the company's value is $90 million. The equity holders' investment banker argues that the company's value is $120 million. If the debtholders' investment banker prevails, old equity will be wiped out. If the equity holders' investment banker prevails, the old equity recovery could be substantial. In other words, to the winner of the valuation fight can go the spoils.

In this chapter, we will discuss various approaches to valuation, including:

- the comparable public company approach;
- the comparable transaction approach;
- the constant growth approach;
- the discounted cash flow (DCF) approach; and
- the leveraged refinancing transaction approach.

To these, we recommend adding a "sanity check," when possible, based on the actual trading of the target company's securities, particularly its debt securities.

In the course of this chapter, we also discuss different tactics used by competing financial advisors to advance their clients' positions.

The foregoing valuation approaches presume the context of the business being a "going concern," either as an operating entity or in a sale of the company. In most circumstances, this represents the highest value achievable for a company. However, if a company is not able to maintain these operating values (due to liquidity problems or otherwise), the company must look to the next best alternative. And that may be a liquidation.

Viewed at its most basic level, a liquidation valuation analysis assumes that the company promptly shuts its doors to stop the cash drain. All remaining assets would be disposed of through auctions or other sales and through attempts to collect on receivables. Specific valuation techniques vary by asset category, and are beyond the scope of this work. But suffice it to say that the recoveries can range from close to par (for very good receivables) to pennies on the dollar (for certain types of fixed assets). And then such aggregate values would need to be reduced by the fees and expenses of the liquidator.

Sometimes, it is also useful to examine whether the basic liquidation analysis can be modified to enhance values. For example, it may be better to continue to run the business in "wind-down" mode for a period of time. If the cash costs of operating the business are less than the increases in business values – relatively worthless inventories being converted into receivables – then such a strategy may make sense. But in any event (unless the company strikes oil under the corporate parking lot), liquidation values will very likely be well below going concern values.

GORDIAN KNOTS/CSG

Valuation determinations can also play a pivotal role in litigation settings.

The Heritage Fund II Investment Corporation, for example, had purchased Creative Solutions Group (CSG) from the Pentzer Corporation. In connection with the sale, Heritage claimed that CSG's prior earnings were materially lower than Pentzer had represented. Gordian Group was engaged as an expert by Choate, Hall & Stewart on behalf of Heritage and CSG in conjunction with litigation against Pentzer to recover damages for the alleged misrepresentations.

Gordian Group conducted its analysis and determined the fair market value of CSG as of the date of the acquisition, using "real" earnings levels. Gordian concluded that the fair market value of CSG was significantly lower than the price actually paid by Heritage, which guided the ultimate favorable settlement.

Valuation Overview

The underlying goal of valuations is to estimate at what price a company (or security) would trade between a willing buyer and a willing seller. In restructuring situations, particularly those not exposed to market tests, the task is more difficult, because the company is typically engaged in an operational turnaround. Accordingly, the investment banker needs to look beyond the current and historical financial performance to future projected periods in which the target company would hope to report significantly enhanced profitability.

As discussed in Chapter 3, the investment banker needs to conduct carefully a due diligence analysis leading to a credible forecast. Without the underpinnings of such a credible plan, the valuations themselves may lack credibility. One major area of spirited debate among financial advisors is the appropriate category of operating statistic(s) to which multiples should be applied to derive implied valuations. We do not favor one category over another, but prefer to look at a range of operating data and multiples. From time to time, certain categories may be more in vogue than others (a favorite these days being EBITDA, or Earnings Before Interest, Taxes, Depreciation and Amortization).

In recent years, many participants in restructurings seem to focus myopically on the question: "What is the *multiple*?," frequently referring to the "appropriate" EBITDA multiple.

In its simplest terms, a valuation multiple is the ratio of price (or value) to some operating statistic, such as earnings or book value. It lets an investor determine how expensive or cheap a particular company's stock is. For example, Company A, with a price/earnings ratio (P/E , or the ratio of stock price to earnings per share, or EPS) of 10 would require 10 years of earnings to earn back the price paid for the stock, assuming no growth in earnings. This is a lot "cheaper" than Company B, with a P/E ratio of 20.

If there are stocks trading at 10 times earnings, why would anyone want to buy one that trades at 20 times? Because certain investors believe that the stock with the higher multiple will have a higher long-term growth rate.

> *Assume both Company A and Company B trade for $10 per share; Company A's initial EPS will be $1.00 and Company B's will be $0.50. Over a 10-year period, no-growth Company A will earn $10.00 per share cumulatively. But if Company B's EPS grows at 15% annually, the 10-year earnings stream will aggregate $10.15 per share. Accordingly, the market balances near-term cash flows against long-term earnings prospects.*
>
> *Valuation multiples come in lots of flavors. The most widely known multiples in the popular press are based on the ratio of share price to a per-share figure (such as EPS or book value). These are known as equity value multiples because they are based solely on the values associated with the stock price.*
>
> *It has become increasingly popular in financial circles to use multiples that relate to the market value of the entire firm – the equity plus the debt, net of cash (the sum of which is called enterprise value). Accordingly, these are known as enterprise value multiples. The most common examples are enterprise value to sales, enterprise value to earnings before interest and taxes (EBIT) and enterprise value to EBITDA.*

Each approach represented by equity value multiples and enterprise value multiples has merit, and we think these methodologies are complementary. From these valuation metrics, advisors extrapolate the recoveries to various of the target company's constituencies based on forecasts of future-year profitability levels.

The very nature of the analytical process lends itself to a wide range of subjective interpretations. Forecasts on which the valuation is based could include base case, low case, high case, or any number of variants. Often, we see the bizarre spectacle of professionals negotiating the recoveries based on highly judgmental business plans – assuming that the "predicted" (and inherently imprecise) EBITDA level several years out is the appropriate metric to which to apply *the multiple.*

Assume, for example, that all the professionals in the case had agreed that the right EBITDA multiple for the company was 8, given current industry dynamics and financial market conditions. One problem with this approach is that multiples should vary based on the underlying facts (including company-specific facts). Now, further assume that the company was contemplating two sets of forecasts – one that involved "milking" the business over time, and the other that involved a substantial investment in activities that would support a high long-term growth rate. In the milking case, the EBITDA level three years out might be $100 million, leading the court to conclude that the future enterprise value would be $800 million. In the investment case, the investment program would likely be a drag on current earnings. If the near-term drag amounted to $20 million, the reduced EBITDA level of $80 million would translate into an enterprise value of only $640 million at the same 8 times multiple.

Does this make sense? We do not think so. The investment program – assuming the money was well spent – would be likely to generate higher long-term earnings growth. Higher growth prospects translate into higher earnings multiples. Assuming the investment program created $100 million of value in excess of that associated with the milking case (in other words, a $900 million future enterprise value), the multiple would increase significantly, from the static 8. The $900 million divided by $80 million would be a multiple of 11.3.

The point is that switching from one type of growth and investment scenario to another should change "the multiple" significantly.

Even if the professionals approach valuation on a more rigorous basis than simply determining *the multiple,* each investment banker could assign different probabilities, risk assessments or discount rates to the achievement of such financial forecasts. Or the investment banker could create different scenarios that might contemplate divestitures of various operations. Such differing subjective interpretations and scenarios could lead to widely varying conclusions.

Sound confusing? It frequently is, as different professionals set forth seemingly cogent arguments to buttress their respective positions. As a result, we think that the outcome of the valuation negotiations sometimes centers not so much on which is the "right" value, but on what will be the most "believable" value in the eyes of a bankruptcy court.

GORDIAN KNOTS/Federal Communications Commission, State of Vermont

Gordian Group was called in to advise the Federal Communications Commission (FCC) in connection with the bankruptcy of certain failed "C-Block" telecommunications licensees that included Next Wave, Pocket Communications and other companies. These companies had won auctions for spectrum licenses, but ultimately had failed commercially, and they owed almost $12 billion through obligations secured by the spectrum licenses.

These matters involved numerous difficult issues such as license re-auction values, merger market issues and valuation of business plans – all in the context of complicated governmental policy goals.

An important part of Gordian Group's assignment was to offer advice to the FCC regarding the realization of value on its claims, in light of government policy objectives and other key matters. Our valuation views enabled the government to stay the course and ultimately prevail both in consensual C-Block restructurings and fraudulent conveyance litigation.

In another instance involving government regulatory authorities and policy objectives, Gordian Group was retained to advise the State of Vermont. The two largest utilities in the state, Central Vermont Public Service and Green Mountain Power, had entered into very high-cost power purchase arrangements, including long-term supply contracts with Hydro-Québec and a number of independent power producers, as well as obligations with respect to the Vermont Yankee nuclear facility. The aggregate value of these "stranded costs" exceeded $1 billion – a huge sum for Vermont.

The State engaged Gordian Group to advise it in connection with the effect on the utilities of various levels of rate relief. Gordian Group analyzed overall values, likely securities prices and solvency under a variety of scenarios that contemplated securitizations, rejections of contracts in bankruptcy and various out-of-court renegotiation possibilities.

The Comparable Approaches to Valuation

As Mark Twain once said, "There are lies, damned lies and statistics."

We believe that the most reliable approaches to valuation generally are based on actual market-related information. The theory underlying these methodologies is that actual money passed hands based on current public securities trading prices or historical merger transactions with similar companies. The financial operations and financial metrics associated with such securities and deals (such as price-earnings or enterprise value-to-operating-profit) are then applied to the target company's operating statistics to determine valuation.

Despite the market-based appeal of these approaches, they suffer from a number of drawbacks, including the selection of the appropriate comparables, the right operating statistics, the dates associated with any comparable transaction, and the presence of fraud or other irregularities. The first opportunity for a major disagreement among advisors using a comparable approach arises in the construction of a "comparable universe." In the ideal world (which never exists, of course), the investment banker will develop a group of public comparables that will be in the same industry and have similar growth prospects to the target. In practice, there may be a dearth of truly similar companies, so "comparables" could be far afield in terms of business, growth and profitability.

The occurrence of such wide comparable ranges creates an opportunity for the varying constituencies' professionals to adopt different clusters of data as the "most comparable." In the most cynical view, the senior classes (which would be advocating a lower valuation to enable them to acquire relatively more stock of the reorganized company than junior classes) would deem companies with low multiples of earnings to be comparable, while the junior classes might conversely strive to find data points with very high multiples.

As a result, the use of multiples – without appropriate judgments layered on – is itself potentially misleading. The potential for mischief abounds.

The comparable multiple may be high simply because the comparable's current earnings are depressed: one way to get a high multiple is through a high valuation and another is to have poor earnings. So, such a multiple may be misleading and its use – generally to apply to "normalized" future earnings of the target – should be suspect.

Even if the comparable earnings multiple is not artificially inflated because of depressed earnings, it may still be inappropriate to apply an historical (or even current) multiple to the target company's future earnings. High multiples are generally associated with high prospective growth rates. If a comparable company or industry is currently experiencing a period of high growth – which is expected to moderate in coming years – then such a company is likely to experience a decline in its multiples over time. As a result, it may be inappropriate to assign the comparable's high current multiple to the target company's future (post-turnaround) earnings.

When using multiples, it is extremely important to understand what historical or forecasted period they are being used for.

Company X (a "comparable" company) has just completed its fiscal year, and earned $0.50 per share. Wall Street is forecasting EPS of $0.75 for next year and $1.00 for the year after. The stock is trading for $10 a share. Arithmetically, Company X is trading at P/E ratios representing 20.0 times latest 12 months (LTM) EPS, 13.3 times next year EPS and 10.0 times the following year EPS.

How are you supposed to interpret all this and then apply it to your target company?

Clearly, the changing multiples for Company X are a function of its growth rate. The analyst needs to incorporate an understanding of Company X's growth profile into the forecasts for the target company. Without understanding how the two companies' growth prospects compare, it would be hard for the analyst to have a view as to whether the multiple applied to the target company should be on LTM earnings (20 times) or two-year-out forecasted earnings (10 times).

A related gambit with respect to the use of comparables is based on the concept of statistical averages. Some analysts may focus on overall group averages, some on a subset of the overall group, and some on only one or two of the "closest" comparables. No single approach is necessarily superior in all cases. We observe a great deal of subjectivity associated with the assembly of the data parameters, which leads to significant opportunity for valuation disingenuousness. Even within a well-defined group, these can be problems. Many analysts use an "average" multiple to apply to the target company. However, if the target is materially better (or worse) than the group, its appropriate multiples may be higher (or lower) than the average.

When using a transactional data set (*e.g.*, comparable merger deals) to determine comparable values, an additional opportunity looms for reaching misleading conclusions. The validity of historical merger multiples is predicated on buyers currently willing to pay what buyers historically paid for similar companies – possibly under different circumstances.

Sometimes, such historical data sets comprise transactions that occurred over a relatively long time period. Certain historical deals may have occurred at times during which dramatically different financial market conditions prevailed. Such deals may have occurred at times when the companies were experiencing different long-term growth opportunities than those currently available – which would have a major impact on multiples.

As a result, these historical transactional multiples are, at best, a guide as to valuation. They also need to be used in concert with market knowledge of the identity of likely buyers and those buyers' financial wherewithal, in order to determine if there is a good fit with the prospective target.

> *Multiples also reflect the amount of control and degree of liquidity that the investor is getting.*
>
> *Prices of publicly traded common stocks typically represent a minority ownership position with relatively little or no control over the decisions of the enterprise, but which can be monetized easily.*
>
> *Frequently, investors hold common stock in public companies that may be restricted from public sale for various reasons. In such cases, the value of the restricted securities is generally significantly below the levels of the liquid stock. Rules of thumb for such illiquidity discounts range from 20% to 50%.*
>
> *On the other hand, prices paid in M&A transactions for control of a company may reflect a premium over prevailing public market prices. The buyer may be willing to pay more than the public market because it can effect changes in the company's operations, such as integrating it with the buyer's own operations to achieve efficiencies. However, if the purchase of a company would subject the buyer to onerous license agreements or non-competes, the merger buyer may not even be willing to pay the prevailing public market price.*
>
> *There are numerous variations on these themes, and the analyst must always understand the context from which the multiples were derived. Applying M&A multiples in a mechanical fashion, without sober reflection and analysis, to a reorganization plan may generate misleading results.*

Constant Growth Approach

Together with the related DCF approach (described below), the constant growth approach is one of the preferred methodologies of the academic world. This method is a prospective approach and determines the value of a firm based upon a mathematical formula:

$$\text{Enterprise Value} = \frac{\text{Cash flow}}{\text{Cost of Capital} - \text{Growth Rate}}$$

Where:

Cash Flow = After-tax unleveraged cash flow (next year's)
Cost of Capital = Weighted average cost of capital (WACC – see below)
Growth Rate = Long-term (perpetual) growth in Cash Flow.

In the previous sections regarding comparables, we discussed the concept of value as the product of cash flow (or earnings) and a multiple. The multiple is embedded in the formula above as follows:

$$\text{Multiple} = \frac{1}{\text{Cost of Capital} - \text{Growth Rate}}$$

Using the comparable approach, we had to determine only one number – the multiple itself. However, with the constant growth approach, we need to determine two parameters.

The company's cost of capital is determined by its cost of equity, its cost of debt, and the relative mix of both. The cost of equity is based on a set of formulas that have earned Nobel Prizes for several academicians. We believe the theory is right. Even so, the real-world calculations of such parameters can be problematic (see Chapter 6).

After determination of the equity cost of capital, the analyst needs to calculate the cost of debt capital. There are various approaches to doing this, but one common methodology contemplates using the pro forma financial leverage characteristics of the target and calculating the cost of the senior debt portion, the cost of any junk bonds, and so on (determining the cost of debt capital is discussed in Chapter 5).

The firm's after-tax weighted average cost of capital (WACC) is calculated from the foregoing components. The equity cost of capital is multiplied by the equity percentage in the pro forma capital structure. The after-tax debt cost of capital is determined by multiplying the debt percentage by the debt cost of capital – and then by multiplying by the complement of the tax rate (100% minus the tax rate) in order to account for the tax shield associated with the deductibility of interest for tax purposes.

The equity component and the debt component are then added together to derive the firm's WACC.

Because of the myriad different statistical inferences an analyst is supposed to make, there are innumerable opportunities for error, and the analyst needs to start with some common sense.

> *In most equity market environments, a useful rule of thumb for the required equity market rate of return is probably 4% to 6% over the 10- or 20-year U.S. Treasury yield, give or take 1%. At a 4% 10- or 20-year Treasury yield, that would imply a 8% to 10% required return.*
>
> *If the target company's securities are expected to be more risky than the overall market, the analyst might want to add one to two percentage points to account for that, possibly through the use of what is known as a "small company premium." Alternately, the analyst can increase the cost of capital for "company specific" reasons. In other words, for restructured companies using this example, 9% to 12% may represent a reasonable expectation. If the statistically calculated results differed materially from such rate, the analyst may wish to re-examine the work.*
>
> *Other factors can significantly affect the appropriate discount rate. Companies with lots of current assets that can be financed with low-cost bank debt may have a lower WACC than originally envisioned. In contrast, a restructured company that is small and illiquid may require a higher cost of equity capital to account for such factors.*
>
> *In any event, the actual derivation of a company's WACC may be more of an art than a science.*

The next step in the constant growth formula is the determination of the perpetual growth rate. As the word suggests, this is the growth rate of cash flows into infinity.

Some analysts attempt to construct this number by estimating the real growth potential of the firm (possibly as a function of population growth or some other metric) and factoring in the estimated long-term inflation rate. Or they try to extrapolate historical trends in the business.

In any event, forecasting into infinity is a subjective matter. But it is necessary for this methodology.

The multiple is the inverse of the difference between the WACC and the growth rate. For example, if the WACC is 11% and the perpetual growth rate is 5%, the differential is 6%. The inverse of 6% is a multiple of 16.7 times.

We fully recognize the limitations inherent in this subjective approach. Nevertheless, we admit to being fans of this constant growth model. Appropriate comparable companies or transactions do not always exist. And if they do, the results may be misleading.

We think that the constant growth model is a good way for an analyst to explore whether the multiples developed through comparable analyses make sense. For example, if "comparables" suggest a high multiple for a low-growth company, the perpetual growth model may be able to lead an analyst to a more reliable conclusion.

Discounted Cash Flow Approach

The basic concept of the DCF approach, which is also prospective in nature, is sound and straightforward: the value of a business is equal to the present value of the after-tax cash flows it is expected to generate in the future. This requires a forecast of such cash flows and a determination of the discount rate needed to calculate their present value. The DCF methodology is subject to substantial subjective interpretation.

The DCF approach is also necessarily dependent upon a believable set of multiyear projections for the target company, and adoption of one set of projections over another could easily have a material impact on valuation. Furthermore, it is impractical to develop a set of projections that stretches into infinity. Financial analysts generally use annual cash flows from a three- to five-year forecast and calculate a terminal value based on the last forecast year's earnings or cash flow.

In turnaround situations, companies frequently generate only modest amounts of cash flow in the initial years after a restructuring. Accordingly, a substantial portion, if not all, of the target company's DCF value may come from the terminal value. This places a huge degree of importance on both the cash flow forecast several years from now, with all its associated imprecision, and the multiple used to translate such cash flow into the terminal value.

The DCF approach is designed to assess value based upon a stream of future cash flows. The formula for the DCF approach is:

$$\text{Present Value} = \sum_{n=1}^{\infty} \frac{CF_n}{(1+r)^n}$$

where
CF = After-tax cash flows
n = period (generally measured in years)
r = required discount rate

However, as a "convenience," the methodology contemplates the use of a terminal value after several forecast years to serve as a proxy for cash flows occurring after that.

As a result, the formula becomes:

$$\text{Present Value} = \sum_{n=1-5}^{5} \frac{CF_n}{(1+r)^n} + \frac{TV}{(1+r)^5}$$

where TV = Terminal Value

Assume that a company will generate $10 million of after-tax cash flow in each of the next five years. Also assume an $80 million terminal value and a 12% discount rate. The DCF value of the company is $81 million. The net present value of the terminal value represents $45 million of this amount, or 56%.

Now assume that the company will instead break even for the first four years, generate $10 million of after-tax cash flow in the fifth year and have the same $80 million terminal value and 12% discount rate. The resultant DCF value of the company is $51 million. The net present value of the terminal value is still $45 million – but now represents 89% of the total value.

This is a relationship characteristic of many restructuring situations. The terminal value accounts for substantially all of (and sometimes more than all of) the overall value. Which means that this is not really a DCF model at all. Rather, it is simply a mechanism for putting a multiple on forecasted cash flow, or earnings, several years out and discounting the result back to the present.

One common way to determine terminal value is to apply multiples to the forecasted cash flows and earnings levels (it is almost always preferable to look at a variety of financial metrics – such as net income, EBITDA and cash flow, as well as revenues – rather than just a single one). Such multiples are generally based in some measure on current multiples derived from the comparable approach. Or the analyst can construct a terminal value based upon the constant growth method.

Leveraged Refinancing Approach

A variant of the DCF approach is to examine the target company in the way that many leveraged buyout (LBO) investors do.

This approach often starts with an assessment of the target company's senior debt capacity. Under most market conditions, this is the cheapest form of financing, and companies may seek to maximize its utilization to decrease overall capital costs. Depending upon market conditions, the facility size may be constrained to that associated with a formula-based working capital line, or to a modest multiple of operating cash flow.

Depending upon the financial and operating characteristics of the target company, there may be an opportunity to raise one or more junior debt tranches. In general, these debt instruments are likely to be considered "high yield" – that is, junk bonds. The financing costs associated with these securities would be predicated on a number of factors, including whether the bonds could be issued in the public markets or if the issuer would have to resort to private sources.

This pro forma capital structure is then evaluated in the context of the target company's business plan. Any excess cash generated during the projection period is generally used to repay debt.

The analyst will determine an enterprise value at the end of the three- to five-year forecast period, possibly by applying an appropriate EBIT, EBITDA, or constant growth multiple. It is also standard practice to evaluate whether the implied valuation makes sense by determining other resultant multiples, such as price-earnings ratios. The net debt at the end of the forecast period is subtracted from such enterprise value to arrive at the terminal equity value.

In private equity capital markets, it is customary to seek relatively high annual returns (at least 25% to 35%) on leveraged investments such as these. Such returns are not necessarily consistent with those associated with the CAPM approach discussed above, which rely on Beta.

Discounting the terminal equity value back to the present at a 25% to 35% return yields a sense of how private financial investors would approach valuation of the target company. Given such investors' high level of importance in the turnaround world, this type of analysis provides as an important benchmark.

Valuation for Fun and Profit

If, after all this work, the investment banker is convinced his or her analysis is "bulletproof" (generally, the younger the investment bankers, the more convinced they are), then he or she can try to take advantage of it. Starting with the investment banker's estimate of enterprise value, she or he can than "distribute" it one layer at a time to the company's varying constituencies in a pro forma analysis.

First, the banker deducts any amounts owed to the DIP lenders and to holders of administrative claims (post-petition trade and professionals). The remainder is the amount available for pre-petition claims and interests.

Then, the banker splits any secured claims into their "money-good" and under-secured portions. The "money-good" portion represents the underlying value of the collateral – frequently calculated on a liquidation basis (see above). In practice, this may be difficult to estimate without detailed information unavailable to the public (and unless the banker is an insider, he or she will have to deal with this information limitation). If the investment banker is looking at a purchase of the bank debt, such information may be available through the selling bank. However, if the investment banker is investigating the value of more junior claims, he or she may elect to make the conservative assumption that the bank debt above such junior claims is all "money good."

The investment banker would then subtract the secured value of the pre-petition debt from the amount available for all pre-petition claims and interests to arrive at the amount available for unsecured claims. If any of the "secured" debt is actually under-secured, such under-secured portion would be added to the total unsecured claims.

Can the investment banker then divide the amount available for unsecureds by the total unsecured claims to determine recovery percentages? Generally not.

Unsecured claims can arise at different legal entities. And each such entity can have materially different relationships between its respective values and claims. There may also be inter-company guarantees and sharing of collateral. And the debtor may elect to reject certain executory contracts – which will increase cash flows, but also increase unsecured claims. The investment banker needs to work through all of these complex interrelationships.

And then there is the fact that many claims are expressly subordinated to others. In a "strict priority" world, the senior claims would have to have a par recovery before the junior claims could get anything. However, as noted elsewhere, we frequently do not live in a strict priority world. In practice, this dynamic is often resolved through a negotiation between the senior and subordinated holders in which the seniors get a relatively higher recovery. For example, seniors may get an 80% recovery and juniors may get a 20% recovery.

And some claims (like trade claims) may forfeit recoveries if they have been found to have received pre-petition preferences. The investment banker also needs to understand how contingent claims (such as environmental or pension obligations) can swell the amount of unsecured claims needing to be satisfied.

Then there is the question of what old equity will receive.

In short, it is a complex exercise. Mistakes in assumptions as to valuation, priority of claims, validity of legal entities and negotiating dynamics can all lead to misleading answers.

A Sanity Check

In connection with developing valuation views, the investment banker should also look at the actual trading prices of the target company's securities.

To be sure, we do not believe that markets are even close to being efficient in all restructuring cases. In numerous instances, common stock prices of bankrupt companies trade at substantial market value levels – in situations where it is inconceivable that the equity could receive any recovery at all.

Nevertheless, we believe that certain securities prices – particularly those of junk bonds – provide a useful window into what knowledgeable market participants believe the target company is worth. These trades have their own drawbacks: they reflect relatively illiquid market conditions, high levels of uncertainty as to the outcome of the restructuring, imperfect knowledge of the company's operations, and the high rates of financial return sought by such distressed debt buyers. In other words, the conclusions of the market reflected in the bond price are not perfect. But they may be helpful.

In order to translate these prices into an enterprise value, the investment banker could multiply the trading prices of one or more impaired classes of unsecured claims by the aggregate amount of those claims. To the sum of such market-adjusted claims, one could add the bank debt or the discounted value of the bank debt, if it were trading at a material discount, and subtract the cash (net of restructuring expenses).

Material differences between the "sanity check" values and the investment banker's value determination can be an opportunity for trading profit if the analyst is correct. Or vice versa. In the event of major differences, the analyst needs to re-check his approach.

CHAPTER 5—DEBT CAPACITY AND VALUATION

Everything else being equal in the everyday world, the after-tax cost of debt is cheaper than that of equity. Debt is higher up in the capital structure, so it requires a lower rate of return than equity. And it also enjoys a significant tax benefit (assuming the company is profitable) – the interest payments are deductible. Therefore, a company's controlling shareholders often like to increase, even maximize, the amount of debt on the balance sheet. This simple truth underlies most major financial train wrecks that we have experienced.

The amount of debt a company can incur from third-party sources is a function of a number of factors, including the quality of its collateral (particularly accounts receivable and inventory), the level of and predictability of its cash flows, its size (a larger company can generally borrow relatively more than a smaller one) and its access to alternate sources of capital, as well as the nature of the company's industry and capital markets conditions at the time.

The pricing of the debt can vary widely – even within the same capital structure. Senior secured, floating-rate debt may carry a cost hundreds of basis points below long-term fixed-rate unsecured bonds. More restrictive financial covenants can result in a better debt instrument and lower interest charges – at the cost of hamstringing the company at a later date if things go wrong. Changes in capital markets conditions can also dramatically affect pricing of various debt instruments, particularly high-yield ("junk") bonds.

The amount and pricing of its debt can affect the overall enterprise value of a company. On the one hand, the tax shield associated with the deductibility of interest can lower the company's cost of capital and increase overall values. However, a high level of debt can result in the need to direct cash flows toward debt repayments rather than to investments that would facilitate growth. In certain cases, high levels of debt may make the company a target for competitors that perceive weakness. Such dynamics would obviously reduce overall values. The tradeoff among these factors is frequently a subject of heated debate among a company's constituencies during a reorganization.

For simplicity's sake, we are confining our discussion of fixed income instruments to bonds, but many of our observations may apply to preferred stock, as well.

Overall Debt Capacity

In restructuring scenarios, knowing a company's debt capacity and pricing is critical. The company and its financial advisors have the ability to incur new debt to refinance the old capital structure. Such new debt can be obtained either through third-party lenders or by giving existing creditors new debt instruments. These parameters may be the subject of intense negotiations in a restructuring – particularly if the new debt instruments are to be exchanged for obligations of existing constituencies.

There is no one simple way to compute debt capacity. Although various market participants frequently use aggregate rules of thumb (5 times LTM EBITDA, for example), such arbitrary guidelines can be misleading – particularly in restructurings where EBITDA levels may be expected to increase dramatically.

Instead, an analysis of debt capacity should be developed, one instrument at a time. The amount of senior secured debt is a function of collateral coverage and perhaps of predictable cash flows. The amount of other debt is a function of overall firm values, interest costs and cash flows. The debt capacity of the firm is the sum of all of the above – after deducting an appropriate liquidity reserve for growth and contingencies. As a sanity check, it never hurts to apply various industry rules of thumb.

Term Structure of Interest Rates

Some interest rates are fixed, some are floating. Some are based on short-term maturities, some on longer-term ones. These differences can make comparisons confusing and misleading.

In most market environments, floating rates are lower than fixed rates. While a fixed rate established now will remain constant over the life of the loan, a floating rate may increase or decrease over time. Accordingly, to state that a company's current secured borrowing cost of 3% (floating) is below its long-term unsecured borrowing cost of 6% (fixed) tells only part of the story. The use of collateral to backstop a secured loan is itself a cost that needs to be factored in (see "Asset-Based Lending" below).

There is no one right way to compare fixed and floating alternatives. However, one useful tool to calibrate such markets is to construct a hypothetical interest-rate swap to turn the floating-rate loan into its fixed-rate equivalent. Such analysis can add several hundred basis points (each basis point is one hundredth of a percentage point) to the "true" fixed-rate equivalent cost of the floating-rate alternative. Although this adjustment will not account for the secured vs. unsecured dichotomy, it does provide a partial "apples to apples" comparison.

Similarly, long-term fixed rates are higher than shorter-term ones under most market conditions we experience. There are various ways to account for this difference, including the use of the differential between U.S. Treasury rates for government bonds of the two different maturities, as well as a similar analysis for corporate bonds. Without such adjustment, stating that one alternative is more or less expensive than another is likely to tell only part of the story.

> *There are a number of different ways to calculate interest rates, and none of them is necessarily the one correct way. Consumer interest may be calculated on the basis of daily compounding, or of simple interest. Some calculations use each day of a 365-day year, while others use 360 – in the form of 12 30-day months.*
>
> *For public bonds, the convention is to use two semiannual periods to calculate the yield. The analyst will calculate the number of semiannual periods remaining (including any fractions of a period), and divide the annual cash coupon by two (to get the semiannual portion). The resultant yield data for this "bond equivalent method" is multiplied by two (in order to annualize) and will be slightly higher than the yield determined by the continuous daily compounding method. In this book, we generally use the bond equivalent method.*

Asset-Based Lending

At or near the top of the capital structure pecking order are the senior secured lenders. In many cases, these lenders will base their loans largely upon the amount and nature of working capital collateral that a company has available – primarily accounts receivable and inventory. In theory, even if the company were to shut down and liquidate, these lenders would be able to collect cash from receivables and to sell the inventory at prices that would make the lenders "whole," net of collection costs.

Lenders may perceive that receivables are generally a company's strongest form of collateral, given that its customers have already accepted delivery of goods or services and that the receivable represents a promise to pay within a month or two. Because of this collateral strength, lenders frequently advance 65% to 85% of the face amount of "eligible" receivables. Such eligible amounts exclude receivables associated with issues like overdue payments and excessively high concentrations of receivables with a single customer or industry.

Such an advance rate range of 65% to 85% is dependent upon specific market conditions at any one time, as well as potential problems related to receivable collections. It is common for customers in certain industries to attempt to refuse payment on receivables owed to bankrupt companies. An automobile manufacturer, for example, may claim that the sheet steel previously shipped by a steel manufacturer has subsequently been found to contain defects. Such claims (whether valid or not) would increase the risk and costs of collection. Accordingly, asset-based lenders tend to use lower advance rates in situations where they find a material likelihood of such prospective collection problems.

In certain situations, it may even be possible to establish a receivables trust or other entity that could issue "receivables-backed" securities. These entities have come to be known as "bankruptcy remote vehicles" (BRVs). We have been involved in restructurings (such as Zale) where this technique was used. The theory behind such financings is that thc BRV is immune to any subsequent bankruptcy of the related company. In turn, this makes the trust a stronger credit, with lower borrowing costs. We acknowledge, however, that in another case (LTV) in which we were involved, the judge ignored the structural niceties of the BRV and allowed the estate to invade it and use the money. Go figure.

Inventories can generally be categorized into finished goods, work-in-progress and raw materials. Depending upon the situation, lenders may give dramatically different advance rates to inventories of different classifications. For finished products that can be readily sold to a large number of customers without further modification, the advance rate might be relatively high. For custom products with a single customer, the lender's willingness to advance much, if anything, may be very limited. For raw materials, advance rates will similarly reflect whether such inventories can be readily sold to other firms in sufficient quantities. For work-in-progress (where additional expenditures would be required to turn the goods into finished products), a lender might not be willing to advance anything.

The company will periodically prepare a summary of eligible receivables and inventories, called the "borrowing base." Against this borrowing base, the lender will apply its respective advance rates to determine the amount that may be drawn at any one time.

Depending upon negotiations between the lender and the borrower, maximum borrowings may be greater or lesser than what the formulas indicate. The lender may initially establish a "reserve" that reduces the formula-derived borrowings to give it more cushion. Conversely, the lender might agree to extend an "overline," which would allow the company to borrow a greater amount for some period of time. The overline might be backstopped by additional collateral, such as fixed assets. To the extent that the overline is more or less permanent, it might be based upon an earnings test (*e.g.*, bank debt should be no more than 2 times LTM EBITDA).

The secured lender may make other modifications to the lending arrangements. Typically, the lender has the right to establish any additional reserves it deems appropriate, from time to time – thereby lowering the amount that the company can borrow.

This type of financing arrangement gives the lender enormous control over the borrower. The lender has a collateral interest in some of the best assets. This can result in a tremendous potential cost for the company if it subsequently needs liquidity desperately (without unencumbered collateral, it may not be able to obtain such liquidity). The lender typically has the unfettered ability to decrease the borrowing availability and may have the contractual right to call the loan at any time. In most cases, the lender will have the benefit of financial covenants that provide even more control over the borrower.

So why would a company want to incur debt on such terms? The answer is twofold – need and cost.

Companies involved in restructuring activities may not have access to such debt on more favorable terms. Their historical track records and prospectively high leverage may preclude them from obtaining unsecured borrowings. Accordingly, the asset-based market may be the only viable source of credit.

Second, for reorganizing companies, these asset-based loans may be the cheapest form of financing by far. The cost of borrowing would be a "spread" over a floating-rate index such as Prime or LIBOR (the London Inter-Bank Offered Rate). In virtually all market conditions, this would result in a savings of several hundred basis points from what the company could borrow on unsecured fixed-rate terms.

Other Senior Secured Financings

In certain restructurings, the company may have already pledged its receivables and inventory as collateral for a loan – or may not have "good" working capital assets at all. Or it may have less working capital collateral than would realistically support a loan of the size it needs. In such circumstances, the company may still be able to obtain a secured facility on more advantageous terms than would be available for a conventional unsecured loan. The issuer can have second lien secured debt, behind "fully secured" first lien debt.

The reserve-based fixed assets of natural resource companies can serve as excellent collateral for a loan. The fixed assets of wholly-owned profitable processing facilities (*e.g.*, refineries) can also be attractive. Until the telecom sector melted down, some lenders readily loaned on the basis of fiber optic cable and other purchased assets. In certain cases, equity interests in profitable joint ventures that are saleable could serve as valuable collateral. The list goes on.

It may be possible to structure a parent-level loan facility that achieves structural superiority without actually granting security interests in assets. Instead, the new loan could be guaranteed by wholly-owned subsidiaries – thereby giving the lenders a better instrument than other unsecured debt at the same parent level.

These types of creative financings for distressed companies are not easily pigeonholed into descriptions of structure, collateral, maturity or fixed vs. floating rate. Given their unconventional nature and the relatively few potential lenders, their pricing tends to be relatively expensive for secured loans – somewhere between the asset-based alternative discussed above and unsecured alternatives.

"Straight" Unsecured Debt

"Straight" debt is just plain debt, without any equity "kickers" or conversion features. It may be public or private, high yield or investment grade, short or long term. It may be senior or subordinated. Generally, it refers to fixed-rate obligations, although there are exceptions.

The fundamental key to the value and pricing of such instruments is the credit quality of the issuer. Credit quality is generally determined by a number of ratios that measure factors such as debt to cash flow, cash flow coverage of fixed charges, earnings coverage of interest, and debt to equity (both balance sheet and market-based). We note that such ratios must be calculated on a "pro forma" basis for a company engaged in a restructuring, because the capital structure is likely to be dramatically different in the future.

> *Financial analysts determine comparable credit statistics for distressed companies in a fashion similar to that used in equity valuation analysis. First, the analyst creates a "universe" of issuers as similar as possible to the company in terms of industry, size and other factors. As there are far fewer issuers of public debt than of public equity, the degree of comparability may necessarily be less than that in an equity analysis.*
>
> *For each company, the analyst calculates various credit ratios based upon historical data (e.g., LTM or three-year average) and compares such statistics to those of the target company (LTM pro forma, three-year average pro forma, forecast).*
>
> *In parallel with the credit comparison, the analyst will calculate various yields for the bonds associated with each issuer, including the yield to maturity (YTM) and the yield to worst (YTW). In connection with this analysis, the analyst will frequently exclude bonds that have significantly different maturities and may exclude bonds that have materially different issue sizes. The analyst will then correlate the various yield data to the credit statistics of the comparable group.*
>
> *Based upon such calculations, the analyst determines where the target company falls within the overall range of credit quality observed. The analyst may also make some subjective assessments of the target company's credit statistics in light of its size and other factors – including whether the bonds are senior or subordinated. This "positioning" will enable the analyst to develop a view of where the target company's bonds would fit in the credit quality vs. yield matrix.*
>
> *As a cautionary note, we point out that yield data regarding "comparable" bonds in the distressed marketplace can be highly misleading. A bond close to default might be trading at 38 cents on the dollar, representing*

a calculated YTM of 40%. Yet, if the bond is really likely to default, the 40% yield statistic is largely meaningless. Instead, the pricing may be more representative of an expectation that the company will be restructured at a future date at a value materially less than 100 cents. Accordingly, analysts should be highly wary of deriving meaning from any public bond yield data in excess of 25% or so.

And, of course, the analyst should look at credit rates and yield data for various broad categories promulgated by the ratings agencies. However, given the reservations we have expressed elsewhere about the ratings agencies, this example may best be viewed as a "sanity check."

No one ratio is necessarily superior to others, and, as with equities, it is useful to look at a number of them at the same time. Moreover, these ratios may produce dramatically different results on a LTM basis vs. projections – given that the target company is in the midst of a financial restructuring.

There are also several less quantitative factors that may be considered in assessing overall credit quality, including the size of the company, its industry and whether it is public.

In credit analysis, size does matter. Larger companies tend to be more diversified and are generally better able to withstand the adverse impacts of a major shock. Accordingly, all else being equal, with two companies having identical credit ratios, the larger company would be considered the stronger credit. Industry conditions also matter. It may be hard to find a stellar, creditworthy company in a troubled industry.

Access to alternate sources of capital is also important. Should a problem arise, lenders appreciate a company's ability to tap the financial markets for additional liquidity. One indicator of this ability is whether a company is public – and whether the ratio of public market capitalization to debt is healthy.

After examining various comparable credit ratios (including those for industry competitors that do not have extant bonds), the investment banker will have a sense of where other companies' ratios lie. This can prove useful in developing a capital structure for the target company. For example, if the company's key competitors maintain an EBITDA-to-interest ratio of 2, this might be a good metric to target in the forecast.

In addition, the company should integrate various pro forma debt levels into its business plan to see how much debt the company can "afford."

This is essentially a solvency analysis. The analyst needs to measure various coverage and liquidity ratios to check that the company will remain healthy, even when downside operating cases are run. The analyst also needs to determine if the company will likely be in a position to effect necessary refinancings down the road.

If the company's pro forma leverage is not "excessive," the restructuring plan can pass muster as to "feasibility." To be "feasible," a plan should demonstrate a reasonable probability that the company will not have to restructure again. Otherwise, it's back to the drawing board. Perhaps to lower the amount of debt. Or perhaps to sell a non-core property to raise more cash. Or perhaps to "tweak" the amount of interim cash interest payments, as set forth below.

Deferred-Coupon Debt

Turnarounds and restructurings are frequently marked by expectations that a company's future cash flows will be substantially greater than those available at present. In other words, the company may not be able to make cash interest payments on debt today, but it may be able to do so in a couple of years. These dynamics create an opportunity for the use of deferred-coupon debt.

In the most extreme case, deferred-coupon debt is a zero-coupon bond – no payments until a final one at maturity. In practice in the restructuring world, however, cash interest payments typically begin within one to five years of the date of issuance because of the perceived risk of waiting longer for any cash payment.

There are various ways to achieve the deferred-interest feature. The most common are payment-in-kind (PIK) bonds and split-coupon bonds.

A PIK bond generally gives the issuer the option of satisfying an interest payment obligation through the issuance of more bonds, rather than cash. For example, a company with a 10% annual coupon on $100 million of bonds could satisfy its semiannual interest obligation through payment of either $5 million in cash or $5 million in face amount of new bonds with identical features. At the end of the PIK period, the company would be required to pay cash interest thereafter.

A split-coupon instrument operates with slightly different dynamics to similar effect. For the initial period (one to five years), no payments are made, in cash or in kind. During this period, the bond acts largely as a zero-coupon bond, with the intent that the value of the security accretes to face value by the end of the deferral period. After that, the bond pays its stated coupon in cash. Its price at such later date would be a function of the coupon rate vs. the company's credit quality at that time and the extant debt market conditions.

> *A zero-coupon bond will trade at a discount to its face value. The amount of the discount represents the aggregate compound interest that the holder will forgo because there are no cash interest payments. For example, if a zero-coupon bond has five years until maturity and requires a 10% interest rate, it would trade at 61.4 cents on the face amount of one dollar.*
>
> *Assuming no change in the required interest rate, that bond would trade at 67.7 cents at the end of the first year, 74.6 cents at the end of the second year, 82.3 cents at the end of the third year and 90.7 cents at the end of the fourth year. At the end of the fifth year, it would be repaid at par.*
>
> *Even in the absence of a default, a zero-coupon bond does not necessarily accrete in value to par in a straight line. In the above example, the bond was initially trading at 61.4 cents under a 10% interest rate environment. However, if the required interest rate increased to 15% at the end of the first year, the bond value would fall to 56.1 cents. By definition, a zero-coupon bond will have a longer duration than a coupon bond with a similar maturity (due to the absence of cash coupons). And movements in interest rates have greater effects on bonds with longer durations. Accordingly, changes in required interest rates affect zero-coupon bonds more than they do cash-payment bonds – which makes the prices of zero-coupon bonds very volatile.*

Issuers should have a slight preference for PIK bonds over split-coupon bonds, because PIK bonds generally give the issuer the option to pay either in cash or in kind. This option can be valuable if the required interest rate on the company's debt falls significantly – as a result either of improved credit statistics or more bullish bond-market conditions. In such case, the debt would be trading at premium levels, either over par (the PIK bonds) or above expected accreted value (the split-coupon bonds).

Assume that the company had issued PIK bonds with a 10% interest rate, but that the required interest rate had fallen to 8%. Assuming the bonds had four years remaining until maturity, the debt would be trading at 106.7 cents on the dollar. So, in contemplating the semiannual interest payment on a $100 bond, the company could pay either $5.00 in cash or $5.34 in value of new PIK bonds. The issuer would probably elect the cash option and save value. Such flexibility would not occur in the split-coupon structure.

Under most market conditions, we believe investors will require a higher yield on a deferred-coupon bond than *pari passu* (*i.e.*, the same seniority and status) cash-payment bonds of the same issuer. Partly, this reflects the longer duration of the cash flows of a deferred-payment bond. Generally, longer-term bonds require a higher rate, as discussed above. Another factor is the higher volatility of deferred-coupon bonds compared to cash-payment obligations. And yet another part is the "trust me" risk of permitting the issuer to keep the cash for longer periods of time.

Hybrid Securities With Equity Features

Frequently, restructurings feature debt instruments with equity components, such as debt with attached warrants or convertible bonds. Such equity components provide additional return to the holders, to compensate them for additional risk – or give the holder an incentive to accept a lower cash coupon than it would with a "straight" bond. Combinations of debt and equity are legion in variety, and some wags call some of the versions "dequity." Most of these instruments, at the core, are either debt-plus-warrant packages or convertible bonds.

A cautionary note: In some restructurings, these hybrid packages form a large portion of the capital structure and may even swamp the size of the underlying common stock. In such cases, it may be necessary to develop an iterative valuation approach in order to achieve the right valuation balance between these various capital layers based on market judgments.

Debt Plus Warrants

Bonds can come packaged with warrants in any number of combinations. The warrants can be attached to the bonds, meaning they can never be separated. Or they can be detached immediately or at some later date. The warrants can represent a large portion of the value, or they can be only a small kicker to enhance the debt return. The warrants may be exercised only for cash, or the investor may have the option of using the bonds as a form of payment when they are exercised.

There are several ways to value these debt-plus-warrant packages (see the discussion of warrants in Chapter 6). One straightforward approach is to aggregate the value of the debt and the warrants to determine the package's overall value. A related approach for a new investment is to subtract the value of the warrants from the money advanced in order to determine the net price paid for the debt – and then to calculate a yield on the debt portion. For each approach, the investor needs the tools to value the warrants independently.

Alternatively, many private investors do not determine a current value for the warrants as independent securities. Instead, they integrate the debt-plus-warrant capital structure into forecasting models for the company. Such investors then estimate any debt repayments and apply terminal values to the remaining debt and the equity (including the warrant portion) at the end of the forecast period and determine the internal rate of return they expect on their investment, based on various forecast scenarios. These investors would then adjust the debt-plus-warrant mix in order to achieve their expected target returns.

Convertible Bonds

Generally speaking, a convertible bond is exchangeable at the option of the holder into a fixed number of common shares of the issuer. Because of the convertibility feature, companies are able to achieve a lower coupon rate then they would with straight debt. Typical variations on the theme include a zero-coupon feature, an early call at the option of the issuer, contingent conversion based on future stock prices, early put provisions for the benefit of the holder, and conversion into equity securities of companies other than the issuer.

These bonds trade on the basis of both their debt and equity characteristics. If the common stock has appreciated significantly, the bond will trade largely based on its equity features. For example, assume that each $1,000 bond has a 10-year maturity, a 5% coupon and is convertible into 50 underlying shares of stock (*i.e.*, a $20 conversion price per share). Assume that the stock has increased in price to $30 per share. Because of the value of the underlying equity, the bond would be worth at least $1,500 (50 underlying shares × $30 per share). It would have a current yield of 3.3%, which would make the bond attractive relative to the stock if the stock bore no dividend. Accordingly, such a bond should trade at a slight premium to the underlying common value. The amount of the premium would be predicated in part on the time remaining until the issuer would be able to call the bond for redemption (at which time the holder would presumably convert into equity and no longer be entitled to the coupon income).

Conversely, if the common stock price has plummeted, the bond will assume debt-like characteristics. Assume that the stock has fallen to $5. The underlying stock value would be $250. Given the company's deteriorated fundamental performance, assume the required bond yield would be a distressed 12%. Accordingly, the bond portion of the value would be $599 – far above the underlying equity value. We would expect the bond to trade at some premium to $599, with the premium representing the value of an out-of-the-money call option (see Chapter 6).

> *Convertibles are complex financial instruments that need to be analyzed across several parameters. The relevant bond-related parameters include* current yield *and* yield to maturity *or* yield to worst). *The bond value (generally determined by the yield-to-worst calculation) should provide a floor on the convertible's price. The current yield – the coupon payment divided by the current bond price – is useful in connection with examining the case where the bond price is driven by the equity component, but where the current coupon provides more of a yield to the investor than the underlying common dividend.*
>
> *The* conversion premium *is the degree by which the bond price exceeds the underlying common value. In our experience, "true" cash interest bearing convertibles have conversion premiums in the 15% to 35% range. Premiums falling much below 15% tend to indicate that the stock has appreciated to the point where the equity features start to dominate. Premiums much above such a range tend to flag situations where the common stock has fallen significantly in value and where the convertible is largely trading on its debt characteristics.*
>
> *Analysts also examine the convertible's* breakeven period. *The breakeven represents the number of years of bond-coupon payments (less any forgone dividend payments on the underlying stock) an investor needs to recoup the conversion premium. For example, a $1,000 bond with an underlying stock value of $800 would have a $200 conversion premium, or 25%. With an annual coupon of 5%, the cash interest payment would be $50 per bond. Assuming no common stock dividend, the breakeven would be $200/$50, or four years.*

The best method of valuing convertibles is to examine comparable publicly traded securities and reach judgments regarding the target company's bonds. Each security needs to be analyzed in terms of credit quality and yield, as well as in terms of its equity and warrant features.

For so-called "broken" convertibles – those with relatively low underlying equity values – pay particular attention to the yield to worst in comparison with other such convertibles with high conversion premiums, as well as to comparable "straight" junk bonds. For bonds trading well over par due to the appreciation of the underlying equity, look at the conversion premium and current yield in relation to other such convertibles. For the convertibles in between, try to look at all such parameters. And in all cases, look at the breakevens.

The use of debt instruments can dramatically enhance a financial restructuring. In general, debt is tax-efficient because of the deductibility of interest. Layering of debt with various collateral positions and relative seniorities can maintain the "pecking order" of certain pre-restructuring constituencies, as well as provide downside protection for various creditors. Because of their equity characteristics, the hybrid debt instruments can turbocharge recoveries.

Much like the punchbowl at a New Year's party, however, debt can easily be too much of a good thing. Excessive debt loads, after all, are a primary reason that many companies have been forced to restructure in the first place. If a restructuring leaves a company with too much debt, it may not be able to access the financial markets to meet future needs, and it may remain a financial cripple.

As in so many other situations, moderation may be a good thing.

CHAPTER 6—COMMON SENSE AND TECHNICAL STUFF

Valuation is as much of an arcane art as it is a science, as we have seen in the previous discussions of valuing equity and debt. That means that investment bankers must use their experience and judgment to translate esoteric theories into the practical realities with which they are dealing. And just like Scotty in *Star Trek* used to make the Enterprise do things its theoretical designers never intended, the investment banker in the real world needs to consider ways to apply theory to problems that the academicians never considered.

In this chapter, we specifically deal with some of the more technical concepts discussed in earlier chapters. Certain of the valuation approaches discussed in Chapters 4 and 5 are predicated upon relatively complex mathematical relationships. Warrants are based on theories regarding volatility of assets. Equity rates of return are based on concepts of diversifiable and non-diversifiable risk. The math behind these principles can be quite dense, but we promise that there will be no quiz on the formulas herein.

In addition to the pure technical material, we set forth our views as to how to approach problems for which textbook answers do not provide pat answers. Instead, we believe the investment banker must adapt relevant, related theoretical constructs to the situation at hand.

Warrants

An equity warrant is basically a stock call option with a relatively long maturity. Its value is primarily a function of:

(i) the relationship between the current stock price and the warrant's strike price (the price at which an investor can purchase the underlying stock);

(ii) the time remaining until maturity of the warrant;

(iii) the possibility that the company's underlying stock price will climb over time and exceed the exercise price;
(iv) interest rates prevailing at the time; and
(v) the underlying dividend on the stock.

Assume, for example, that a warrant strike price is $10 per share. In other words, the investor can exercise the warrant for $10 and own a share of stock. If the stock were trading at $100 per share, the warrant would be said to be far "in the money" and would have an "intrinsic value" (the difference between the stock price and the exercise price) of $90 per share. Conversely, if the stock were trading at $5, the warrant would have no intrinsic value and would be considered to be "out of the money." In a third scenario, if the stock were trading at $10, the warrant would have no intrinsic value and would be considered to be "at the money."

If the warrants in each scenario expired immediately, their values would be equal to their intrinsic value – one worth $90 per share and the other two worthless. But if the warrants did not expire immediately, each would have value in excess of their respective intrinsic values. The question is how much.

Financial professionals have tools to analyze the theoretical values of warrants, based on the popular Black-Scholes model and similar "black boxes." In addition to the exercise price and the current stock price, the analyst inputs several factors, including the maturity, the underlying stock volatility (which generates a probability that the stock price will increase over time) and a risk-free interest rate. The model then generates an answer with great precision – but often with surprisingly little real meaning.

> *Option pricing models such as Black-Scholes attempt to measure the value of an option (or warrant) through a series of statistical procedures. Until these models were developed, conventional wisdom generally held that a warrant's value (over its intrinsic value) was directly related to the company's future earnings prospects. The thinking was that the greater the future earnings, the higher the future stock price and the greater the warrant value.*
>
> *Black-Scholes and its brethren threw that conventional wisdom out the window. Nowhere do these models account for earnings expectations. Instead, they assume that stock prices will simply fluctuate up and down. If*

the fluctuations (or volatility) are large enough, or if the time factor is long enough, the probability increases that the stock price will rise to the point where the warrant will have significant intrinsic value. The mathematical formulas in these models determine warrant values based upon a wide range of these possible outcomes.

While these models may be theoretically correct, in the real world they are potentially misleading.

Aside from the relationship between stock price and exercise price, most of the remainder of theoretical warrant value is built from the relationship between volatility and maturity. How these parameters are determined can be deeply flawed.

The conventional method of determining volatility is to examine historical volatility for the underlying company's stock. For a company engaged in a restructuring, there is no reason to expect that historical volatility would be a proxy for future volatility, given the changes in capital structure, improved stability in operations and the potential, continuing shift in ownership.

Volatility may also not capture all the upside potential of the warrants. The theoretical models were originally developed to value shorter-term options, rather than longer-term warrants. Thus, we believe such models miss the differential between expected long-term equity returns and the risk-free rate. This is particularly true if the target company transitions from losses to profitability.

The warrant maturity itself is uncertain. For example, the company could be acquired years before the warrants would otherwise mature. This scenario – called "event risk" – could dramatically reduce the value of the warrants by removing their time value.

Many option pricing models assume that the writer of the option is a third party, rather than the company. If warrants issued by a company represent a large part of its capitalization, the model results may be skewed.

At best, we believe, these theoretical models provide no more than a benchmark by which to approach warrant value.

In order to avoid such false precision, analysts need to exercise a great deal of judgment in applying these models. An easy way to produce a grossly misleading answer is to use an artificially high historical volatility based only on recent trends. The analyst should keep in mind that any extraordinary volatility patterns at the time of the restructuring will probably calm over time – making it necessary to modify any volatility inputs based on subjective judgments about volatility conditions for comparable but more seasoned stocks.

Another common way to get a misleading answer is to assume blindly that the warrants will remain outstanding for their stated maturity. Any company could be acquired – and thus the life of its outstanding warrants would be shortened. Given the ownership structure of many recently reorganized companies and their stockholders' desire for liquidity, it is more likely that a company emerging from reorganization will be acquired in the ensuing years than the average public company. The analyst needs to acknowledge this reality by considering a range of potential shortened warrant maturities.

Perhaps the best way to check the output from these black boxes is to use common sense and to analyze other warrants trading in the marketplace with similar parameters. Consider the three scenarios outlined above, with stock prices of $100, $10 and $5.

The ***in-the-money*** warrant will trade similarly to the underlying common stock. In our example, the intrinsic value of the warrant is $90 – based on a $100 stock price and a $10 exercise price. The chief difference between this warrant and the common stock is that the investor not need pay the full $100 for the stock now – saving some interest costs for the life of the warrant. Accordingly, the warrant should trade at some premium to the $90 intrinsic value, but well below the $100 stock price.

The ***at-the-money*** warrant would benefit from any appreciation in the stock price above $10. Assume the stock is likely to appreciate by 10% per year (with no dividends paid) over the next five years (the stated maturity of the warrant) and that the required discount rate on the warrant would be 12% (the required warrant return would greater than the stock return). That means the expected stock price would be $16.11 in five years (a $6.11 gain). The gain would have a present value of $3.47 – or about 35% of the current stock price. We know this computation violates a number of the precepts behind the option pricing models, but we believe it serves as a useful common sense check on the "black box" approach.

The ***out-of-the-money*** warrant is a more speculative instrument. The stock would have to appreciate as much as 20% per year from the $5 level for the warrant to have any significant value. At the end of five years at such 20% rate, the stock price would be $12.44 – representing an intrinsic value of $2.44. Given the increased riskiness of this warrant return, we could discount the $2.44 back to the present at an assumed rate of 25% or higher. This implies a warrant value of $0.80. This approach, too, is theoretically flawed but serves as a common sense check on the "black box."

Equity Cost of Capital

A substantial portion of modern finance theory is based on the Capital Asset Pricing Model (CAPM). One key tenet behind the CAPM is the notion that if you want higher returns, you must endure higher risk – the old question of whether you want to eat well or sleep well.

Another key tenet is less obvious. The CAPM says that not all risk is created equal: there is diversifiable risk and non-diversifiable risk. The diversifiable risk of a stock relates to the ups and downs of a particular company that are unique to that company. In theory, in a carefully balanced portfolio of stocks, the individual up-and-down effects would be largely offset against each other. The non-diversifiable risk relates to the degree to which an individual stock moves in concert with the overall market (generally, as measured by the S&P 500 Index). If a stock were to move twice as far as the market – in either direction – then the CAPM would say that stock is relatively risky.

The degree to which these stocks move relative to the market is statistically determined using a correlation measure known as Beta. If the stock behaved exactly as does the market, it would have a Beta of 1.0. If the stock was a stodgy blue chip that moved only a little bit, it might have a Beta of 0.75. A high-flying tech stock might have a Beta of 2.0.

The CAPM integrates these concepts through an incremental build-up. It starts with the risk-free rate, below which theoretically no one should want to invest. In other words, why would an investor willingly take both additional risk and a lower return?

The CAPM then layers onto the risk-free rate the incremental return (over the risk-free rate) an investor should want for bearing the market risk. The sum of the risk-free rate and this increment is exactly the expected market return. The CAPM then adjusts the market portion of the return calculation to incorporate additional risk characteristics (measured by Beta).

CAPM is a compelling theory. In practice, however, the determination of required returns for specific securities can be materially off the mark because of sometimes misleading statistics.

According to CAPM, the firm's cost of equity is:

Rf + *B* × (Re – Rf), where
Rf = the risk-free rate
Re = the market cost of equity
B = Levered Beta, or a measure of the stock's riskiness.

We note that some analysts may "tweak" this theoretical model to account for certain empirical observations, For example, smaller companies have correlated with higher returns. To account for this, analysts sometimes add a percentage point or more (sometimes a lot more) to the CAPM results to deal with this small company effect.

The risk-free rate is generally considered to be either the five- or ten-year U.S. Treasury rate and is readily determined. However, the cost of equity for the market as a whole (the S&P 500) is not so easily calculated. Many analysts have used long-term rates of return for the market, as published in various sources. Using historical rates of return, however, is a bit like steering a car solely by relying on the rear-view mirror.

Given the still relatively lofty level of the markets and the expected long-term growth rates of the economy, we do not believe that the market will experience the 11% to 12% long-term results it has historically enjoyed. This view of prospective lower equity returns is increasingly prevalent. As of the date of this writing, various respected academicians have been estimating the S&P return as being in a range of 400 to 600 basis points over Treasuries.

Accordingly, we think that any investment banker determining the weighted average cost of capital, or WACC, needs to develop a contemporaneous estimate for overall market returns. Relying solely on market history will no longer do.

As difficult as the determination of overall market returns may be, the calculation of Beta can be more difficult still. As we have noted, the historical Beta for a company in restructuring may not be relevant, given that the restructured company will have a completely different capital structure and possibly a different operational profile than before. In order to determine the appropriate pro forma Beta, analysts frequently examine the Betas of stocks deemed to be comparable to the target company.

When Betas are calculated for individual stocks, they are "leveraged" Betas. Just as the related common stocks reflect the effect of their respective companies' leverage, so do the Betas. In general, more-leveraged companies are likely to have higher Betas than less-leveraged companies.

The target company we are analyzing is quite likely to have a different degree of leverage than comparable companies. As a result, it is necessary to adjust the comparable leveraged Betas in order to translate Beta into a meaningful statistic for the target company. Traditionally, this is done by "unleveraging" the comparable universe Betas, and then "re-leveraging" such statistics to comport with the target company's pro forma capital structure.

The formula for determining unleveraged Beta is:

$B_U = B_L / [1 + (1 - t) \times D/E]$ or, transposed to calculate leveraged Beta:
$B_L = B_U \times [1 + (1 - t) \times D/E]$, where
t = tax rate
D = net debt
E = equity value (valued at market, not book)

In order to make this data useful for the target-company analysis, it is necessary to unleverage the Betas. The financial advisor will then select the appropriate unleveraged Beta, and re-leverage it using the pro forma financial leverage characteristics (based on market values, rather than book values) of the target company.

One more thing. Over time, the Beta of a company is expected to converge to 1.0, the market's rate. In order to account for this, analysts frequently create "Adjusted Betas," which arithmetically shift to calculated Betas closer to 1.0.

We find numerous problems associated with the calculation of Beta. In practice, it is quite common for a group of relatively similar companies to have dramatically different Betas. These differences may arise from occurrences that affect one company more than another or the market as a whole – for example, a change in the management team, a company-specific earnings or accounting surprise, or a recent acquisition or divestiture.

So, how does an analyst derive a cost of equity capital out of all this mumbo-jumbo? Let's look at a few examples.

Remember we said that the long-term historical 11% to 12% return for the market was too high? Let's use 9% as an expected market return for illustrative purposes. Then look in the newspaper for the 10-year Treasury yield. If it were 4.0%, then the market equity risk premium would be 5.0%.

What if you were looking at a high-growth technology stock? It would likely make larger up-and-down movements than the market as a whole. Say it had a Beta of 1.5. Then its equity return would be 11.56% (4.0% + 1.5 × (9% – 4.0%)). Conversely, a stodgy utility with a Beta of 0.75 would have an equity rate of return of 7.75% (4.0% + 0.75 × (9% – 4.0%)).

Finally, how can we be certain about the overall market's required rate of return of 9%? Obviously, we can't derive it directly, but a sanity check helps. Remember the constant growth valuation approach from Chapter 5? The multiple was:

$$\frac{1}{\text{Cost of Capital} - \text{Growth Rate}}, \text{ or transposed}$$

$$\text{Cost of Capital} = \frac{1}{\text{Multiple}} + \text{Growth Rate}$$

Therefore, one way to look at the market return is to take the inverse of the market multiple, and to add the economy's nominal (*i.e.*, including inflation) growth rate.

At a 16 P/E multiple (making the assumption that earnings equal cash flow), its inverse would be 6.25%. With an assumed 3% long-term nominal GDP growth rate (unfortunately, we are growing more slowly than we used to), the implied market return would be 9.25%.

Using Common Sense

One of our basic rules is that few things are more dangerous in finance than a 23-year-old with a spreadsheet. Accordingly, we cannot stress enough the importance of using plain old common sense to verify the output. Whether investment bankers use a "black box" to obtain the answers to questions arising earlier in this chapter or to conduct more fundamental financial analyses, it is critical that they have a sense of what the right answer should be before allowing associates to start turning the crank on the computer. We cannot mention the number of times that key mistakes have been made as a result of trusting a computer printout.

But common sense can do a lot more than simply prevent calculation errors. A myriad of problems arise in the real world for which the academicians have not provided a ready recipe in their textbooks. For these issues, the investment banker must develop a common sense approach using appropriate theoretical constructs.

For example, assume that a company has been spun-off from its parent. As part of the spin-off transaction, it has committed to forgo the sale of assets for a couple of years in order to comply with applicable tax regulations. If this subsidiary is cash-starved, it may actually need to consider selling such assets. How should the investment banker take these restrictions into account? One approach may be to analogize the situation to that of a holder of restricted stock. Clearly, an asset that can be sold is more valuable than one that cannot be sold until much later. The discounts observed on restricted stock studies can be applied to the near-term realizable value of the restricted assets.

Or, what if the investment banker is able to demonstrate that a certain group of comparables exhibits an explainable excess return, perhaps not otherwise explainable by theoretical factors? Small company risk premiums can be an example of this. But there may be other situations, such as companies new to the public markets, or those that have certain geographic exposure, or any number of factors. If there is a real correlation here, banker take note. In finance theory, there should not be a free lunch. With excess return comes excess risk. This might be a reason to consider increasing the WACC.

The point is that the investment banker should fully grasp finance theory. And then have the judgment to know how to apply it to the situation at hand – whether some academician has been there before, or not.

CHAPTER 7—FRAUDULENT CONVEYANCE, OTHER RELATED CAUSES OF ACTION, AND OPINIONS

In financially distressed situations, creditors often pursue litigation strategies in order to bolster their recoveries. Of such legal strategies, fraudulent conveyance is perhaps the most utilized "big gun" insolvency tool in the creditors' arsenal.

The targets of fraudulent conveyance litigation are generally groups that obtained some benefit prior to bankruptcy, and may include secured lenders that received paydowns or collateral grants, stockholders that received large dividends or third parties that may have bought assets from the company. Situations have arisen, for example, where a private-equity firm makes a large and controlling investment in Company X, then ensures that the company returns big dividends to it. Should Company X become insolvent, the creditors might well seek to have the dividends disgorged.

All these target groups should have a thorough understanding of how fraudulent conveyance litigation might affect them, and that understanding should guide them in designing how certain transactions are structured.

A financial transaction can subsequently be voided if the company had an actual intent to defraud creditors. That "badge of fraud" is not necessary, however, for determination of fraudulent conveyance. Its name notwithstanding, "constructive" fraudulent conveyance can be deemed to have occurred even without fraudulent intent.

For plaintiffs to win such a suit, they must pass two tests. First, they must prove that the debtor received less than reasonably equivalent value for the assets that it transferred or the obligation that it incurred. If that hurdle is cleared, the plaintiff need then demonstrate that the company was actually insolvent, either immediately before or after the transaction.

While the tests of insolvency vary somewhat from state to state, they are largely based on Section 548 of the Bankruptcy Code. Definitions of "insolvency" typically include such concepts as (i) the value of assets being below the level of liabilities, (ii) the company being unable to pay debts as they become due and (iii) the company being left with unreasonably small capital with which to conduct its business. Individual states have different lengths for their statutes of limitations, which range up to six years.

Courts have almost uniformly determined solvency based upon what was *known* or *knowable* as of the relevant transaction date (a historical perspective). This places the burden on the plaintiffs to show that the ensuing business failure was not the result of some unforeseen problem or one that occurred after the transaction date. Defendants may point to the existence of rosy projections at the time of the transaction, "demonstrating" clear solvency. To prevail in their suit, the plaintiffs and the professionals they employ must be able to discredit such projections as being unreasonably and imprudently optimistic in light of the circumstances known at the time.

Of course, courts may take a different tack in assessing solvency. After all, the elephant in the courtroom is generally a dismally failed, bankrupt company. And it found its way into bankruptcy, somehow. In one situation (Sealed Air Corporation), the court took into account subsequent contingent asbestos liabilities, even though such obligations were not known at the time of the relevant transaction, which made the plaintiff's case much easier. Liability may depend upon individual courts, at least in part.

If this area appears to be arcane and complex, it is. And it involves difficult issues arising from the interplay of solvency, valuation and fairness of consideration. We believe that this area is one of the most specialized and challenging in all of finance.

The implications of fraudulent conveyance law are profound. Years after a transaction occurs, a court can examine the deal with 20/20 hindsight. Good faith participants in the original transaction can suffer large economic losses resulting from the litigation.

Investment bankers play key roles in fraudulent conveyance litigation, and their influence will be the focus of much of this chapter. Financial analyses of valuation and solvency are important elements of court determination of the existence of fraudulent conveyance, as well as its magnitude. That investment bankers have "real world" experience in doing transactions lends their testimony far more credibility than consultants brought in with an "ivory tower" perspective.

In addition to being key players in fraudulent conveyance litigation, investment bankers can play an instrumental role in the initial structuring of a transaction – in order to minimize subsequent problems that might occur. Having an investment banker issue a solid fairness opinion can be an important piece of evidence in demonstrating adequacy of consideration. Similarly, a solvency opinion can be a critical independent determination at the time of the deal. In either case, the opinion needs to be backed by a credible analysis – with the assumption that it will be subsequently examined by a court.

Many types of corporate transactions can give rise to subsequent claims of fraudulent conveyance. All share certain characteristics.

On the one hand, money is transferred out of the company or the company assumes more liabilities. On the other hand, the company may receive assets in the transaction – but at a valuation level lower than the consideration paid. The combination of these factors creates a decrease in shareholder value.

The other key element of the fraudulent conveyance analysis is that the shareholder value at the end of the transaction is *negative*, or so marginal that the company will not be in a position to pay its debts as they come due, or be able to refinance them at maturity.

Within this analytical framework, let us examine several forms of fraudulent conveyance.

The Dividend. From a value received/value obtained standpoint, dividends are straightforward. Cash goes out of the company, with nothing in return (the goodwill of stockholders is not a tangible benefit, in this analysis). If the dividend is large enough, it can create financial problems for the company. This can occur in connection with a greedy parent looking to milk its subsidiary, or in connection with a leveraged recapitalization, an LBO or a leveraged spinoff, in which the company incurs a significant amount of debt in order to pay a one-time cash dividend to its parent. If the incurrence of the new debt renders the company "insolvent," the dividend transaction can be attacked as a fraudulent conveyance. If there is no new debt, but rather simply a dividend that leaves the company insolvent (or if the company was insolvent already), it can also be attacked as a fraudulent conveyance.

However, we hasten to add that fraudulent conveyance actions may not be straightforward. Some courts have held that if new money comes in at or near the bottom of the capital stack in connection with an arguable fraudulent conveyance (such as a leverage-fueled dividend), then the transaction may be permissible. The legal theory is that the newly purchased securities that are part and parcel of the overall deal would have "cleansed" the transaction; the company could not have been insolvent in an efficient market if someone simultaneously purchased equity securities. We understand that courts nationally are wildly split on this issue.

The company's estate could, in theory, pursue such claims on behalf of creditors that were harmed by the transfer. Such creditors could include trade claimants and holders of bonds at the time of the transaction. The litigation would be likely to follow the money and target the beneficiaries of the dividend (*i.e.*, the stockholders that received it). In cases where ownership is concentrated, such litigation can be very effective. But if the company were widely held and public, such litigation might encounter significant collection risks. It is basically problematic to collect a judgment against thousands and thousands of relatively small shareholders in a transaction that occurred a long time ago.

The estate could also bring a fraudulent conveyance action against any lenders that obtained collateral in connection with funding the transaction. The goal of such litigation would be to set aside the collateral grant, treating such creditors as unsecured. If successful, this argument would decrease the recoveries of the secured creditors in favor of the unsecured claimants bringing the fraudulent conveyance litigation. In our experience, many such threatened actions are a "stretch," but depending on the facts they can nonetheless be useful in gaining negotiating leverage with secured creditors.

Distressed Asset Sale. A more complex situation arises when a good faith buyer purchases a business from a distressed company. In contrast to a dividend, mutual consideration changes hands. And there may actually have been a competitive process run by the seller – giving the transaction the patina of procedural fairness. But such a fact pattern does not guarantee the successful buyer quiet enjoyment of the purchased assets.

Assume that the seller uses the sale proceeds to repay debt or to reinvest in its remaining businesses – but nonetheless, a year later, needs to seek bankruptcy protection. Assume further that the plaintiff creditors bring litigation a few years later, and have a strong case for showing that the seller was insolvent at the time of the sale (after all, the company did file for bankruptcy 12 months later).

At that point, the buyer must respond to the plaintiff's assertion and attempt to demonstrate that the seller was solvent at the time of the transaction or that the sale price represented "equivalent value." Failure to defend this would result in the buyer losing the case. In theory, the transaction could be "unwound," and the buyer would have to return the business to the seller and receive an unsecured claim from the bankrupt estate. In practice, "unwinding" would be unlikely due to the complexity of unscrambling an omelet – the businesses would have long since been operationally intertwined. What is more likely to happen is that the buyer may have to contribute funds to the estate, representing (at least a part of) the difference between what the buyer paid at the time of the transaction and what (with 20/20 hindsight) the business is determined to have been worth at the time of the sale.

Leveraged Asset Purchase. A company can buy a business, finance the purchase price with debt and then subsequently go broke. The creditors of both the company and the acquired business may then bring fraudulent conveyance actions regarding the transaction.

To be successful, the plaintiffs will first need to show that the company (and/or the acquired business) was rendered insolvent at or immediately after the transaction. They will also need to show that the company overpaid for the acquisition. If the plaintiffs were indeed successful in these attempts, then they still would have to be able to collect from the beneficiaries of the purchase – a difficult endeavor with publicly owned sellers.

To some observers this outcome is alarming. After all, if the business was marketed through an auction process, isn't the measure of fair value the purchase price itself? And if so, how can there have been inadequate consideration?

Nevertheless, courts have indeed made these determinations. When the Federal Communications Commission auctioned wireless telephone spectrum licenses to small "independents," the value for such licenses plunged between the auction date and the dates on which the transactions were to close. These independents were therefore rendered insolvent. And a federal court found that inadequate value was received at the actual closing (in another FCC-related matter on which we consulted, however, the lower court decision based on a similar line of reasoning was overturned). The moral of the story for a seller is that having a solvent buyer is important. Otherwise, a seemingly high sale consideration can backfire down the road if the buyer is too highly leveraged.

And the Beat Goes On. Many other permutations and combinations of fact patterns can give rise to credible fraudulent conveyance claims. If a parent company "spins out" a subsidiary to its shareholders, and the subsidiary later falters, its creditors can claim that the parent burdened the subsidiary with too much debt at the outset. There can be intra-creditor squabbles about whether certain creditors were advantaged *vis-à-vis* others as a result of a company's refinancing and ensuing paydown of a variety of creditors. A parent company can receive a material loan, and in connection therewith burden its subsidiary by granting to the lender a subsidiary guarantee or collateral for the loan. In such case, the subsidiary arguably has given up something of great value (its guarantee of parent obligations) and not received anything, much less reasonably equivalent value, in return. A parent company can direct its troubled subsidiary to upstream a material dividend that might cause the subsidiary to be insolvent, or occur at a time when the subsidiary was already insolvent.

What could the parties have done to protect themselves in such scenarios? And what can plaintiffs and defendants do in lawsuits to advantage themselves? The investment banker should play a central role on all these fronts.

Scope of Services

An investment banker can become involved with fraudulent conveyance in several ways:

- up-front, in advising transacting parties as to the most desirable way to structure a particular transaction (including, but not limited to, the sale of assets from a distressed company, a financial recapitalization, spinoff or LBO);
- up-front, by rendering a "solvency" opinion in order to provide participants in a transaction with a contemporaneous due diligence defense against later-arising allegations of fraudulent conveyance (to give comfort that the company is not, and after the transaction would not be, insolvent);
- up-front, by rendering a "fairness opinion" in order to address the issue of adequacy of consideration, which provides a due diligence defense to "reasonably equivalent value" arguments; and
- after the fact, as an expert witness on behalf of either plaintiff or defendant, rendering views on solvency or reasonably equivalent value as of the time of the transaction.

We are regularly involved in fraudulent conveyance litigations and have the opportunity to observe after-the-fact challenges to major transactions. We often encounter situations in which transaction participants stand to lose tens, if not hundreds, of millions of dollars in these actions. Yet, in virtually every case, these participants were not adequately advised by financial or legal insolvency professionals at the time of the transaction.

Would such advice change the outcome? It well could. Contemporaneous solvency and fairness opinions can be important determinants in any ensuing litigation. Advice as to modification of transaction terms or to sale process can materially alter the solvency or procedural fairness of any deal. Why, then, if the benefits are so potentially great, do companies regularly ignore hiring professionals to advise them on lowering the risks attendant to fraudulent conveyance? Part of the answer lies in the cost. In many, many cases, this desire to avoid the cost amounts to being "penny wise and pound foolish." Seasoned advice up-front that avoids a back-end fraudulent conveyance problem would save millions and millions of dollars in litigation costs alone.

In many other cases, the answer may lie with conflicts of interest. Many major investment banks whose M&A departments are hell-bent on getting a deal done want nothing to do with issues of solvency – particularly given that such "bulge bracket" firms do not render solvency opinions. They cannot profit from the opinion, and it only represents an impediment to getting a deal done.

Opinions – in General

Fairness, solvency and valuation opinions have uses apart from fraudulent conveyance concerns. The advent of Sarbanes Oxley and related corporate governance concerns have given rise to increased demands for comfort for boards of directors, and financial opinions are a linchpin of that.

Opinion-rendering is one of the most stressful and demanding aspects of our business. Clients often have time-sensitive needs, and the opinion-giver must do the requisite work to enable a defensible opinion. Moreover, the various constituencies involved simply want the result they want – while the opinion-renderer must get to the "correct" result. Emotions can run very high. Firms that provide "turn-key" opinions or opinions that say whatever the client wants them to say, irrespective of the facts, will put themselves and the client at risk of ensuing lawsuits.

We firmly believe that unless the opinion-renderer is both an investment bank and a firm tested in the crucible of litigation, the opinion is likely not to be particularly effective in giving true comfort to the recipient. Not every firm can do this well, all the more so under extreme deadlines.

In a sense, an opinion is an insurance policy – and as in insurance, many people and businesses deem the price of the insurance policy too expensive until and unless the underlying coverage is actually needed.

GORDIAN KNOTS/Morrison Knudsen

The Morrison Knudsen Corporation, a large engineering, construction and mining management services company that was facing insolvency, struck a complex deal with its banks and with surety companies that had provided it with performance and completion bonds. After an unsuccessful sale process, MK transferred certain assets and contracts relating to the manufacture of mass-transit vehicles for various municipalities into a newly-formed limited liability company established for the benefit of the sureties. In turn, MK received cash and was released from certain financial obligations in this spinoff transaction that had an aggregate deal value of more than $200 million.

Gordian was retained to render an opinion that the transaction was fair to certain creditors, because of our significant capital markets and opinion experience, and our ability to perform a massive amount of due diligence, valuation, solvency and other work in a very short period of time.

Gordian's work involved examining the transaction (and the alternatives thereto), the implications of a bankruptcy on the claims (secured and otherwise) of various creditors, together with the valuations and financial obligations of the other MK entities. The desired transaction closed successfully.

GORDIAN KNOTS/Silicon Gaming, Inc.

Silicon Gaming was a startup company engaged in the design, manufacture and sale of innovative electronic-based slot machines. After spending $100 million in the development and early manufacturing phases, it had exhausted its financing options. These illiquidity problems occurred simultaneously with product problems and significant management turnover, leaving the company at the precipice of a "meltdown."

> In order to provide sufficient financing to save the company, its major lender offered to advance monies, subject to a conversion of its existing exposure into a majority of the pro forma equity. In addition, management proposed that it receive almost 40 percent of the pro forma equity as part of its restructuring incentive package. These proposals would have diluted the existing non-management shareholders' equity to a *de minimis* position, and Gordian Group was retained to render a fairness opinion with respect to the impact of the proposed transaction on the old stockholders.
>
> Gordian Group concurred that Silicon Gaming had significant, imminent liquidity problems – but that, if the problems were overcome, there was a significant upside in the stock. Moreover, based upon our views of valuation and of what could happen favorably to old equity in a Chapter 11 scenario, even assuming the imminent liquidity issues, Gordian Group negotiated a new structure with management and the major lender that provided for materially more common stock and warrants to be allocated to old equity. These negotiations were heated – but resulted in a transaction now largely immunized from attack on fairness grounds, precisely because of the vigorous negotiations.

Contemporaneous Analysis

Performing work at the time of a contemplated transaction – when the company's management team is available – is the "normal" way of doing business in investment banking. The bankers have the opportunity to evaluate management's plans, as well as management's capabilities. If questions arise, the bankers have the ability to ask management to alter their business plans to measure sensitivities to various elements of risk in the plans. In practice, these sensitivities are measured in the form of "stress tests," in which bankers determine how far a company has to miss its plan in order to fail. These stress tests can be based on various benchmarks, including historical operating ranges unique to the company or to its overall industry.

Further, the bankers must examine the company in terms of its ability to live within its capital structure (including its covenants) and its ability to access additional funds in the future – whether to refinance or to grow its operations. Part of this analysis involves understanding of the capital markets. Another part involves judgments regarding the company's working capital requirements, given the degree to which trade creditors will extend credit to a leveraged company.

In terms of valuation, the bankers will examine various metrics such as comparable company analyses, comparable transaction analyses, perpetual growth analyses and analyses of discounted cash flow.

After examining all of the foregoing, if the margin of safety is too low with respect to the impact of the contemplated transaction, the banker should determine that the company could very well be, or become, insolvent as a result.

In cases involving an actual sale of assets, the bankers will also examine the process by which the sale took place to determine whether it was conducted properly (an indicator of "procedural fairness"). Or whether a sale was required in the first place (perhaps value could have been enhanced through retention of the asset coupled with a debt restructuring). Or whether the involvement of insiders in the transaction creates the appearance of impropriety.

This examination can provide invaluable feedback. A business plan that is too aggressive for the capital structure can be changed. Or the capital structure can be changed to be less leveraged. Or if the buyer's advisor deems the purchase price to be "too good" for his client, the buyer can demand that the sale be conducted through a Chapter 11 process, which can insulate the buyer against subsequent fraudulent conveyance litigation. Such changes can mean the difference between viability and failure of the enterprise. They can also mean the difference between success or failure in dealing with fraudulent conveyance.

Ex-Post Analysis

In theory, the types of analysis conducted in the contemporaneous mode would be relevant to the "ex-post" analysis – after the litigation is brought years after the transaction. However, the ex-post analysis is a much more difficult task for the investment banker. This analysis is hampered by any number of factors, including lack of management input (management themselves may be embroiled in the litigation), uncertain provenance of projections and other internal financial information discovered in various files, and by the passage of time itself (rendering participants' recollections unreliable).

As a practical matter, this means that the investment banker must become somewhat of an investigator as well. Using experience, the banker must be able to evaluate projections in light of the reasonableness of, or the motivation behind, the assumptions that underlie them. The defense will of course seek to argue that the projections were reasonable at the time and supported the capital structure – therefore, the company was solvent. In such circumstances, it is incumbent upon the plaintiffs to demonstrate that the projections were fundamentally flawed, based upon "irrational exuberance" or other factors.

In any case, the investment banker engaged at this point in the litigation will need to assess valuation and financeability as of the historical period. Experience, therefore, is critical. The banker will need to understand merger market, public market and private market conditions as they existed at the time – and, in particular, for the subject company. Failure to bring such experience to bear will result in just another inadequate "ivory tower" expert witness analysis.

Other Related Causes of Action

Other distress-related causes of action that an investment banker needs to be cognizant of include the "Zone of Insolvency" theories.

In essence, "Zone of Insolvency" litigation is an attempt to get creditors of a financially troubled company a seat at the negotiating table and an ability to hold boards of directors accountable earlier than they otherwise might be. Many courts have historically expressed the view that when a company becomes insolvent, the fiduciary obligations of its directors shift. Depending on the court, that shift can mean a board is now responsible to the company (in a way that loops in its unsecured creditors), in addition to being responsible to the company's shareholders.

In any event, the judicial move from a strict "insolvency" to the "Zone of Insolvency" concept is analogous to enlarging the golf hole on the green. One still needs to sink a putt, but it has now become easier.

To illustrate the impact that the "Zone of Insolvency" can have on a company and its investment banker, recall the example in Chapter 3 of a company that has a pile of cash at the same time its bonds are trading at distressed prices. The company is arguably prepared to pursue strategies that might seek to hit a home run for its shareholders and risk recoveries for the bondholders. However, the bonds are not in default, and the bondholders, by the terms of their indenture, have no seat at the table to seek to influence the board. The bondholders could, however, sue the board of directors on the grounds that the company, if not insolvent, is at least within the "Zone of Insolvency." Their suit could seek to enjoin the board from taking actions at odds with its fiduciary obligations to the bondholders. While many legal and business defenses are available against such a suit, we will again focus on the investment banker's role.

One potential defense is if the board used its business judgment, based on advice of outside advisors (including an investment banker), to determine that its proposed course of action was reasonably calculated to improve recoveries for all creditors and security holders.

As an advisor to the company, the investment banker's view may be solicited on several matters. First, the board of directors should be quite interested in its investment banker's take on the relative merits of the proposed course of action to increase the company's overall value – the same course of action that may be opposed by the creditors. Second, the board will likely wish to know if the investment banker has a view on whether the company is insolvent.

Groups of creditors may also claim that other creditors (pre-petition banks, for example) took inappropriate steps to advantage themselves vs. other constituencies. If proven, these "lender liability" allegations can lead to various judicial remedies against the miscreants – including "equitably subordinating" their claims to those of creditors.

Given what is at stake when fraudulent conveyance suits and other related actions are brought, it is clear that all participants in corporate transactions – at the time of those deals – should have anticipated potential future litigation and acted appropriately to buttress their evidence of why the transaction made sense.

CHAPTER 8—THE *STATUS QUO* APPROACH

Faced with some combination of impending liquidity and capital-structure crises, companies and their boards of directors may consider multiple options, as we have seen in Chapter 3. One option is to maintain the "Status Quo," and do nothing. It's roughly analogous to the physician's credo of "first, do no harm." In effect, this strategy plays for time (liquidity permitting), in the hope that market forces or operational initiatives can adequately address the capital structure challenges that have arisen because of the mismatch between leverage and operational performance.

In this scenario, the company will monitor the situation, perhaps trying to improve liquidity internally but without seeking new financing. It may not hire restructuring professionals (in our view, a mistake, as set forth below) and is not likely at this juncture to develop, much less implement, a financial restructuring plan. Status Quo must always be considered in conjunction with other potential courses of action, in part because the company and its various constituencies will have different perspectives on the rewards and the risks of the Status Quo approach.

The Company

Management teams and boards of directors are never eager to admit to problems and never excited about the prospect of interviewing, engaging and paying high-priced investment banking and legal talent that specializes in distressed company problem-solving. Moreover, because capital structure and liquidity issues in the distressed context are almost invariably linked directly to operational challenges, management needs to be spending all its time on operations – leaving precious little time, and likely having little inclination, to focus on capital structure issues. Thus, to these parties, the advantages of maintaining the Status Quo are:

- management's time can be spent solely on operations, and not on the development, negotiation and implementation of a financial restructuring;

- the company can avoid the expense of hiring restructuring professionals; and
- If the company's operations do turn around in a dramatic fashion, this alternative (which involves no dilution) can result in the best outcome for old equity.
- The disadvantages of the Status Quo approach include:
- Sticking with the Status Quo too long may preclude a later sale process, or it may delay a sale beyond the point of peak value. "The sooner the safer," Jack Dempsey, the heavyweight champion, once said when he was asked why he sought to knock out his opponents as quickly as possible. The sooner a company begins to address these financial issues, the more financial restructuring options it will likely have;
- this approach can turn into a "bet the ranch" strategy, as the company risks waiting too long to act and losing the ability to maximize its value, and perhaps save itself;
- it does not take advantage of any mismatch between the market's pricing of the bonds and the company's prospects;
- the company is likely to find itself at a competitive disadvantage with rivals that have greater financial wherewithal; and
- management will be functionally working for the benefit of creditors until and unless the company can grow back into its capital structure.

Secured Lenders

Once a company stumbles financially, it will generally be in at least "technical" default under its credit agreement – and may be in payment default as well. This technical default signals a covenant breach, and (outside of Chapter 11) gives the secured lenders the right to call their loans. In practice, this gives the secured lenders the ability to approve or disapprove the company's course of action.

At their core, most secured lenders are concerned with minimizing their loan losses. Generally speaking, if the Status Quo alternative will permit a secured lender to ratchet its exposure down without precluding other options, the secured lender is likely to be supportive.

Accordingly, the view of this type of secured lender will be highly influenced by several factors:

Can the company continue to service its secured debt?

A secured lender – particularly a traditional secured lender, as opposed to a vulture investor – is motivated in part by maintaining a performing loan on its books. If the borrower's cash flow is such that it is in a position to make principal and interest payments – or at least interest payments – on its secured debt, lenders may support the Status Quo.

However, the secured lenders' view is likely to be unfavorably biased if junior constituencies would also be receiving major paydowns (see below). In such case, the secured lenders may argue that Chapter 11 is a better option, since pre-petition unsecured liabilities would be frozen.

Similarly, if a borrower is unable to make even secured interest payments, that augurs poorly for a Status Quo approach. Operations may be beyond salvage and may require more immediate and drastic courses of action (for example, a sale or liquidation of the company).

Is the company going to require near-term additional liquidity beyond that supported by the existing borrowing base?

This is a threshold issue for secured lenders as a borrower starts to hiccup or stumble. Status Quo is much more acceptable to a secured lender when a borrower remains in or close to formula. A borrower that requires additional monies to operate and maintain its existing capital structure will find it difficult to enlist enthusiastic secured lender support for the Status Quo program – unless the borrower can credibly demonstrate that Status Quo is likely to prove to be superior to the alternatives.

What about subordinated bond interest payments? As part of a Status Quo approach, the borrower may want to make a scheduled bond coupon payment. Clearly, if the company has run afoul of covenants in its Credit Agreement, the secured lenders should be able to block a subordinated coupon payment. And even if the company is not yet in such technical default but needs, or is likely to need, additional operating liquidity, the secured lenders will still have leverage on this decision, albeit not as much as if the company were actually in default.

Circumstances always differ in terms of how the secured lender will react to a discussion of whether to permit a bond coupon payment. Generally speaking, secured lenders do not like to see material payments to junior creditors if the secured lenders believe that a creditor compromise is foreseeable.

On the other hand, if the payment is made, then the bondholders will not have a seat at the table for at least six more months (most corporate bonds pay on a semiannual basis), and the secured lenders will be able to influence what happens to the company unfettered by the views of the junior creditors. In our experience, secured lenders generally care more about the cash going out the door than about whether the bondholders are in default (*i.e.*, "show me the money").

How comfortable are the secured lenders with their liquidation analysis for the "worst case" scenario?

To the extent that the secured lenders feel comfortable with their views of liquidation results (to wit, that they will comfortably come out whole), they will be far more comfortable with the Status Quo than if they are beginning to believe that the borrower's asset mix is starting to degrade to levels where the secured lenders may not come out whole. Once the secured lenders' recovery becomes problematic, behaviors can change. At collateral values close to the loan amount, the lenders may force a liquidation or other liquidity event. Conversely, at low recovery levels, lender reactions can vary greatly, including "playing ball" with the debtor if the upside scenarios are believable.

How comfortable are the secured lenders that the Status Quo approach will not preclude a viable sale strategy down the road?

Because the secured lenders almost always view a going concern sale process as superior to a liquidation, the secured lenders will usually need to be convinced that if the Status Quo continues, it is not likely to lead to liquidation. Secured lenders will want to know that if operations do not rebound as management projects, time will still be available to implement a going concern sale process that will get the secured lenders out whole.

"Loan-to-Own" Secureds

We want to point out that not all secured lenders are patient and constructive. Far from it. In particular, there is a type of secured creditor that thrives on crisis and insolvency. These "loan-to-own" lenders will take advantage of a distressed situation to try to convert their secured positions into as much value as they can. They don't need to have purchased at a discount to par to be successful in their endeavors. All the loan-to-own players need is an opportunity to act quickly in the absence of viable alternatives for the debtor.

When faced with loan-to-own lenders, the "Status Quo" may not be an option for the debtor. If a company finds itself it this position, it needs to engage financial professionals to develop alternatives as quickly as possible.

Bondholders

Bondholders seldom have a real say in determining whether a company embarks on a Status Quo approach. Instead, they are more or less there for the ride – unless the company misses an interest payment.

If the company is indeed able to make the coupon payment, the bondholders will likely have no immediate seat at the company's restructuring table. Because the company has remained in compliance with the terms of the indenture, the bondholders have been effectively sidelined for at least another six months, until the next payment date. On the other hand, they will have pocketed a coupon payment that perhaps they never anticipated the company would be in a position to make.

However, it is worth noting that bondholders may have another weapon at their disposal – but one that is rarely, if ever, used. If a company has a large cash position, has been burning cash through its pursuit of its business plan and continues to pursue strategies aimed at benefiting shareholders while putting bondholder and other creditor recoveries at high risk, we believe the bondholders could bring a credible lawsuit seeking to derail the company's strategies. The lawsuit would argue that the company (and its board) is dissipating assets and not acting in the best interests of creditors at a time when it is in the Zone of Insolvency. There can be meritorious defenses to such a lawsuit, but filing such a suit might give bondholders a seat at the table, through settlement discussions, that they might otherwise not have. This dynamic is discussed at greater length in Chapter 3.

Trade Creditors

A company needs to be very concerned about the impact on its trade creditors of pursuing the Status Quo alternative – because this approach likely leaves the company over-leveraged and with its liquidity constrained, at least until operations rebound.

In fact, it is the trade that will often derail a company's efforts to pursue the Status Quo alternative. The trade may become increasingly skittish about being stretched and about the company's wherewithal and leverage (especially the collateral position of the banks).

Loss of trade support is a common reason for a company to abandon the Status Quo in favor of other strategies.

Equity Holders

Old equity is the constituency that can potentially gain the most, but also is the one likely to be most at risk under the Status Quo approach. Old equity's appetite for risk will dictate its views of the Status Quo.

The advantage to old equity is that if the company can avoid a financial restructuring and "grow back" into supporting its existing capital structure, old equity should again be in the money and recognize great value. Avoiding a financial restructuring is frequently to the benefit of old equity – but only if the ship is able to right itself in a timely fashion.

Similar to those for the overall company, the potential disadvantages to this approach for old equity include:

- it places equity value in a precarious position, as the outcome for shareholders is in the hands of the general economy, the vagaries of the marketplace and the company's operating performance;
- if operating performance declines further, the company's financial restructuring alternatives are likely to dwindle further, to the probably permanent detriment of shareholder value and recoveries;
- should the company fail to grow back into its capital structure, old equity is likely to have done better if the company had pursued alternative restructuring or sale strategies earlier;
- if operating performance improves, the company's bonds, not the common stock, will "soak up" most of the initial economic gains, until and unless the bond price nears 100 cents on the dollar (meaning management is essentially working for the benefit of only the unsecured creditors until then); and
- it does not permit equity to take advantage of any mismatch between the existing price of the bonds and the company's prospects.

Making a Decision

Companies rarely make a proactive decision to pursue the Status Quo alternative. Instead, they end up pursuing Status Quo as a result of <u>not</u> making a decision. Unfortunately, this places the company in a reactive mode where it may need to adopt one or more restructuring strategies in a crisis atmosphere.

It does not have to be that way. Ideally, a company (or its advisors) should be able to identify the early signs of trouble outlined in Chapter 1. And having recognized the symptoms, it should analyze the alternatives available – starting with maintaining the Status Quo.

Depending upon the circumstances, we can be big fans of a Status Quo approach. We just think that a company should make a deliberate and well-reasoned decision to pursue it – rather than choosing that approach out of simple inertia.

CHAPTER 9—EXPLORING THIRD-PARTY OPTIONS

Almost invariably in restructurings, companies and their constituencies will consider exploring the values that may be attainable in the M&A or private equity marketplaces. They may not embark upon, much less consummate, a sale process as part of a reorganization, but their assessment of a third party outcome is a critical benchmark against which to measure other alternatives. The focus of this chapter is largely on the concept of a sale to a third party. However, the same general principles as to negotiating dynamics apply to situations where private equity investors make an investment for less than 100% control.

As in the contemplation of other strategies, the various constituencies in a restructuring are likely to have differing perspectives about a transaction with a third party.

One of the most important aspects of a consummated third party M&A transaction is its relative *certainty.* The company receives cash and other, hopefully valuable, consideration in exchange for businesses that may have been operating sub-optimally. In contrast, if the company were to hang onto its assets, it would preserve the upside potential, but at a substantially higher risk.

In other words, a sale may well provide lower value than a restructuring through a compromise of creditor claims into equity (*e.g.*, an "internal" reorganization, discussed in Chapter 10). To the financially savvy, this may come as a bit of a surprise. The conventional wisdom in investment banking holds that merger transactions are generally consummated at a premium to public or other market values, because of operational synergies, elimination of overhead costs and other factors. (From time to time, of course, stock market conditions can become so bullish that valuations are bid up far in excess of what a cash bidder would be willing to pay in the merger market, as the Internet bubble demonstrated.)

In the restructuring world, however, things are a little different:

- Buyers may not be willing to pay for the potential of an operational turnaround. The company's constituencies must decide between a bird in the hand (the merger consideration) or a possible two in the bush (the value of the reorganization securities should the turnaround succeed);
- Financial and other data may be unreliable because of poor MIS and other factors (as noted in Chapter 3). Moreover, the seller may not be around later to stand behind its representations and warranties. In a number of important aspects, these are "as is, where is" deals, which frequently are consummated at lower prices than a "fully repped" deal;
- As we have pointed out, fraudulent conveyance may represent a risk to buyers;
- People being what they are, a distressed seller is a vulnerable seller. While the effect of this vulnerability can be mitigated (more on this below), it is quite common for buyers to offer "low-ball" bids or to try to "re-trade" the deal at the last minute at a substantially lower price. The end result is that distressed sales can occur at lower prices than if they were conducted without a whiff of financial trouble; and
- If a company is deteriorating rapidly, there may be little remaining value unless the business can be preserved while the assets are marketed and sold expeditiously (the "melt-down" scenario).

On the other hand, Chapter 11 provides certain tools that allow for the removal of onerous contracts, the granting of clean title (perhaps the cleanest known to man) and elimination of fraudulent conveyance risk. These factors can enhance purchase prices.

How do the various constituencies view the M&A transaction? It depends upon where they sit in the company's capital structure relative to the values.

Assume that a company has $50 million in bank debt and $150 million in subordinated debt. Assume further that a buyer is willing to pay $100 million in cash for the company. In this case, we would expect the banks to embrace the deal, although they might be relatively indifferent about the choice between the sale and an internal reorganization, if they were reasonably certain their bank debt could be refinanced in an internal plan. If the banks were concerned about the refinancing risk, they might have been pressing for a sale, and the likelihood of consummating an internal plan might be diminished.

The subordinated debtholders, on the other hand, would have to do quite a bit more homework. In a "strict priority" sense (in which the stockholders would receive nothing), these junior creditors would receive $50 million, or 33% of face, in the M&A transaction. These creditors would need to compare that recovery to their assessment of the risks and rewards associated with achieving recovery through an internal reorganization – including the prospect that the company could be sold into the merger market at a later date.

Now assume that the buyer lowers its bid from $100 million to $75 million. The bank group may not change its view (although it may grow more nervous about the seeming loss of implied value coverage). However, the subordinated debtholders may very well change theirs. Their 33% recovery has now sunk to 17%. What happens in such a case? It depends upon various factors – each of which may mean different things to different individual members of the creditor class.

What is the risk-adjusted expected realization from an internal plan? Will the buyer try to re-trade again? Can the buyer be made to pay more? How long will it take to consummate the sale transaction compared with the time needed to execute an internal plan? Vulture investors with high IRR targets may have relatively short time horizons – and may choose a quicker outcome, even if it results in a lower absolute recovery.

The smaller the recovery for the subordinated notes, the more incentive such holders have to "roll the dice" to see if they can achieve a higher recovery through an internal plan.

And what about the equity holders? In the above examples, we have assumed that the old equity is "out of the money." In general, we believe that old equity is better off with higher long-term potential values and more time to achieve higher values – which translates into a likely preference for an internal plan that contemplates an operational turnaround. Roughly speaking, these concepts correspond to the volatility and duration of a call option; in essence, old equity is functionally an out-of-the-money call option in most restructurings.

In contrast, a sale at a value materially below the face amount of the debt can easily translate into no recovery for old equity, unless it has made alternative arrangements. One alternative would be if old equity could reach an agreement with its creditors before embarking on a sale process. Such an agreement could contemplate a pre-agreed split of proceeds, according to a formula based upon recoveries or otherwise. The creditors could offer such a deal to old equity, which may well control the debtor because of exclusivity provisions or simply by being outside of court, in exchange for agreeing to market the company – which might be difficult for the creditors to effect unilaterally. In other words, the allocation to old equity would be the "price of peace" for pursuing a sale alternative. We note, however, that old equity must be particularly careful about such agreements because of the potential pitfalls regarding the enforceability of any such agreement against the creditors. We used this strategy successfully with Petsec Energy and with Osyka Corporation, to old equity's advantage.

Alternatively, the company could initiate a sale unilaterally, and it could specifically request that potential buyers set aside an allocation for old equity as part of their proposals. The company could then enter into definitive purchase and sale agreements with the high bidder that provided that old equity would actually receive such allocation – or no transaction would occur at all.

Pursuant to this approach, the company would try to provide the creditors with a "take-it-or-leave it" alternative. Although the creditors would likely respond by refusing to go along unless the buyer or old equity would change the deal in the creditors' favor, the tactic can be a powerful negotiating tool for old equity. One of us advised Amoco with respect to this approach in connection with its successful purchase of Dome Petroleum.

Timing

One key driver in the timing of a sale is liquidity. And that is frequently a function of the company's relationships with its secured bank group. If the company has adequate liquidity – through out-of-court funding, a DIP line or sufficient cash collateral availability – then the company may have the luxury of considering the appropriate time to enter the merger market. Conversely, if the secured banks are legitimately concerned that the company is bleeding cash or collateral value and if no additional collateral can be provided in replacement, the company's ability to continue to operate (not to mention its ability to choose the time of sale) is questionable.

In such a case, the secured banks are essentially in command of the situation, because they can control decisions to fund or to stop operations. The banks do not necessarily have unfettered control; other constituencies and the court itself could weigh in on any decision. At the end of the day, however, if the company has no other source of liquidity but the secured banks – and the banks are being impaired through deterioration in the collateral base – the conditions that the banks impose upon the reorganization will largely control the process. Put simplistically, they can choose between liquidating all or a portion of the company, supporting an operational turnaround or pursuing a merger market transaction. These alternatives need not be all or nothing; some assets could be sold in the merger market and others liquidated.

Any such decision needs to be made in consideration of the likely recoveries through each alternative, together with assessments of timing, cash burn rates and other risks. If the banks could get out whole through shutting the doors and liquidating the collateral, and continuing in business (either to effect a turnaround or a sale) would erode the collateral base through ongoing cash losses, the likely outcome may be a liquidation.

Conversely, if the collateral liquidation values would be insufficient to repay the banks in full (as is frequently the case), the banks need to consider other alternatives. In such cases, the banks are likely to demand that the company begin to market all of its businesses and assets immediately, while in return the banks agree to continue to fund operations. The banks may try to confine the time frame for sale in order to limit the cash burn. The banks can then compare the results of the M&A process (or the interim indications) to their other alternatives. The bank group does not necessarily need to wait until the buyer is ready to sign a definitive agreement before making a decision. If there is lack of buyer interest at levels that would materially beat liquidation, the bank group may curtail the M&A process early. And if the secured banks do not like the price being obtained in an auction in court, they can "credit bid" their claims (generally valued at par) to buy the assets themselves.

GORDIAN KNOTS/Riedel Environmental Technologies, Inc.

Through a series of acquisitions financed largely with debt, Riedel expanded its business to become a vertically integrated provider of environmental services. Riedel's operating performance significantly

> declined because of slower-than-expected spending in the remediation of Defense Department and Energy Department sites and weak enforcement of environmental regulations in the commercial sector. As a result, Riedel faced a severe cash crisis.
>
> Riedel engaged Gordian Group to assist in restructuring its debt at a time when Riedel was within days of liquidation (which would have generated insufficient proceeds to cover the face amount of the secured debt and left nothing for the bondholders and other unsecured creditors, not to mention shareholders). Before Gordian Group's arrival, the bank had been preparing to force Riedel to liquidate, even though it knew it would take a haircut in a liquidation. Gordian Group convinced the senior secured bank to extend additional credit to enable the company to conduct a sale of substantially all of its assets. As Gordian Group demonstrated good progress on the sale process, the bank continued to cooperate.
>
> By running a skillful and competitive process, Gordian Group was able to assist Riedel in selling its primary operating business outside of Chapter 11 at a highly advantageous price, thereby maximizing the recovery for both the bank (which was paid in full) and the unsecured creditors. Gordian Group also provided the company with a fairness opinion regarding this complex sale effort, which involved multiple competing bidders using different forms of consideration.
>
> The sales effort produced sufficient value so that even old equity holders were able to obtain a recovery, even though unsecured creditors received considerably less than 100 cents on the dollar.

If the banks do not drive the push for an M&A process, then the junior creditors frequently do. The motivations for this vary but include a desire to compare "actual" M&A values to reorganization values, the preference of some creditors for cash rather than speculative reorganization securities, and the prospect of achieving an earlier resolution of the case.

But to a junior creditor (or an equity holder, for that matter), the alternative to a sale in large or middle-market companies is generally not liquidation – it is reorganization. And that gives rise to some important dynamics.

The fact that a company launches an M&A process does not necessarily mean that it will ultimately consummate a sale, unless the values compare favorably to those of an internal reorganization. For that reason, many sale processes are now called "market tests," in order to distinguish them from an "everything must go" sale process. In these market tests, the company makes very clear that the buyers will be competing with the internal plan values.

Moreover, reorganization constituencies are acutely aware that the alternative to selling now is not necessarily no sale at all. It could very well be that value could be maximized by waiting to sell at a later date, after operations have stabilized in a post-reorganization environment.

Third-Party Recapitalization

Plans of reorganization can be utilized to sell a company, to recapitalize it or to reorganize internally.

GORDIAN KNOTS/Office of Thrift Supervision

Gordian Group advised the federal Office of Thrift Supervision (OTS) in connection with the restructurings of both CalFed and GLENFED, two large, failing savings and loan institutions.

The OTS believed that the government could save significant taxpayer resources if the institutions were restructured commercially, rather than seized by the Resolution Trust Corporation. As a large contingent creditor, the government was seeking to maximize the values associated with the continuation of these entities as going concerns.

Gordian Group provided advice to the OTS with respect to implementation of its policy and economic objectives through negotiations in a commercial context. Frequently, Gordian Group needed to respond to government requests for information and recommendations on an immediate basis, given the tight time frames involved and the difficult dynamics associated with a multiple-sided negotiation involving the OTS, the institutions, existing security holders and new money participants.

Specific topics on which Gordian Group advised included the structure of exchange offers of newly-issued equity securities for outstanding debt obligations, negotiation with bondholder groups, development and analysis of financial and legal alternatives available to the government and assessment of the institutions' ability to raise capital.

> Gordian Group was also asked to make recommendations regarding the government's decisions as to continuation of capital adequacy waivers. Without such forbearance, these institutions would likely not have had time to reorganize.
>
> Both CalFed and GLENFED were successfully recapitalized through external capital infusions and compromise of pre-existing debt and other claims. The intangible assets associated with continuing lending operations were preserved, and taxpayers were relieved of the significant potential expense that would have ensued as a result of the alternative to these restructurings – seizure.

The Process – the Big Picture

One goal of the process should be to achieve maximum value in the face of all of the company's problems. These typically include liquidity and time constraints, uneven operating results, employee defections, incomplete financial and operating data, and other general problems associated with being a distressed seller. The mix of these various challenges is generally somewhat different for every company and demands that each M&A process be tailored to the specific needs of the client.

We cannot stress enough the problems that flow from being a distressed seller. Potential buyers can try to "re-trade" the deal by lowering the price at closing, or some other time – a not-so-subtle bait and switch – if they think they can get away with such ploys. Frequently, buyers try to invoke the "material adverse change" clause of the purchase agreement. Given that many distressed companies do not <u>experience</u> a material adverse change, but rather <u>are</u> a material adverse change, some buyers can have a high degree of confidence that they are well-positioned for a re-trade down the line. Accordingly, sellers frequently try (with varying degrees of success) to eliminate or limit the scope of the material adverse change clause.

The best way to fend off re-trades and other such hardball tactics is to develop alternatives. And the best way to do that is to create competition. Conversely, the buyer's goal is to end-run a seller's competitive process.

The "self-help" form of seller competition is a viable internal plan of reorganization (which will be discussed in detail in the following chapter). To be credible, this internal plan needs to be feasible, meaning that it is likely that the exit financing can be obtained in an amount sufficient to fund any required refinancings, and that the company will be financially stable after the reorganization. Further, the company needs to be able to articulate – with a straight face – that the values in such a plan are at least competitive with certain merger market alternatives.

Done appropriately, this can place a floor under third-party bids. This is particularly true when there are significant unfunded liabilities that a buyer may perceive differently than the company itself. For example, if unfunded pension plans could be maintained through an internal plan but would need to be terminated in a sale, the pension laws create a dynamic where the liabilities increase more in a sale. Similarly, buyers may view potential environmental liabilities as being more onerous than does the company already saddled with them.

External competition entails a contact program with appropriate strategic and financial buyers. The first step is to identify and prioritize the likely buyers based upon business fit, acquisitiveness, ability to do distressed deals and financial wherewithal. Although it is tempting to conclude that the desire for competition translates into "the more the merrier," that is not always the best course. More participants require more human resources to handle them. And management may not have the bandwidth to be able to deal with a huge number of potential buyers. A more judicious initial approach calls for a considered winnowing process.

We frequently encounter requests from potential buyers for an "exclusive" arrangement, whereby they can have a period of weeks or months during which they are the only buyer allowed to pursue a transaction with the company. Such an arrangement, they say, is the only way they would be willing to spend the time and money to work with the company. Generally, we do not find this argument persuasive. While in some cases (such as joint ventures), the transactions are so complex and so specialized that only one or two industry players could even think about participating, more often the erstwhile buyer is just trying to get a leg up on the competition – and to take advantage of the distressed seller. In effect, the potential buyer is hoping that its head start will chill competitive bidding. Granting the bidder this advantage generally translates into an equal and opposite disadvantage for the seller.

Another key potential buy-side tactic is to purchase sufficient claims within creditor classes to enable the buyer to achieve blocking positions (in terms of voting to approve a plan of reorganization) that may derail the debtor's goal of consummating a plan of reorganization without the buyer's consent. However, in the event that the purchaser of such claims does not ultimately succeed in its effort to buy the company, it takes the economic risk on its ownership of the debtor's securities, including the risk of cram-down.

The number of potential buyers contacted should be a function of:

- the diversity of the company's businesses (the more disparate the businesses, the wider a variety of buyers that may be required);
- the potential impediments to closing (the more contingent liabilities or other problems, the wider the net that needs to be cast); and
- the relative attractiveness of the property (the uglier it is, the more potential buyers that are needed).

In this contact process, the seller and its investment banker need to think through such issues as confidentiality agreements, the extent and timing of materials that will be distributed to prospective buyers (see below), the structure of the winnowing process, the conduct of additional due diligence, and the strategy for achieving a closeable deal.

One key early decision the seller needs to make is whether to insist on confidentiality agreements. On the one hand, these agreements confer tremendous advantages to the seller in addition to simply requiring erstwhile buyers to keep the information they receive confidential. For example, the successful bidder will be able to rely on such agreements after the sale, providing an additional layer of protection with respect to intellectual property and potentially increasing the price the buyer would be willing to pay in the absence of such agreements.

Moreover, confidentiality agreements can be used to enhance the seller's control over the process. The agreement can be structured to limit sharply the erstwhile buyer's ability to circumvent the rules that the seller and its investment banker establish. Sometimes referred to as "anti-bear hug" provisions, these restrictions can prohibit a potential buyer from acquiring securities or other claims on the company, from attempting to influence the restructuring process, or even from talking to creditors without the company's permission. Such provisions can prevent the buyer from trying to cut a deal with one or more of the company's constituencies or from acquiring a major position in the company's claims or securities in order to gain a leg up on the process.

On the other hand, confidentiality agreements take time to negotiate and execute. If the seller is under severe time pressure, these agreements may not be practical in all cases. Many buyers refuse, as a matter of policy, to enter into confidentiality agreements – particularly those with anti-bear hug provisions. Many strategic buyers may refuse to enter into confidentiality agreements because of thorny issues with respect to hiring of employees and use of competitive information gleaned during due diligence.

Another nuance of the confidentiality agreement process is that many buyers are reticent to enter into such arrangements without first having seen some preliminary information regarding the company. Many sellers and their investment bankers address this with "teaser" packages of non-sensitive information that the erstwhile buyer can evaluate in connection with its decision to enter into the company's process. At the beginning of the process, the seller and its investment banker need to weigh the trade-offs and make a decision regarding the relative merits of using these confidentiality agreements, including, perhaps, a toned-down version.

We also note that bankruptcy courts do not always look kindly on financially troubled companies that force prospective buyers to enter into confidentially agreements – on the theory this both takes time that a distressed seller cannot afford and may chill buyer interest.

We shall never forget the chief judge of one of the nation's bankruptcy courts some years ago as he addressed this issue during our testimony about a sale process. When we came to the part about the confidentiality agreement process, he threw down the sports page he was reading (truly!) and exclaimed, "Confidentiality agreement? Confidentiality agreement? That's like saying you've been gut-shot, and you're lying in the emergency room on a gurney, but when the nurse comes over to evaluate your status you're too modest to let her peek under the sheet. Sheesh!"

Key considerations the seller and the investment banker need to evaluate in developing a sale strategy include:

- **Strength of the internal plan alternative.** A distressed sale process is all about alternatives and perceived weaknesses. If a potential buyer believes that it is competing not only against other buyers but against a high-value, credible internal plan, its own price thinking and bidding strategy are likely to be impacted. Conversely, if the seller has no viable internal plan or the plan is simply akin to a "Potemkin village" – the elaborate empty shells of homes that were constructed to mislead Catherine the Great about the prosperity of some regions she ruled – the buyer may choose to pursue a "low-ball" pricing strategy or attempt a last-minute re-trade.

- **Relative attractiveness of the property offered for sale.** Just because a business is being sold in a distressed context does not mean that it is a dog. We have been involved in many situations in which the seller was perceived by the buyer group to be a valuable strategic asset, despite its recent history of losses. Having an investment banker that is able to recognize the relative strength of the property is a critical part of strategy development.
- **Quality of the buyer list.** The seller's investment banker needs to assess the number of potential buyers likely to have significant interest in all or part of the seller's businesses, as well as the ability of such buyers to consummate a deal.

If time and liquidity permit, it is generally useful to winnow out obviously uncompetitive buyers early in the process. If such buyers are likely to fail in their quest to acquire the company – as a result of relatively low price thinking, inadequate financial wherewithal or other factors, culling them will free resources to devote to buyers more likely to be able to close at higher prices. In a distressed environment, such culling streamlines the process so that a transaction can occur faster (sometimes, however, there is no time to winnow or cull).

A wide variety of winnowing processes are available. The most common is a bidding technique in which the seller's investment banker tells the potential buyers (generally, as they receive an initial information package) that there will be an initial round of bidding based upon the material distributed to all buyers. There is no one "right" time frame in which to call for such initial bids. In distressed situations, the deadline may need to be only a few weeks from initial distribution of information. Note, too, that if time permits, the culling need not occur until after potential buyers conduct on-site due diligence.

Upon receipt of preliminary indications of interest, the seller and the investment banker can determine which subset of buyers is most likely to be able to close at an attractive price. In certain situations, the culling process is repeated more than once, which can serve both to increase overall bidding levels (by creating an impression of intensified competition) and to eliminate bidding stragglers. Be aware, though, that buyers can rapidly tire of such techniques and perceive that they are being gamed by the seller. The seller's investment banker needs to be aware of such tradeoffs and act accordingly.

Once the buyer group is at a manageable size (whether culling is used, or not), the seller and its advisor can begin to work closely with each potential buyer. This allows the potential buyer to obtain more in-depth due diligence information through meetings with management and interaction with the seller's professionals. In a distressed situation where information may be suspect and where the seller's post-closing indemnities may be questionable, the willingness and ability to provide extensive due diligence can materially improve the prospects for obtaining a higher price.

At this point in the process, the seller and its team are likely to have a reasonably good sense of which buyers are likely to go forward, as well as of what their likely price thinking is. Indeed, it is quite common for the seller's investment banker to provide price guidance to buyers during this period.

And the mechanisms must be established for consummating the deal. As discussed in Chapter 3, an evaluation must be made of whether to effect a Chapter 11 sale through a Plan of Reorganization or through a 363 Sale. As we have said repeatedly, no single approach fits all situations.

GORDIAN KNOTS/Pinnacle Holdings

In the case of Pinnacle Holdings Inc., we were called in to explore, under strict time constraints, a variety of alternatives to assist in Pinnacle's restructuring.

Pinnacle leases and maintains space on a portfolio of owned, managed and leased communications sites that are primarily composed of towers and rooftops where wireless communication providers can locate their antennas and equipment. Pinnacle created a portfolio of wireless communications site clusters in markets including Atlanta, Birmingham, Boston, Chicago, Dallas, Houston, Los Angeles, New Orleans, New York, Orlando and Tampa.

During the course of its rapid acquisition program, Pinnacle had accumulated a significant level of debt, and eventually it violated certain financial covenants and defaulted on an interest payment on its convertible notes. It engaged Gordian Group when it was at risk because of its inability to comply with the requirements of its senior credit agreement.

Pinnacle generated annual revenues of approximately $180 million and annual adjusted EBITDA of approximately $80 million. Prior to its restructuring, Pinnacle had net debt outstanding of approximately $892 million, and its Net Debt/EBITDA ratio was 11.1x. Among the alternatives that we examined were raising additional capital to effect a paydown of Pinnacle's credit facility, development of an internal restructuring or recapitalization, and exploring M&A alternatives with potential financial and strategic buyers.

Gordian Group, in connection with Pinnacle's management and counsel, was able to recapitalize and restructure Pinnacle successfully through a plan of reorganization under the protection of Chapter 11. The plan of reorganization was funded by an aggregate equity investment of $205 million by the new investors and a significantly reduced, amended and restated credit facility provided by the existing senior credit facility lenders.

Pinnacle's senior discount noteholders received a recovery of approximately 35 percent through a combination of new common shares and cash, at the noteholders' election. Pinnacle's junior convertible subordinated noteholders received a *de minimis* recovery through cash and warrants for shares of the reorganized Pinnacle and despite the very modest recoveries of Pinnacle's subordinated creditors, Pinnacle's common stockholders received a recovery through warrants for shares of the reorganized Pinnacle.

GORDIAN KNOTS/Pentacon, Inc.

Pentacon, Inc., was one of the largest distributors of fasteners and small parts to original-equipment manufacturers in the aerospace and industrial markets. It served approximately 7,500 customers that manufacture a wide variety of products including diesel engines, locomotives, power turbines, motorcycles, telecommunications equipment, refrigeration equipment and aerospace equipment.

Pentacon had borrowed heavily to complete two acquisitions that did not produce the expected return on investment. Given the leverage resulting from these acquisitions and the subsequent downturn in the aerospace industry, Pentacon was unable to finance its operations and service its indebtedness.

Gordian Group was engaged by the Company to explore a variety of alternatives to address Pentacon's leverage and liquidity issues. These included raising mezzanine financing in conjunction with a tender offer for Pentacon's senior subordinated notes, negotiating an internal restructuring with Pentacon's senior subordinated noteholders and exploring M&A alternatives with potential financial and strategic buyers.

Working with Pentacon's management and counsel and its creditors, we determined that a pre-negotiated Chapter 11 all-cash sale of Pentacon's assets to Anixter International Inc. (a Fortune 500 company) provided the highest and best recovery to all constituencies. There is a somewhat reduced competitive dynamic though a sale via a POR, and it takes longer than a 363 – but the advantage is it wraps up all loose ends in the case and usually affords more stability for the underlying business.

Similar tradeoffs must be weighed in out-of-court transactions, as well. These considerations are relevant for both the buyer and the seller, and the seller should have a pretty good feel for the needs of each buyer with respect to these key structural issues. Armed with knowledge regarding all these issues, the seller can set the stage for the final episode in the sale process.

A distressed sale process frequently requires the consent of one or more impaired classes. These consents are generally not granted overnight. Moreover, there are rules in bankruptcy auctions that require an open, transparent sale process. These dynamics can cause the sale approval process to go on for quite a while. And, therefore, to cause friction between buyers and sellers.

When a buyer enters into a definitive contract, it wants the seller bound to the deal. Unfortunately in situations involving widespread creditors and bankruptcy court approvals, that ideal may not be possible.

On the other hand, the seller will want the certainty of having a buyer committed to closing a transaction. Among other benefits, a firm purchase contract provides a floor under the restructuring values. And if a higher bidder emerges, so much the better.

These conflicting goals are generally accommodated within the restructuring world through offering "bidder protection" to a chosen "lead bidder". This "lead bidder" (sometimes referred to as the "stalking horse") may be the highest bidder, may offer the best combination of price and certainty, or may simply be the best bidder willing to enter into an agreement with the seller.

In order to provide incentives to such a lead bidder to play ball with the seller, professionals have several tools at their disposal. In view of the fact that the lead bidder will have to allow its bid to be shopped (either actively or merely by having the world be aware of it), the seller can grant the lead bidder a "break-up" or "topping" fee.

The structure and amount of such break-up fees vary widely, but may aggregate 1% to 5% of a transaction's total consideration. The fee may also contemplate reimbursement of certain of the bidder's out-of-pocket costs.

Another form of bidder protection can grant the lead bidder the right to beat another bidder simply by matching the latter's bid. This can be important in situations where the court-determined minimum bidding increments are large. Or where the court imposes a rule that other bidders use the lead bidder's exact purchase contract as the template for their own bids. Or where the court allows the lead bidder to use the amount of the break-up fee as "green stamps" toward the determination of bid value.

The list can go on. But with creative professionals and a constructive bankruptcy court (which needs to approve these provisions), lead bidders can indeed obtain advantages. In turn, such advantages can make it compelling for them to assist the seller by providing a floor price – rather than just opportunistically waiting on the sidelines.

Bringing It Home

At this point, the goal of the M&A portion of the process is to get one or more definitive agreements with as few "outs" as possible. The company can then choose to enter into one of these agreements and move toward closing – or to reject the offers if the internal plan is more compelling. This is perhaps the trickiest part of the whole process, because a host of problems inevitably crops up when the parties start negotiating the details.

Here, too, no one path is "right." However, in dealing with distressed companies where time is at a premium, it is extremely useful to provide the potential buyers with a draft purchase and sale contract before the final round of bidding. We recognize that the typical non-distressed M&A protocol calls for the buyer to provide the initial draft of the purchase and sale agreement. But in distressed situations, we have observed that when the seller creates these, time is saved, key issues important to the seller are highlighted and competing bids are more easily compared (because the buyers are at least starting from the same agreement).

The buyers can then fill in the blanks with respect to price and form of consideration and can mark up the document with respect to the terms of sale with guidance that the race will go to the buyer with the best combination of higher price and fewest deviations from the contract as drafted.

Each deal is different, and the parties can be at loggerheads over any number of issues, including environmental problems, pension accruals, employee retention programs, and so forth. Assuming that the buyer does not drop out because of concerns over such issues, the differences are typically resolved through negotiation of the purchase price in the definitive agreement.

But some issues can creep into a definitive agreement, and that can lead to a major re-trade or other problems near closing. Two such common issues are "material adverse change" (MAC) outs and buyer closing contingencies, such as a "financing out." Simply put, a MAC clause allows the buyer to drop out of the deal if a major problem emerges with the seller's business (and sometimes even its "prospects"). Obviously, a distressed company is no stranger to MACs, and the occurrence of such an event would effectively give the buyer a "free look" at the business with an opportunity to re-trade the deal. A "financing out" gives the buyer the ability to walk away if it is unable to obtain financing on acceptable terms. This also gives the buyer an opportunity to re-trade the deal.

In an ideal world, the seller's investment banker would refuse to allow such provisions into a contract because of the uncertainties they create. But the investment banker to a distressed seller rarely lives in a perfect world.

When they have the luxury of competing bids, the seller and its advisors need to evaluate the proposals across a number of parameters – not just price. The best bid may not be the highest cash bid. In some situations, though, cash may be king, and alternate forms of consideration just may not cut it. The concept here is that the investment banker must analyze which bid is the "highest and best." A "highest-and-best" valuation analysis must take into account the two key goals of a distressed sale, which do not always neatly dovetail: (1) maximizing value to the estate and (2) achieving relative certainty of results.

Across another dimension, the company needs to consider the value of the stated bid against the likelihood of consummating the deal. This is where the issues of material adverse change, financing contingencies and other outs come into play. In a situation where the inability to close could cause real damage (as in a distressed sale), the possibility of achieving a premium price may not be worth the incremental risk of the "outs."

As we have observed, a bird in the hand is often worth two in the bush. The non-price aspects of the definitive agreement underscore the importance of trying to keep as many bidders involved in negotiating definitive agreements until the very end. The best way to achieve the tightest definitive agreement is to conduct the negotiations in as competitive a manner as possible, so the "winning" bidder doesn't believe that it can hold the seller over a barrel.

The Nuts and Bolts

However good the strategy may be, it is also necessary to execute the due diligence and documentation tasks well. Given the tight timelines frequently encountered in distressed M&A, it may be of critical importance to think through – in advance – all the major items likely to come up. If a buyer is likely to need before closing an environmental study that might take weeks to prepare, and the seller has not thought to commence such a study earlier, the closing could be delayed significantly. Such delays can be disastrous to a distressed company.

One of the first tasks in any M&A process is the development of data and marketing materials. In distressed M&A, the time available is frequently materially less than in a conventional M&A assignment. In fact, in a few "Hail Mary" situations (as last-gasp, desperation plays are called in the sports world), we have had a week or less to assemble a marketing package, compared with the two months or more common to conventional transactions.

GORDIAN KNOTS/Colfor and Colmach; Intelogic Trace

Colfor and Colmach were related companies that had combined annual sales of $90 million to the automotive OEM marketplace. Colfor and Colmach were not reorganizable, and their customers – the automotive OEMs – required that they be sold quickly. We were retained to do this shortly after an involuntary bankruptcy petition was filed against each company.

All buyers were aware of the debtors' vulnerability, and many were prepared to sit back to see whether there would be a liquidation at bargain prices. Because of this buyer "fence-sitting," Colfor and Colmach faced the unpleasant prospect of having lender and customer support withdrawn, facing near-term deadlines with the bankruptcy court and not having a lead bidder in hand with which to file a sale motion. Gordian Group had no time to prepare a "book."

Gordian Group crafted a unique solution tailored to these circumstances and was successful in creating an auction sale environment that drew seven bidders from the sidelines within a month or so. Moreover, Gordian Group orchestrated a process that forced buyers to submit "highest and best" offers and that resulted in a significant increase in consideration from the opening bid. The companies signed a contract with the highest bidder, which was presented to and approved by the court.

An even more dramatic case involved Intelogic Trace, a company that provided computer, telecommunications and other electronic equipment installations and support services. The company found that it was unable to service its indebtedness and effected a restructuring in bankruptcy with its key creditors.

Shortly after it emerged from bankruptcy, Intelogic Trace engaged Gordian Group to provide advice regarding maximizing shareholder value. We immediately discovered that, unbeknownst to the bankruptcy court that had just blessed the reorganization, Intelogic Trace did not have enough money to stay in business. It should never have come out of bankruptcy in the first place. The company's new owners were equally surprised by the news and were willing to provide only a relatively small amount of incremental liquidity.

We knew we were in a race against the clock, and that we had to develop marketing materials and contact buyers. We had to negotiate definitive purchase and sale agreements, and we had to obtain an agreement by the buyer to provide needed DIP financing through closing.

The nature of Intelogic Trace's business was such that its value was largely associated with intangible assets, such as service contracts. A severe liquidity problem would materially and adversely affect the company's ability to operate, and would result in major losses for all of Intelogic Trace's constituencies.

In order to preserve values for these constituencies, Gordian Group had to move extremely quickly to preserve and maximize the company's intangible values. Almost immediately, Gordian Group negotiated with the company's lenders to obtain new capital and certain other concessions. Shortly thereafter, Gordian Group:

- contacted more than 100 potential purchasers;
- obtained a buyer for the company's assets prior to filing for protection; under Chapter 11 for the second time;
- arranged for the lead buyer to extend immediate credit; and
- assisted counsel in orchestrating a second Chapter 11 filing to implement an emergency asset sale

Less than three months later, Intelogic Trace was sold in a bankruptcy court sale. The proceeds were sufficient to repay the secured creditor in full, and to provide some recovery for unsecured claims. The emergence from the first bankruptcy to a closed M&A transaction for the whole business in a subsequent Chapter 11 took four months, including the negotiation and execution of a stalking-horse contract within 10 days of the buyer's commencement of due diligence. A real "Hail Mary" success story. The judge in the case commended us for our successful efforts in this very difficult matter.

The primary objective of the marketing materials is to encourage potential bidders to delve more deeply into the company, rather than to provide a comprehensive opus. The trick is to strike the right balance between early-stage disclosure and time constraints and to be creative and pragmatic in light of exigent circumstances.

GORDIAN KNOTS/Allied Digital Technologies, Inc.

Allied Digital Technologies, Inc. (ADT) was formed through a merger of Allied Digital, Inc. and Vaughn Communications, and was one of the nation's largest independent multimedia manufacturers and providers of supply-chain management services and videotape duplicating equipment, with $200 million in revenues. The merger was financed by bank debt and equity provided by a major private equity sponsor.

> Hoped-for synergies from the merger failed to materialize, and within months of closing, the deal sponsor engaged a crisis manager, as well as Gordian Group, to seek to effect a sale of all or parts of ADT. The bank lenders were strongly encouraging of a sale process, particularly given that ADT was in a liquidity crisis, although they openly questioned whether a sale could be effected under such circumstances.
>
> Within a matter of months, Gordian Group prepared a comprehensive Confidential Information Memorandum in conjunction with management, identified and contacted about 100 potential strategic and financial acquirers, developed and implemented a strategy to split ADT into two component parts to enable a sale either of the whole or of component parts of ADT and consummated, through several bankruptcy section 363 sales, a sale of one part of ADT to AmericDisc (a Canadian strategic buyer) and a sale of the other part of ADT to a financial buyer.
>
> The sale process was complex and competitive. As a result of the highly successful sale process, values at ADT were maximized.

The development of these marketing materials needs to occur in concert with the decision about a confidentiality agreement. If a confidentiality agreement is used, the marketing materials may contain significant sensitive information. At the same time, the seller is likely to have to create a "teaser" memo that deletes such sensitive information in order to give the prospective buyer a basis on which it can elect to enter into the confidentiality agreement. If there is no confidentiality agreement, the seller may insist that the initial marketing materials contain relatively less sensitive information. .

On the one hand, a good rule of thumb is to treat all buyers equally, on a level playing field. On the other hand, when a seller is dealing with direct competitors, it might withhold proprietary information (*i.e.*, cost data and customers) from such competitors until late in the process, when the seller is certain the competitor is a viable bidder – and not just a "tire kicker."

Buyers will certainly want more information than what is presented in the initial marketing materials – no matter how extensive such materials are. Such requests can be accommodated in various ways. These days, the most efficient is to establish a "virtual," online data room. The contents of the data room typically include corporate organization materials, detailed historical financial statements, budgets and projections, customer and supplier information, appraisals and engineering reports, and employee data. Prospective buyers can log in and review the material and obtain copies of documents. We reiterate that the seller's team must anticipate the need for reports that take time to prepare, such as environmental assessments. Planning can save a lot of time between entering into a contract and closing.

When representing buyers, we have sometimes found these data rooms to be disorganized and lacking requisite information. This disarray creates the impression that few competitors have expressed interest in the property – because if they had, the data room would surely run more smoothly from the experience of dealing with other buyers' requests. Accordingly, the seller's investment banker should take care to avoid this perception.

Once an interested buyer has digested the marketing and due diligence material, it is likely to request meetings with management. This can be a highly sensitive time in the process.

The buyer's goal is to get a detailed picture of operations, prospects and risks from the key management personnel. Certain buyers may want highly specific information, digging deep into the organization. Most buyers will want to assure themselves that key members of management will stay on after the transaction. And that can entail conversations directly between the buyer and management regarding future compensation. Unsurprisingly, such conversations may not be consistent with the seller's goal of maximizing value in the sale (see Managing Agendas, below.)

The company's investment banker must know at least as much about the company as the buyer universe in order to be able to outflank competing buyer strategies.

GORDIAN KNOTS/Hooked on Phonics

Hooked on Phonics, a well-known consumer education company, was a high flier that ran into difficulties and filed for bankruptcy. Gordian Group advised a prominent buyout fund in connection with its interest in buying the company. The company's creditors opposed a quick sale to the Gordian Group client and sought instead a competitive auction process to maximize value. As advisor to the buyout fund, Gordian Group's goal was quite the opposite: to end-run that process and acquire the business as quickly and as inexpensively as possible.

> During its due diligence, Gordian Group determined that the entrepreneur who had founded Hooked on Phonics was the owner of the famous 1-800-ABCDEFG telephone number that the company used as a marketing tool. The entrepreneur licensed use of the number to Hooked on Phonics. In order to give its client a "leg up" on the process, Gordian Group encouraged it to enter into an option agreement with the entrepreneur, enabling its client to have the exclusive right to own the telephone number – whether or not it was the successful buyer. This tactic was successful, insofar as it significantly reduced other buyers' enthusiasm for the property, and Gordian Group's client was able to buy Hooked on Phonics on desired terms expeditiously.

After due diligence is largely completed, the seller can enter the next phase of the process, which entails transaction documentation. By now, the seller and its advisors will have a reasonably good idea of the key issues and uncertainties surrounding the deal. This gives the seller's professionals the ability to draft comprehensive documentation, including the purchase and sale agreement. As noted above, the purchase and sale agreement can be used by the seller to elicit final bids from potential buyers and to focus their thinking along transactional lines desired by the seller.

Accordingly, careful preparation of the purchase and sale agreement is an essential element of a well run process. Without showing such leadership, the seller is likely to see the process degenerate into a free-for-all, with different types of contracts promulgated by different groups.

Managing Agendas

In a distressed situation, many employees are understandably concerned about retaining their jobs. The advent of a buyer with its own agenda adds to that uncertainty. This can result in attrition, as the better employees jump ship while they can, or poor productivity, as dispirited workers worry about their own situations and neglect their duties. Accordingly, many sellers try to maintain an internal communication program to keep their employees informed and at the same time establish a wall between midlevel employees and the buyer, hoping to minimize the disruption of misunderstandings and rumors.

With key senior-level employees, the stakes are higher. Many buyers will insist on management continuity as part of any transaction – and that gives the senior management enhanced negotiating leverage. This is particularly true in industries where key talent is at a premium. In certain cases, this can create a substantial problem for the seller, should the managers and the buyer "conspire" to take value away from the seller.

Assume that the buyer is willing to pay $25 million for a business, based upon "normal" management compensation levels. If the transaction is conditional upon management's continuity, management may be able to negotiate a better-than-normal deal for itself. If management insists on a package worth $10 million in excess value and the buyer is not willing to increase its price, that $10 million might come out of the seller's pocket.

This risk cannot be eliminated, but the seller can take steps to mitigate it. One way is to provide management with incentives, such as a percentage of the purchase price. The higher the price, the more management gets. Another is to forbid the buyer from one-on-one compensation talks with key managers – at least until very late in the process. Instead, prospective buyers would be invited to submit management compensation plans in connection with their overall bids.

The best defense on this front is, in fact, one that should have been in place long ago – the company should install, maintain and nurture a management team with a strong ethical streak.

Implementation

Once the buyer is in place, how does the company actually get the deal done? With respect to the sale of an asset in court, it can be done through a plan of reorganization, or through the orchestration of a Section 363 sale in order to provide a high degree of competition.

Ideally, there would be multiple back-up bidders to compete with the lead bidder. The company's professionals could assess which particular assets might be of more interest to one group than another. Depending upon the buyers' individual interests, by breaking the bidding into various "lots," the professionals can create value for the estate.

Before the bidding gets started (or even afterward in some cases), the professionals can work with the court to fine-tune the bidding procedures. For example, incremental round-by-round bidding may be the way to go. Or, if the professional is aware that most bidders have maximum bid limits, the incremental approach may not be best. After all, it is the second-highest (or "cover") bidder that will determine this type of auction price, not the highest. In such an instance, it may be advisable to have bidders place their best and final offers on the table. For a well-financed buyer that has to have the asset, this may be the best way to elicit the maximum price.

We used this technique to our clients' advantage when we were running the Colfor/Colmach auction process, discussed earlier in this chapter. When incremental bidding was about to stall as buyers reached their price limits, we convinced the court to switch to a sealed "best and final" format. One buyer was desperate to have the asset. The value received by the estate was much greater than it would have been. Fluidity in exigent circumstances is a great asset.

In an out-of-court asset sale scenario, the same concepts apply. Except (as noted in earlier chapters) certain buyers will require "proof" of fairness and the seller's solvency to effect the transaction outside of Chapter 11.

With respect to simultaneous M&A/restructuring transactions, the game becomes more complex still. Once the buyer is placed in this position (*i.e.,* needing concessions from creditors without bankruptcy implementation tools), the implementation mechanics are very similar to those used in an out-of-court "internal" reorganization, discussed in the next chapter.

CHAPTER 10—INTERNAL PLAN OF REORGANIZATION

An internal plan of reorganization (IPOR, or "stand-alone plan") is, put simply, a "self-help" remedy for a debtor. While other approaches involve outside parties, an IPOR does not necessarily require material new equity financing and does not involve the sale of substantially all of the debtor's assets (although it may very well contemplate a debt refinancing).

Done well, an IPOR can be used offensively or defensively. Knowing in advance what "self-help" options are available can greatly inform a company's strategic thinking regarding third-party transactions or negotiations with its own constituencies.

Strictly speaking, an IPOR can be effected only in a Chapter 11 setting. However, an internal financial "restructuring" that is functionally similar can be effected outside of Chapter 11. The general parameters are similar for both – a distressed company must establish valuations for all its various units across a range of contingencies and combinations, develop a business plan and establish the company's debt capacity (all the elements of strategy discussed in detail in Chapter 3). Developing an IPOR is thus an opportunity for management and its financial advisors to consider what assets to retain, what perhaps to sell and what the optimal capital structure for the reorganized entity might be.

It is never too early for a financially challenged company to contemplate what an IPOR might look like, and one particular advantage to an early start is that the IPOR can be a powerful viable tool in selling assets or the entire company, or in negotiating with third-party new money (see Chapter 9). If a company is unable to develop a competitive auction dynamic for its business, and sale of such operations at a certain minimum price is essential to the success of the overall restructuring, the debtor has a real problem. Being able to offer up a credible and seemingly viable IPOR almost takes the place of another "live" bidder, by creating or maintaining a competitive dynamic. So long as the bidders believe that the debtor and its constituencies are able and willing to act on the self-help program of an IPOR, the bidder is likely to feel pressure to bid higher.

Additionally, developing the structure of an IPOR and getting at least informal creditor concurrence enables a distressed company, should it file for Chapter 11, to be well-prepared. This concurrence might take the form of having sufficient votes up-front for a "prepackaged" POR or sufficient support for a "pre-negotiated" POR.

In-Court vs. Out of Court

Whether in-court or outside the court, the key feature of an IPOR is to recapitalize the company's balance sheet. But meaningful differences exist between the in-court and out-of-court experiences. Most significant, of course, is that outside of court, a company is generally better able to control its own restructuring process, as no judge sits as the ultimate arbiter of the process and the outcome.

One key difference is that an IPOR confirmed in bankruptcy court will bind all members of a class of creditors. If, among those actually voting, 50% of those voting in a creditor class accept an IPOR, and they hold more than 67% of the face amount of debt voting, every member of that class, including dissenters, will be bound by the terms of the IPOR. No holdouts are permitted. Conversely, outside of Chapter 11, holdouts can indeed occur. The degree of problems with such holdouts varies by transaction type.

A company developing an IPOR out of court leaves its officers and directors with significantly less protection from disgruntled creditors than they would have under the protection of the bankruptcy court (this bankruptcy protection is not for actions taken prior to Chapter 11, but for actions taken post-filing). As a result, outside of Chapter 11, officers and directors can be much more sensitive to creditor threats of litigation in connection with negotiating a restructuring proposal. Independent directors (*i.e.*, those with no equity ownership or management position), in particular, will usually be less willing to keep the company outside of Chapter 11 if negotiations are not going smoothly.

Relatedly, inside Chapter 11 an IPOR is able to give releases and indemnification to officers and directors for these types of causes of action. Releases and indemnification are not automatic, of course, but it is certainly possible for them to be negotiated and included in an IPOR. The SEC, in public situations, may well object to these sorts of protections, although its objection may be overruled by the bankruptcy court. Also, an IPOR will bind all members of a creditor class if the IPOR is confirmed.

Outside of Chapter 11, it is possible to build in releases in a restructuring plan, but there are likely to be creditor "holdouts" to a restructuring plan, as discussed above. With respect to the liability issue, this means that not all creditors will be bound by the releases contained in the out-of-court restructuring plan.

Out-of-court, there is no mechanism to deal with contingent claims in a restructuring plan. Conversely, a bankruptcy plan will be able to compromise most contingent claims (with notable exceptions such as environmental liabilities). Among other differences are that, outside court, a distressed company:

- can proceed with its strategy and the attendant negotiations relatively quietly, outside the fishbowl atmosphere of a Chapter 11 filing, and
- does not have to organize its creditors in formal fashion, as it must in Chapter 11. A company may ask its creditors informally to organize, and may offer to pay the costs of their advisors – but only if it wishes to negotiate with them. The company could also tender for or exchange for bonds without holding negotiations with creditors, if it so chose.

As Lewis Carroll's Cheshire Cat reminded us, it does not matter which road you take, if, like Alice, you do not know where you want to go. Defining the goals of the restructuring will shape the structure and effectiveness of any alternative. And the extent of these goals can run the gamut from a "Band-Aid" to a complete rehab.

Probably the least "invasive" form of restructuring is out-of-court covenant relief. If the company is out of compliance with its bank agreements, it may request a waiver or amendment. In turn, the banks may require fees, higher interest rates or additional collateral to do this. The percentage of banks required to approve a waiver or amendment for this varies according to the documentation, but is at least 50%.

The company may also be nearing non-compliance with certain covenants in public bonds (such as limits on capital expenditures). In order to get relief, the company may conduct a "consent solicitation" of its public bondholders in order to modify the covenants. Typically, a company would offer a cash incentive for approving bondholders – generally a minimum of 50% to 67% of the issue is needed for such approval.

Another relatively "low impact" restructuring approach is an out-of-court "stretch-out." The company may not be able to repay its banks or its trade on the original terms. In such case, the company would approach these creditors and ask for more time. Any creditor concessions may come at a price of transaction fees, increased interest rates or even the grant of collateral interests.

However, unlike with covenant relief, it may not be possible to impose the terms of a stretch-out on all affected holders. The holdouts that resist can keep their original payment rights. This creates a serious negotiating problem for many out-of-court restructurings. The more concessions the creditor group as a whole makes, the stronger the company. But any holdouts would benefit from such concessions as well – giving them the economic incentive to hold out. Accordingly, most out-of-court restructurings limit the percentage of affected creditors that can hold out to a relatively small number (*i.e.*, 5% to 10%).

Sometimes, even more drastic restructuring steps are needed, such as a massive creditor "haircut." In this case, the economic incentive to hold out is obviously even stronger than in a stretch-out. The company likely will need to develop a "carrot and stick" approach to deal with the problem.

One such mechanism is an exchange offer in which tendering bondholders would receive a lower principal amount of new bonds for their old bonds. But (subject to evolving law about public indenture modifications) the new bonds might be backstopped by collateral. Depending upon legal issues specific to the indenture, it might be possible to "gut" the old indenture provisions, and even make the new bonds senior to the old ones. This technique leaves bondholder holdouts with the prospect of having their instrument fall much lower in the new capital structure.

GORDIAN KNOTS/Anker Coal Group, Inc.

Anker was a producer of coal used principally for electricity generation and, to a lesser extent, for steel production. The company owned substantial coal reserves and operated a diverse portfolio of eight non-union deep and surface mines in West Virginia and Maryland. Because of operating problems and a revised operating strategy, the company

> experienced severe liquidity problems under its outstanding public senior notes and senior secured revolving credit financing.
>
> Gordian Group was engaged to advise the company with its assessment of the financial alternatives available and to assist it in negotiating the restructuring of all or a portion of its existing indebtedness and obtaining supplemental credit facilities. Over the next several months, Gordian Group reviewed the company's operating plan, developed views and financial alternatives for presentation to the board of directors and engaged in discussions with representatives of a group of noteholders and the company's senior secured lenders.
>
> These negotiations culminated in a creative private exchange offer with a group of noteholders, the private placement of additional notes and enhanced availability from the senior secured lenders. This increased liquidity allowed management the capability to implement its new operating plan and strategy. The exchange offer dynamics developed by Gordian Group strongly "encouraged" recalcitrant bondholders to exchange for fear of what would happen to their position in the capital structure if they did not.

A variant of this approach is to borrow additional secured monies and use the cash proceeds to tender for the public bonds at a discount. Any remaining bonds will then be behind such new bank debt. This approach can be made even more effective through the use of a "Dutch auction" structure for the tender. Pursuant to this format, each bondholder informs the company of the number of bonds to be tendered and the minimum price it wishes to receive from the company. This can create somewhat of a "prisoner's dilemma" for a fragmented bondholder group.

However, these "carrot and stick" approaches are far less effective when the company needs to convert its debt into equity. In such cases, the holdout problem can become intractable.

It is worth noting that the out-of-court techniques are not limited to internal plan alternatives. If a buyer wishes to compromise the claims of creditors outside of Chapter 11, it will likely have to negotiate with each and every creditor group. This is what happened in the Amoco/Dome Petroleum transaction noted in Chapter 9.

Industry Dynamics

We are specialists in solving complex financial challenges, irrespective of the industry. We often work in "new" industries, and after more than 250 engagements our firm has covered most of the industry waterfront. We prefer to avoid situations where bodily harm is threatened, but sometimes even that cannot be avoided.

GORDIAN KNOTS/Keene

Keene, Inc., a diversified manufacturer of industrial and aerospace products, had become seriously embroiled in asbestos-related litigation. Its asbestos liability arose from a 1968 acquisition of a small fabricator of acoustical ceilings, ventilation systems and thermal insulation products, a small percentage of which contained some asbestos. This company ceased using asbestos in 1972, and Keene sold the business in 1974.

Despite this long-ago tangential involvement with asbestos, Keene became the target of a multitude of lawsuits. The liabilities and litigation expenses associated with these lawsuits overwhelmed the company, and ultimately caused it to file for bankruptcy.

Gordian Group was engaged by Keene to assist in its reorganization efforts, including the development of a plan of reorganization, and in negotiations with the attorneys representing the asbestos claimants and with other constituencies. Together with counsel, Gordian Group negotiated a solution that provided for Keene's old equity constituencies to receive almost half of the reorganized company's equity. This stands in stark contrast to many other asbestos-related cases in which the old equity constituencies were wiped out.

But passions ran high, and in connection with the confirmation hearing, certain Gordian Group professionals received death threats (fortunately, not carried out).

Prepackaged and Pre-Negotiated Plans

If the holdout and consent problems prove to be insurmountable, the company must then consider Chapter 11 alternatives. Obviously, the company could simply seek bankruptcy protection right then and there (and many do). But we think it is far wiser to enter Chapter 11 with a solution in hand – rather than in search of one.

A prepackaged plan of reorganization ("pre-pack") is generally established as a parallel path to an out-of-court exchange offer. Creditors chose whether to exchange their bonds for the exchange consideration (new common stock, new bonds, cash). Solicitation of notes is conducted out-of-court pursuant to applicable securities laws. If those electing are greater than the minimum tender condition (*e.g.*, 90% or 95%), then the company can pursue the out-of-court path. But if such minimum is not reached, then each creditor's favorable election would count as a vote for a bankruptcy restructuring with similar economic effect. If 67% of the bonds voting and half of the creditors voting were in favor, then the prepack could be effected in Chapter 11.

A prenegotiated plan is less formal and less binding. The company and its major creditor constituencies agree in principle on a restructuring plan, and agree to implement it in Chapter 11.

The advantages of a prenegotiated plan include greater speed and reduced complexity – largely because the company does not have to undertake the task of an SEC-approved solicitation with a document as thick as a telephone book. On the other hand, creditors cannot be legally bound in a prenegotiated plan (unlike a pre-pack), and the company can be re-traded after it enters Chapter 11.

GORDIAN KNOTS/Mayflower Group, Inc.

A well-known moving and contract-bus company, Mayflower was taken private in a leveraged buyout. Primarily as a result of a downturn in the economy, the company was unable to service its indebtedness.

The creditors retained Gordian Group to advise them in assessing the value of the businesses and in structuring and negotiating the terms of a restructuring with the company, its banks and the stockholders in order to maximize the creditors' recovery.

The company and the creditors reached an agreement in principle, which was implemented through a "pre-packaged" bankruptcy plan approved by more than 95 percent of the creditors. Mayflower emerged from bankruptcy, just four months after filing.

Exit Financing

A company's emergence from Chapter 11 pursuant to an IPOR is usually dependent upon receipt of financing that will permit it to (i) have sufficient wherewithal to operate post-Chapter 11, (ii) replace whatever existing credit facilities must be addressed pursuant to the terms of the IPOR (and/or the DIP agreement), (iii) have sufficient cash to "sprinkle" over certain classes of creditors, like trade creditors or "convenience" classes (a slice of creditors that is small enough to be dealt with through a *de minimis* amount of cash) and (iv) pay "administrative" claims incurred while in bankruptcy.

This type of financing is referred to as "exit financing." Providers of exit financing range from parties already at the table to lenders who specialize in making loans to companies emerging from Chapter 11. Thus, existing bondholders and the existing DIP lenders in a given situation may well wish to be considered for exit financing. Of course, such willingness may be contingent on the IPOR (and creditor recoveries) being shaped to their satisfaction.

By contrast, third-party lenders who consider providing exit financing are not likely to be concerned with an IPOR's creditor recovery percentages, but rather only with their place in the post-Chapter 11 capital structure and the viability of the borrower. The cost of exit financing is market-driven, and the more speculative the turnaround and "risky" the perceived credit risk of the borrower, the higher the cost will be.

"New Value" Plan of Reorganization

Strictly speaking, a "new value" plan of reorganization does not belong in a chapter on the internal plan of reorganization, as it expressly provides for new equity capital. But because the money fueling the plan comes from parties at the table, we will address it here.

A new value IPOR can be one where old equity sponsors the plan of reorganization. Facially, such a plan permits old equity to recover not on account of its existing equity position, but rather on account of the "new value" that it provides, usually in the form of fresh capital. However, a "new value" IPOR can be tough to implement.

In fact, old equity is discouraged from utilizing its control of the process to promulgate its own new value plan. This was recognized in a seminal decision of the U.S. Supreme Court in 1999, in *Bank of America National Trust and Savings Association v. 203 North LaSalle Street Partnership*. The

Court held that in order for old equity to have the opportunity to sponsor a plan of reorganization, its control over the process would effectively need to end. Thus, the debtor needs either to end exclusivity or run a wide-open process that permits creditors and other interested parties to present their own valuation and plans of reorganization. And may the highest value plan carry the day. Or shop the company so broadly that the insiders' deal is demonstrated to be clearly superior.

There are, of course, creative ways to achieve old equity's goals.

GORDIAN KNOTS/Waste Systems International, Inc.

A public, regional waste-management company, Waste Systems International (WSII) had expanded rapidly through various "roll-up" acquisitions. WSII had acquired seven transfer stations, four landfills and one recycling plant located in the Northeast and Mid-Atlantic States, in addition to acquiring dozens of trash-collection routes. These acquisitions were largely financed through bond issuances and other unsecured borrowings. Failure to integrate these new assets efficiently led to a change in senior management and then a liquidity crisis, and Gordian Group was engaged by the board of directors to advise on the restructuring of the company's capital structure.

Gordian Group first assisted WSII in addressing the time-critical liquidity issues, and then was Instrumental in developing and exploring various restructuring alternatives and capital structures. It advised the board of directors regarding restructuring alternatives and negotiating the company's plan of reorganization with holders of the various claims and interests.

WSII's plan of reorganization provided for compromise of more than $100 million in debt through cash payments funded by WSII's controlling shareholder, who retained control of the reorganized business after the reorganization was approved.

Disclosure Statement

The disclosure statement, and attendant plan, is essentially the bankruptcy version of an offering document. It contains the requisite information required for creditors and interest holders to make a decision as to how to vote for the plan of reorganization. The investment banker is involved in certain aspects of drafting the disclosure statement, whose key sections often include:

- Summary of Proposed Transaction
- Background
- The Company and Its Business
- Explanation of the Company's Liabilities and Their Treatment Under the POR
- Projections
- Tax Consequences
- Alternatives to the Plan

In out-of-court scenarios, the offering documents will look very much like a bankruptcy disclosure statement. And for Chapter 11 reorganizations involving a sale or other third-party proponent, the disclosure statement will be used to solicit votes in the same way as within an IPOR.

Complications in Exiting From Chapter 11

There can be many deviations, speed bumps and complications as a company prepares its business plan and establishes its debt capacity, conducts negotiations with key constituencies, accesses exit financing and emerges from Chapter 11 as a viable and profitable reorganized entity.

Creditors and others can object on multiple grounds to the confirmation of the plan of reorganization, and this often happens even when the overall process has gone smoothly. If the debtor has run a good process and encouraged the support of its key constituents, hopefully the disgruntled objectors are small creditors whose objections can either be addressed or dismissed without serious alteration to the otherwise agreed-upon IPOR.

In some situations, however, a debtor will have votes and support to meet the statutory voting approval requirements for confirmation of an IPOR but will still face challenges at confirmation on, say, valuation grounds, from a significant creditor. This is a much more serious challenge, and could force the court to take testimony on the issue and make a decision that could derail the debtor's exit plans.

In addition, should negotiations with creditors stall and a court refuse to extend exclusivity, multiple IPORs could be proposed and come up for judicial approval. In such circumstances, the IPOR approval process will be fraught with uncertainty and take on the appearance of a judicial circus.

The investment banker's role, in the center ring, will be to testify on one or more key issues at the confirmation hearing. Some of the most important issues involve valuation, for the court must be assured that the valuation set forth by the debtor underpinning the IPOR (and the estimated recoveries to creditors) is valid. This can be highly contested and litigated.

The court will often take testimony on whether creditors are receiving more than they would in a liquidation (the "best interests of creditors" requirement of Section 1129 of the Bankruptcy Code), and this, too, is usually an investment banking function. The investment banker may also be asked to testify about the terms of any controversial exit financing, including the type of process that was run to source and negotiate it and whether the terms are fair under the specific circumstances. Section 1129 also mandates a judicial finding that the IPOR is "feasible," which, in lay terms, means that the court needs assurance that the debtor is not likely to return to the court as a "Chapter 22." From time to time, the investment banker may be asked to opine on feasibility, although this may also be a role for management or crisis managers.

Litigation can also be a complicating factor in effecting a restructuring.

GORDIAN KNOTS/Alert Centre

Alert Centre, one of the nation's largest home and commercial alarm-monitoring companies, raised more than $225 million through the sale of limited partnership units and more than $100 million through borrowings. Such funds were used largely to acquire alarm-monitoring accounts.

As a consequence of poor acquisitions, operating difficulties and allegedly fraudulent activities, Alert Centre and the limited partnerships filed for Chapter 11 protection. Previously, certain class actions were filed against various prior officers, directors and shareholders, claiming securities law violations with respect to the sale of limited partnership interests and other problems.

The Official Limited Partners Committee engaged Gordian Group to assist in analyzing Alert's business and to develop and negotiate a plan of reorganization. Gordian Group was instrumental in effecting a plan of reorganization, together with a simultaneous resolution of the various class action suits. This settlement provided significant value to the bankruptcy estate. Alert Centre emerged from Chapter 11 with the Limited Partners owning approximately 97 percent of the company's pro forma stock, and the subsequent sale of Alert Centre resulted in the Limited Partners enjoying one of the best equity recovery results we ever experienced in a restructuring.

The Need to Work With Other Constituencies or Creditors

Restructurings necessarily involve having different constituencies alter their economic rights. This can be done consensually or non-consensually (see "cram-down," Chapter 3). We believe that the consensual approach should be the desired goal and the right place to start.

And it is impossible to develop a consensual IPOR without extensive negotiations among the company's various constituencies. A debtor needs to be strong, with a clear vision about where it wants to go and how to get there. Creditors respect credibility on the part of the debtor, and as long as a debtor and its advisors maintain their credibility, the process has a strong chance of success.

One of the many examples of our experience in consensual IPORs was our work for London Fog Industries.

GORDIAN KNOTS/London Fog

A leading designer, marketer and distributor of quality men's and women's rainwear and outerwear in the United States, London Fog owns one of the most recognizable brand names in the world. Through its wholly-owned subsidiary Pacific Trail, it also markets and distributes casual, active and performance outerwear for men, women and children.

But London Fog suffered from over-leverage and poorly performing retail operations. It commenced a comprehensive review of its operations and financial condition, and engaged Gordian Group to advise the board of directors regarding various business plan options, restructuring alternatives and negotiating and structuring a plan of reorganization.

> London Fog filed for Chapter 11 protection in order to avail itself of certain benefits, including shutting operations and rejecting leases. Through management's efforts to improve and restructure the operations, London Fog was able to demonstrate to its creditors that a valuable core operation remained. In particular, Gordian Group's valuation work was pivotal to London Fog's gaining consensus among its various constituencies with respect to a consensual plan of reorganization.

Negotiations among the debtor and its key creditor constituencies will center on several main areas:

- agreement about the business plan;
- acceptance of the projections;
- concurrence about the debt capacity;
- agreement about valuation;
- agreement regarding allocation of value; and
- agreement about exit financing.

It is not always possible to reach agreement on all of these matters, and that is why all parties will seek to find or create negotiating leverage, in its many forms, in order to be able to encourage a consensual resolution. The debtor and its investment banker, together with counsel, act somewhere between an "honest broker" vis-à-vis the various constituents and *in paterfamilias*, seeking to drive the process to a desired result. Investment banking creativity and experience can provide the debtor with successful strategies to reach its goals.

One strategy is to formulate separate negotiating strategies for each major constituency, and to negotiate with each of them separately. Keeping the various constituencies "in separate rooms" for as long as possible permits the debtor to guide the proceedings. This is much preferable, and leads to superior results, than does unorchestrated mayhem.

At some point in many IPOR negotiations, however, the debtor may become "irrelevant" in the eyes of its creditor and other constituencies, and the parties with the economic interests will seek to cut their own deal themselves. The shrewdly advised debtor will try very hard to avoid this result.

From the perspective of the investment banker, the beauty of this whole, complex process is that there is no cookie-cutter set of standard solutions to negotiating a successful IPOR. The more creative and experienced the investment banker, the greater the likelihood of the debtor achieving its goals in this critically important effort.

CHAPTER 11—EPILOGUE

In the Dickensian era, bankrupts went to debtors' prison. Ebenezer Scrooge's behavior was shaped because his father went to jail for his debts in little Ebenezer's formative years. Times have certainly changed.

Today, resolution of insolvencies, through bankruptcy or otherwise, is increasingly viewed as relatively commonplace – and even necessary for the functioning of the banking system. It allows (and even forces) the banks to deal with their nonperforming loans. To be sure, there is still some stigma to being associated with a busted company. But this is nowhere close to the moral shame people felt only a generation ago. Then, insolvencies were associated with something going horribly wrong. Why the change? Some bankruptcies are still associated with horrendous mistakes and fraud (Enron and Refco, for example). But many more insolvencies are of a far different stripe. Insolvency is merely the flip side of the entrepreneurial dream. Entrepreneurs are encouraged to take chances to grow and become great. The ranks of entrepreneurs have grown enormously in the last generation or two, due in part to massive funding from the venture capital community. Even in large corporations, executives are motivated to become entrepreneurial through large stock option grants – further swelling the list of the entrepreneurial-minded.

In most cases, the entrepreneurs are able to limit their own personal liability by using corporate or other "limited liability" structures. When coupled with debt that is non-recourse to the owners themselves, this limited liability system creates a powerful incentive to take risks. It's called Playing With Other People's Money. Another way to express this is "freedom to fail": Some entrepreneurs make it, and some do not. (One of the authors' grandfathers made it big twice and lost it twice, before succeeding the third time; another made and lost several fortunes). And many of these entrepreneurial failures end up in bankruptcy.

Viewed in this light, a "high" level of insolvencies is not particularly alarming. With more business start-ups, there will be more failures. We encourage talented people to start new businesses, just as we encourage our kids to try new sports.

But, people ask, do these bankruptcies have to be "so big"? Again, the only reason some of these failures are large is that the capital markets have provided these companies with tons of money – all the failed telecom companies, for example. We are not particularly big fans of establishing a capital markets "traffic cop" to tell investors where they can and cannot put their money. Similarly, we are opposed to efforts such as the government-led bailout of the auto companies. The government can too easily tip the economic scales in favor of whoever the cronies of the party in power happen to be.

And what is to be done with those miscreant companies that actually do commit fraud? Call us cynical. Sure, Congress passed Sarbanes-Oxley to combat all sorts of corporate misdeeds. But in big bull markets, the temptation to do evil deeds is just too great for some people. It happened in the 1920s, it happened in the 1990s, it repeated in the mid-2000s, and it will happen again. Viewed from this perspective, the collapse of a fraudulent scheme is just another form of business failure.

What is common about all of these reasons that help explain insolvencies? The human factor. People in our culture are driven to succeed, to take risks. And few people turn money down when it is being thrown at them. Some people's greed takes them further, into criminal activities. As long as you have human beings in proximity to capital markets, there will be insolvencies. And large ones at that.

So, we think that the tide of insolvencies in recent years will continue. Efforts to curtail it will indeed be very much like pushing water uphill.

Instead, we think, efforts to improve the system should be focused on ways to mitigate some of the damage caused by corporate failures. This damage gets more and more severe as the company slides further into insolvency and its financial alternatives dwindle. Just as with a cancer patient, where early detection and treatment can save lives, early recognition in the corporate setting can save jobs and economic value.

The problem is that corporations generally do not have the right incentives to recognize the handwriting on the wall and to act with deliberate speed. Instead, they are more likely to fiddle while a lot of Other People's Money burns. This situation has been exacerbated by the flood of money that has been made available in the recent low interest rate environment. We harbor little hope that the corporate culture will change to the point where early problem recognition becomes the rule, rather than the exception.

As we noted at the beginning of this book, failing companies damage many of their constituencies (while presenting opportunities for savvy putative acquirers and vulture investors). Trade and financial creditors may experience significant losses. Shareholders may be wiped out. Many employees may lose their jobs. Current and former employees may lose their pensions or life savings. Directors will wish they had never taken a board seat.

That is not to say there is no hope. In theory, all of the laws Congress passes to address "excesses" should fix this problem. But it has not yet, and maybe never will. Perhaps more boards will get religion when many lawsuits are successfully brought under new legal theories. Or if organized labor takes up the cudgel early enough to save cash flow and jobs. Or if the Pension Benefit Guaranty Corporation acts quickly enough to prevent untold billions of dollars of pension underfundings from becoming taxpayer liabilities. Or if companies' legal and financial advisors educate boards on the merits of addressing issues early on. If any of these serve to move boards into action, then the out-of-court avenues and other less severe alternatives we address in this book could still be available to the companies.

And that is what we hope for: early problem recognition and acknowledgment, advice sought and followed on minimizing the pain, and better strategic thinking and action for companies that are drifting, or sliding, or rushing toward the Zone of Insolvency.

APPENDIX A: OLD EQUITY'S CHESSBOARD – A THEORETICAL VIEW

We are fierce advocates for achieving recoveries for old equity constituencies. And we start from a premise that is controversial to many: *What is in the interests of the company is not necessarily in the best interests of stockholders.*

We do think that stockholders can benefit greatly from boards' attempts to enhance business value, stretch out the creditors and obtain the deepest discounts from creditors as is possible. Common sense and theory both tell us this. In the rest of this book, we discuss how the company can address maturity extension issues through exchange offers, cash incentives and other mechanisms. Extensions of maturities enable boards to have the opportunity to try to build business values. And we have elsewhere discussed the relative merits of taking out debt at various discounted prices. But interests can diverge.

A clear illustration of the dichotomy between the interests of a company and its stockholders involves the issues of reducing a company's debt burden. In theory, this sounds great less debt is better than more debt for a distressed enterprise. In this context, many of our clients frequently ask us if they should effect transactions or otherwise access capital markets to address or even chip away at "Mount Debt." The answer is not as straightforward as it might seem – it depends on whom you represent and what you want to achieve.

We often like to tell our debtor-side clients that it is a mistake to reduce debt at par if the company is insolvent in the first place. Assume the company has $9 worth of assets and $10 face amount of liabilities. The equity value is 10% under water. Then the company sells $5 of assets to raise cash and repay debt. Now the company has $4 worth of assets and $5 face amount of liabilities. The equity value has dropped to being 20% under water.

We believe that this value destruction can be measured through the use of option theory. The equity of a company whose enterprise value is less than the face amount of its debt can be viewed as an out-of-the-money call option. For illustrative purposes, we assume that this "option" relates to a company with $10 in debt (the strike price) and $9 in asset value (the stock price). We further assume that the option is American-style, that the volatility (see Chapter 6) would be 40%, and that the effective yield on the debt would equate to a 10% underlying common stock cash dividend. Importantly, we use only a two-year life for the warrant, given the time limitations imposed on most restructurings. In this instance, the "black box" option model would spit out a price of $1.10. Using this output, the ratio of debt at face to debt plus equity market capitalization (in this case, market capitalization being the option value) would be 89%, which is certainly consistent with what we regularly see in terms of actual equity trading prices of distressed companies.

Now, let's start selling assets to pay down debt at par. Selling the first dollar of assets would produce total debt of $9 and asset value of $8. The option model indicates that the option price would have decreased from $1.10 to $0.95. We have shown the relationship of such an asset sale program on these option values across a range of sale assumptions in the chart below.

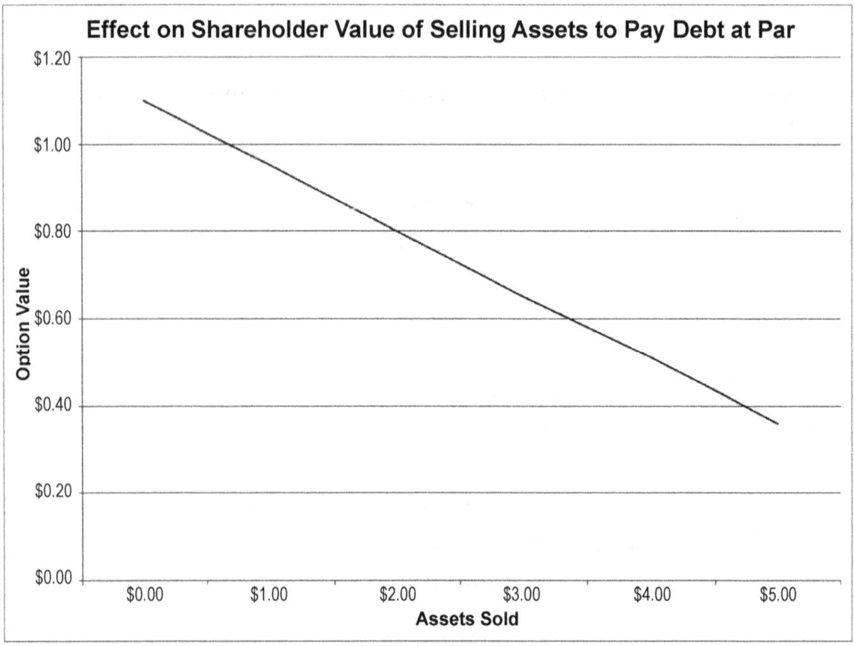

What is happening is that the absolute differential between debt and asset value remains static, while the percentage differential is increasing. When all other factors are held constant (as we have done), the decline in the absolute numbers is translating into a smaller absolute option value, which is exacerbated by the increasing percentage of being "out of the money." Said another way – at least from the perspective of stockholder value – you can't shrink your way to greatness. After all, wouldn't you rather have $9 of asset value that can be doubled to $18 than $4 that can be doubled to $8?

We have found that this logic resonates with our clients. But CEOs with publicly traded stock (or private equity owners that want to get rid of the annoying creditors) also want to know why they can't simply issue additional equity and use the proceeds to repay debt, possibly at a big discount. The short answer is that they can (assuming that the company is adequately disclosed through any needed SEC filings), but that a huge part of the benefits would accrue to the debtholders. Meanwhile, option value held by old equity gets destroyed in the process.

Let's start with the foregoing hypothetical involving a company with a business worth $9 and financial liabilities of $10. For sake of simplicity, we will also assume that the financial liabilities are all *pari passu*. A casual reader skipping the previous paragraphs might wonder what we are talking about in terms of equity values. Why would a company's stock price have any value under these circumstances when the debt exceeds currently realizable asset values? But an observer of distressed companies would know differently. Distressed underwater companies frequently have significant public equity values. And option values are a big part of the reason.

Now, let's repay $1 of face amount of debt with $0.90 of new money (*i.e.*, at a 90% price) from sale of new equity securities. The pro forma amount of debt at face value would now be $9, and the asset value would remain at $9. Keeping the other option assumptions static, the black box model would yield a pro forma equity value of $1.41 (which implicitly includes the $0.90 of new equity that just went into the company). In other words, the pre-transaction equity value decreased from $1.10 to a net of $0.51 (excluding the $0.90 that was invested). As the chart below shows, the fate of Old Equity gets worse as more money is raised until the trend finally bottoms out at some point.

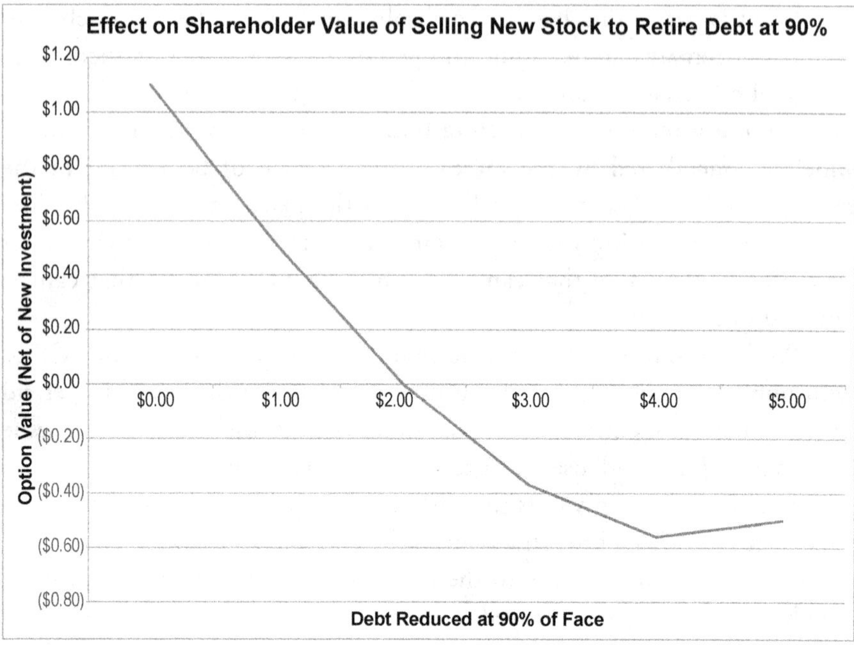

At this point, take a deep breath. The company has raised equity money (even ignoring fees and expenses), retired debt at a discount (again ignoring expenses and taxes on debt cancellation) and has managed to increase its equity value by an amount materially less than the amount it raised. In other words, our hypothetical company managed to *decrease* pre-transaction stockholder wealth, at least in a theoretical sense. Meanwhile, the creditworthiness of the remaining debt would have improved (due to a lower amount of debt in relation to the same amount of assets). In other words, old equity has injected money to strengthen the company – but the creditors have reaped most of the benefit.

The clever reader may ask whether we sandbagged the analysis by limiting the discount to only 10% (*i.e.*, a 90% purchase price). Just to show that we didn't, we looked at the effect of increasing the purchase discount for a $1 debt retirement, everything else held equal. As the chart below shows, things get better with a bigger discount. But they don't get back to the "do nothing" level of the option at this discount level. In order to make sense for old equity, the discount may need to be so great that it would be wildly impractical to achieve with $9 of realizable asset value.

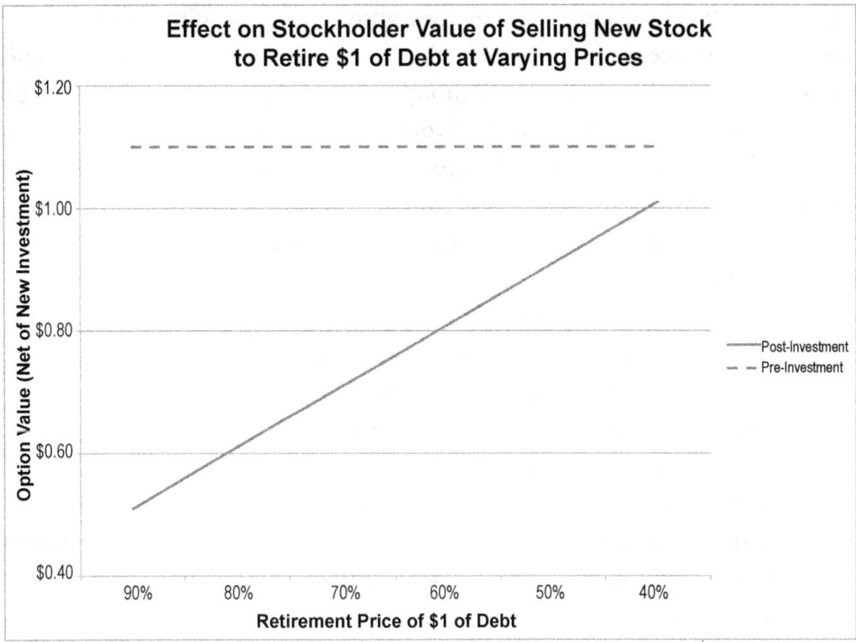

Astute readers will also know that trying to base restructuring strategies on option analysis alone is very risky business. Any financial assumptions going into the model, not to mention the option methodology itself, are open to serious question. Nevertheless, it is critical to take note when theory so strongly confirms our "gut feel" conclusions that selling assets or raising equity simply to repay debt may not be a good idea.

Please understand that the "gut feel" determinations that we have may not be the same as that of others who do not till these fields. Our compass direction is influenced by our experience that old equity constituencies do much better if debt is not retired through asset sales or injection of new money until the end of the restructuring process. Further, depending upon a debtor's cost of capital, a stretch-out in which the debt remains outstanding can be superior in many situations to even retiring debt at a big discount.

Of course, the analysis simply puts a finer point on our "gut feel." And of the two ways to fund debt retirement, the analysis indicates that indiscriminate use of new sales of stock is even worse than an asset disposition program. Of course, when faced with no alternative, sometimes companies have to take such steps just to save the company, although existing stockholders may suffer as a result.

Given the mathematical exercises above, it is clear to us that there are numerous scenarios in which the company itself may benefit, and the stockholders may lose out. Among other things, asset and stock sale programs effect a wealth transfer from stockholders to bondholders. To the surprise of many lawyers, this concept applies to fairness opinions for companies and transactions in this context. As we indicated above, what is a fair restructuring transaction to the company may not necessarily be fair to its stockholders.

In our simple example above, it seems to us that old equity could obtain a better result for itself if it directly purchased the debt at a discount, rather than have the company effect the repurchase. Old equity could potentially benefit from an enhanced control position through ownership of the debt. Initially at least, if the debt remained outstanding, old equity would benefit from any excess of value over purchase price on the debt. Moreover, since the capital structure would be unchanged, so would option value as it related to the common stock itself. In other words, in a strict sense old equity would not be in a worse position, and actually could be in a better one.

On the other hand, due to the purchase of the debt, old equity (viewed from the entirety of its debt and equity holdings) would have increased its "skin in the game." This actually could create problems for old equity in pursuing various aggressive negotiating strategies. Moreover, there are risks involved if a court found that old equity acted inappropriately and imposed penalties (such as subordination of recoveries on its debt ownership position) on old equity.

Despite these very real drawbacks, old equity may find that making a debt repurchase on its own could be a wise decision. Having ownership at various levels in the capital structure can potentially outweigh any such risks.

If you agree with our logic, the board may not always be in the best position to take up the cudgel to promote old equity's interests. It may do what it can, but beyond a certain point, the tools available to the board may advance old equity's cause only so far. Old equity needs its own tool kit.

The tools we would choose for old equity include the following:

- Board control. The ability to be at center stage, be privy to financial and other information and to be able to make corporate decisions as to bankruptcies or sales is of incalculable value. Until this control is changed (*e.g.*, by a court), whatever demands are made by other constituencies can be countered with conditions and counter-demands from the board. Of course, indiscriminate use of board control can be criticized and can get the control person in hot water.

- Money. Particularly as long as old equity controls the situation at the board level, any money the company has (or can raise through a rights offering or otherwise) can potentially be used effectively. If old equity determines that a direct investment in the company to repay debt would be inefficient, old equity could buy the debt itself as a discount and use it as currency in the restructuring. Or it could initiate creative exchange transactions to the same effect.
- Tax Losses. In many restructuring situations, the company has lost money for years and the cumulative tax loss can be a valuable asset. Old equity can influence whether the value of this asset is diminished through a "change of control," particularly in an out-of-court context. Frequently, this can be a significant incentive for the creditors to want to negotiate directly with old equity.

All too often, we see boards try to do the right thing for old equity constituencies, and try to chip away at the debt with the expectation that the benefits will accrue to the stockholders. Unfortunately, the beneficiaries tend to be the holders of the debt, rather than the equity.

We are big believers in advancing old equity's cause, and think that old equity should focus on developing – and using – its tool kit.

APPENDIX B: VALUATION FIGHTS THROUGH THE LENS OF GAME THEORY

In many U.S. restructurings, junior constituencies that may be considered "out of the money" attempt to wrest value from the more senior constituencies – which may not themselves receive 100% of their claims in the restructuring. We believe that this behavior can be expressed in terms of game theory, and that the game can be explained through a concept known as "Nash Equilibrium."

John Nash's theory was penned in the early 1950's and brought to broad public attention in Sylvia Nasar's book *A Beautiful Mind* and the subsequent film. In essence, a game will reach a Nash Equilibrium point if no player can achieve a better result than it currently has by incrementally changing its strategy. This may not be the best result possible for the players, if they had perfect knowledge and the unfettered ability to collude to reach an optimal outcome. But it is a stable outcome, and better than non-collusive alternatives.

Imagine two creditor constituencies in a restructuring involving a bankrupt company, SubmarineCo, which is likely to be below periscope depth in terms of covering the value of its debts. However, valuation is an art and uncertainty exists about the amount of the value in relation to the debt.

One creditor constituency is the Super Seniors, a group of first lien secured creditors which have agreed to convert 100% of their claims into 100% of the new equity of SubmarineCo. The Super Seniors do not believe that they will receive a par recovery, although they do expect to get an initial recovery in the neighborhood of 60 to 80 cents on the dollar.

The other creditor constituency is the Jilted Juniors, which are also secured, but which are slated to get no recovery at all in the restructuring because their second lien stands behind that of the Super Seniors. Because they have contractually agreed to subordinate their recoveries to the Super Seniors until the Super Seniors receive payment in full and because the debtor actually believes that the restructured equity value is less than the face amount of the Super Seniors, the debtor's plan gives all of the equity to the Super Seniors. The Jilted Juniors are arguing that the value of SubmarineCo. is actually in excess of the face amount of the Super Seniors, so that the Jilted Juniors should get some recovery (although far less than their full par amount).

The Game

In essence, the argument is over how the economic pie is divided. And should the parties bargain out a settlement or litigate valuation in front of the bankruptcy judge? The negotiating game ends should a settlement be reached or when the judge's gavel comes down.

We believe that the parameters forming the "rules" of this game can be viewed from the standpoint of a cost-benefit analysis:

Professional fees. Both sides will need to absorb the costs of their respective legal and financial professionals needed to advance their arguments. Even if the estate hires professionals to assist the Super Seniors, the Super Seniors will view the costs as coming at least partially out of their pockets (after all, they believe that the entirety of the economics of the debtor will belong to them). Unless the Jilted Juniors can find an Official Committee to carry their water for them, the Jilted Juniors will have to absorb their own professional fees. The longer the process continues, the more it costs. In a litigation, the final steps can cost a great deal more than any initial moves due to the expenses involved in a contested valuation fight in court.

Business damage. If the valuation fight is prolonged, SubmarineCo.'s business may be adversely affected due to customer and employee attrition, competitive pressures and other factors. To the extent that the time value of money costs exceeds any cash generated in excess of bankruptcy expenses, these time-related costs would go into this particular bucket as well. However, because the Jilted Juniors would have received nothing in the absence of a fight, these costs are mostly borne by the Super Seniors.

The lottery element. We would expect each side to put on compelling evidence in court as to why its valuation is the "right" one. But at the end of the day, the court will determine its view of value – hence the "lottery" reference, because the outcome is ultimately out of the control of either the Super Seniors or the Jilted Juniors. And because the Super Seniors are not entitled to get more than par (other than accrued interest and the like), it is entirely possible that the Jilted Juniors will achieve a recovery.

Assume that, whatever the judge says, the "true" value of SubmarineCo. is V. Further assume that, at the end of any trial, the judge will tell the litigants that the Jilted Juniors will receive α% of V, where $0 \leq \alpha \leq \beta$ and β is the largest minority ownership stake reasonably imaginable that the Jilted Juniors could receive. Also assume that any reimbursements of the Jilted Juniors' professional fees are embodied in α. At the outset of the game, α is unknowable, but can reasonably be bounded with probabilities. As we will discuss below, the participants' understanding of what α may be can improve due to "guidance" given by judges, mediators or others.

To set up the equations, we will call P_s the remaining professional fees of the Super Seniors and P_J the professional fees of the Jilted Juniors. We will also call D the business damage that is being largely borne by the Super Seniors. All of these fees and damages are also functions of time. We will also assume that V will not increase over the near-term, due to any profits being chewed up by reorganization costs.

The payoff equation for the Super Seniors is then:

$$[(1 - \alpha) \times (V - D)] - P_s$$

And the payoff equation for the Jilted Juniors is:

$$\alpha \times (V - D) - P_J$$

Let's look at some examples, in which V is always \$100 million and the incremental costs of litigation through the bitter end are always \$1 million more for the Jilted Juniors than for the Super Seniors. We have assumed that this litigation cost differential occurs because the Super Seniors benefit from the debtor itself absorbing at least some of the cost of litigation (funded, as observed above, by the company's operating profits). Meanwhile, the Jilted Juniors must bear their portion of the costs of their fight alone. We have assumed that if the Super Seniors are aggressive, they spend \$2 million; otherwise, they spend \$1 million.

The Super Seniors should be willing to settle the case for as much as the sum of (i) their remaining litigation out-of-pocket costs plus (ii) business damages plus (iii) the expected value of litigation damages. The formula would be: $P_S + \acute{\alpha} \times V + (1 - \acute{\alpha}) \times D$ for the Super Seniors (where $\acute{\alpha}$ is the expected outcome of the to-be-adjudicated α).

Assume that both sides believe that V is truly less than the aggregate amount of the Super Seniors' claims, and that the judge would ultimately agree with this reality. Accordingly, both sides would really view this as a "nuisance suit," and assign a value to α of 0%. Also assume that the business is very stable, so that D = 0. Therefore, here the Super Seniors should be willing to settle for, say a small amount, say \$0.5 million. In this case, the payoff matrix (the convention is that the first number in the parentheses is the payoff to the Super Seniors, while the second is the payoff to the Jilted Juniors) is (in millions of dollars):

	Jilted Juniors Seek to Settle	**Jilted Juniors Litigate**
Super Seniors Seek to Settle	(–\$0.5, \$0.5)	(–\$1, –\$2)
Super Seniors Litigate Aggressively	(–\$2,-\$3)	(–\$2, –\$3)

The dynamics here are interesting. The Jilted Juniors must be willing to threaten litigation (in which they would spend – and waste – at least \$2 million) in order merely to put themselves in position to extract money from the Super Seniors. And clearly, the Super Seniors should be willing (leaving the precedential impacts aside) to pay up to \$1 million to make the whole thing go away.

In this case, we agree that the Settle/Settle cell is a Nash Equilibrium point, and that outcome should obtain. If the Jilted Juniors chose to litigate instead, they would be out of pocket at least \$2 million, a whole lot less than the +\$0.5 million they would receive in a settlement. The Super Seniors cannot really hope to do better, either. Hence, (–\$0.5, \$0.5) is a Nash Equilibrium point.

Now assume that the business is shaky, and that the decline in value, D, caused by prolonged litigation could be \$10 million. However, both sides believe that an adjudicated α still would equal zero. In other words, this would still be a "nuisance suit," but the stakes would be higher than before. In such case, the payoff matrix is (in millions):

	Jilted Juniors Seek to Settle	**Jilted Juniors Litigate**
Super Seniors Seek to Settle	?	(–\$11, –\$2)
Super Seniors Litigate	(–\$12, –\$3)	(–\$12, –\$3)

We left the outcome in the Settle/Settle cell undetermined, given the potentially wide range of settlement outcomes. Note that any dollar settlement in this cell with a value greater than zero and less than D + P_S is a Nash Equilibrium point (we can argue certain values less than zero are also equilibrium points, but we won't go there because we don't think the Jilted Juniors realistically would pay money to go away).

What is a Nash Equilibrium outcome, assuming the Jilted Juniors won't actually accept a negative number? Any positive number under $11 million. This clearly implies that the Jilted Juniors may have far more negotiating leverage over the Super Seniors in situations involving fragile businesses. It also implies that a key piece of information for the Jilted Juniors – to know and communicate to the Super Seniors – is how badly the business could fare under protracted litigation. There is no one "right" outcome, and the Jilted Juniors do not really have an incentive to mediate. Their best strategy may be to hold out until the Super Seniors put a number between $5 million and $10 million on the table.

For the next example, let's change the assumption for D back to 0. However, now assume the Super Seniors truly believe α = 10% and the Jilted Juniors truly believe α = 20%. The expected payoff matrix, based upon the differing expectations is (dollars in millions):

	Jilted Juniors Seek to Settle	**Jilted Juniors Litigate**
Super Seniors Seek to Settle	N/A	(–$11, $18)
Super Seniors Litigate	(–$12, $17)	(–$12, $17)

In this case, there may be no Nash Equilibrium point that would lead to settlement due to differing views of α. The Jilted Juniors should not want to settle for much less than $18 million, while the Super Seniors should not want to pay much more than $11 million, due to their *a priori* beliefs. The case moves toward litigation.

Now assume that after each side has spent $0.5 million to litigate part of its case, the judge holds a chambers conference and advises each constituency on what the court's views are. The court informs both groups that its preliminary views are that α is *at least* 10%. Also assume that each group assumes that "at least 10%" really means 15%. At this point, the negotiating positions change. If they proceed with litigation, the Super Seniors will lose the $15 million in damages and the $0.5 million minimum of additional litigation costs. Ignoring the $0.5 million that has already been spent by each group, the ongoing payoff matrix is now (in millions), giving effect to the guidance:

	Jilted Juniors Seek to Settle	**Jilted Juniors Litigate**
Super Seniors Seek to Settle	?	(–$15.5, $13.5)
Super Seniors Litigate	(–$16.5, $12.5)	(–$16.5, $12.5)

In this case, the Settle/Settle cell result would fall into a relatively tight $13.5 million to $15.5 million range, ignoring the $0.5 million already spent by each side. And the court gets to move onto other work.

Implications

For rational participants in the "game," there are some key takeaways. Even when one side is really out of the money, a plausible valuation case can result in a settlement payment approximating the costs of defending the litigation. We have referred to this as "nuisance value." And when there are legitimate disputes over valuation, it still can make a lot of sense to settle promptly, given the costs of fighting.

However, in cases where there is true business risk (*i.e.,* D >> 0), the Jilted Juniors have a decided advantage in moving toward litigation, particularly when α is close to zero. If the mere act of going to court and having a valuation fight substantially reduces the recoveries of the Super Seniors due to the collateral damage from protracted litigation, there is a large incentive to settle at a relatively high value.

GORDIAN KNOTS/Alpha Media Company

A multimedia publishing company, Alpha Media was acquired in a transaction partially funded by a big tranche of First Lien Debt.

Gordian Group was retained by the counsel to the junior holders to maximize their recovery. The company had seen a reduction of profitability as a result of operational issues, which coincided with a massive downturn in the media space. At the time of our retention, our valuation of the company indicated that the First Lien Lenders were "under water," further indicating a dismal result for our clients.

The company, its advisors and the First Lien Lenders were very concerned that Alpha Media would suffer greatly from a highly publicized bankruptcy and attendant court fight. Because the First Lien Lenders were pressing so hard for an out-of-court restructuring, it was readily apparent that the perception of potential business damage, D, was great. Given this reality regarding the size of D, Gordian Group and counsel took steps to develop negotiating leverage with the company and the First Lien Lenders, including the development of an alternative business plan that would aid in a potential contested valuation contest.

Ultimately, the parties were able to effect a successful out-of-court restructuring that allowed the company to delever – and which provided our clients with an advantageous outcome in light of the valuation dynamics. Despite the magnitude of below-par First Lien Debt ahead of our clients' claims, we were able to obtain an outcome where (i) all existing debt was forgiven and (ii) the old First Lien holders allowed our clients to obtain new common stock and a very meaningful recovery.

On the other hand, one participant can truly misunderstand its negotiating position. Consider the first, simplest hypothetical game example above. The Jilted Juniors are looking at an expected value of $\alpha = 0$, and the Super Seniors are expecting virtually no business damage (*i.e.*, $D = 0$). It this case, the game is all about a bluff and the potential avoidance of litigation costs. As the payoff matrix we developed suggests, the game should settle at relatively modest recoveries for the Jilted Juniors, and should not advance very far into litigation.

However, in practice, this result does not always obtain. Human factors – hubris, overselling of a litigation strategy, lawyers' desire to litigate with their clients' money – enter the picture as well. As a result, cases that should settle early sometimes become pitched battles, wasting clients' resources and the court's time.

GORDIAN KNOTS/Spansion, Inc.

Spansion is a $1 billion manufacturer of flash memory components. The company filed for bankruptcy due to its overly-aggressive expansion program, which resulted in over $2 billion of liabilities.

Gordian Group represented the debtor and worked to craft a plan of reorganization that refinanced the secured liabilities and converted unsecured liabilities into equity. Spansion's reorganized business was targeted at a shrinking niche of the flash memory market, and we believed that the company's enterprise value was in the range of $900 million. As we discussed in Chapter 4 of this book, prospective growth is a key ingredient of enterprise value. If the business is in long-term decline, values will be relatively low.

The implications of our valuation determinations were that the recoveries would stop within the unsecured classes. This valuation view was shared by many other constituencies in the case, including the Senior Noteholders (analogous to the Super Seniors).

However, such valuation would have resulted in no recovery for the Convertible Noteholders (analogous to the Jilted Juniors), which were subordinated to the Senior Noteholders. The Convertible Noteholders launched a highly aggressive valuation fight, even though the enterprise value necessary for them to even be in the money at all was approximately $1.5 billion. Moreover, the company's business was relatively strong and was not at immediate risk of "melting down." Most companies in bankruptcy – particularly technology companies – suffer from the stigma and uncertainty associated with financial distress. Spansion was no exception. However, most of the damage that was going to happen had already occurred. A delay caused by a valuation fight would be painful, but not ruinous. In other words, both α and D were small, if not zero.

According to game theory, the Convertible Noteholders should have been content to walk away for a relatively modest recovery in the order of magnitude of the single-digit millions of dollars that litigation would cost. For whatever reason, the Convertible Noteholder coalition conducted an all-out valuation fight and refused to settle for what theory would have otherwise indicated.

After a fiercely contested valuation fight, the judge found that indeed the Convertible Noteholders were far out of the money and deserved to have a recovery of zero. Clearly, the lawyers and their clients overplayed their rather poor hand.

In a world where all litigants are well advised and there is a competent jurist, we believe that the game should settle out at a Nash Equilibrium point (or if more than one, at least at one of them). Further, we note that even if the game gets "stuck" due to the parties' differing views as to the value of α, the competent jurist could "unstick" the game by communicating with the various constituencies and changing their *a priori* assumptions.

We have the following "takeaways" from this:

- Professional, talented financial and legal advisors are key – both offensively and defensively. If the goal is to at least prevent the other side from "pulling a fast one" on the court, the professional team needs to be on its toes at all times.
- Similarly, the professionals need to be able to convince the other side's professionals of the relative strength of their legal and valuation positions. The professionals also need to undertake the due diligence necessary to develop valuation views which will in turn determine the value of relevant inputs, particularly α and D.
- But the professionals not only need to be focused and honest with the court. They need to be candid with the clients and with themselves. In situations like this, experience and judgment are needed to overcome the massive egos and "love of the litigation itself." Clients are ill-served if their professionals are viewing the situation solely as a jousting match.
- The court needs to be effectively communicated with by the professionals, and the professionals need to communicate with one another. In situations like this where miscommunications can lead to protracted litigation, serious senior lawyers and financial advisors are required. This communication can be enhanced if the respective sides' professionals have experience with one another.

In sum, in order to play the game correctly, the professional team needs to (i) develop valuation views that will inform the clients, the other side and (if necessary) the court, (ii) analyze potential weaknesses in such views that could affect a court's view, (iii) determine if the business will suffer greatly from protracted litigation and (iv) develop a negotiation strategy that – if necessary – can be flipped into active litigation mode. And then be prepared to make mid-course corrections if other facts come into evidence or if the court gives "guidance" down the road.

Conclusions

We believe that game theory offers a robust tool with which litigants – and courts – can gain valuable insights into the junior vs. senior negotiating dynamics within U.S. restructurings. In the illustrative examples we used, we focused on a two-player game with a relatively few moving parameters. In the real world, there are many players with many objectives and a myriad of moving parts. Nonetheless, complex negotiations can be separated into discrete component segments. And these components do indeed lend themselves to traditional game theory analysis.

We have limited our analysis to the U.S. context because of the emphasis of U.S. law on restructuring the ongoing business. In other countries, where the assets are marshaled and sold, the forgoing game may not generally be available to junior constituencies. No game, no negotiated recovery.

The game also begs another question. Is the game itself a good thing? From one standpoint, it sounds like it can be a bit like highway robbery. But we take the view that (other than the occasional abuse of the legal system), these games are indeed good for the restructuring process. They keep the process honest, and avoid the situation where the Super Seniors can collude with the company's management to illegitimately take value away from the junior constituencies. And from this perspective, the game is totally in sync with the spirit and letter of the Bankruptcy Code.

APPENDIX C: FINANCIAL STATEMENT ANALYSIS – THE FOUNDATION OF AN INVESTMENT BANKER'S VIEWS

Without being able to understand financial statements, the investment banker cannot develop views on valuation, credit capacity and other key concepts. Period, end of story. While volumes have been written about financial statement analysis, our goal here is modest: to describe financial statements, review tools to analyze them and then discuss five common pitfalls in this type of analysis.

Financial Statements

Viewed in their most basic light, financial statements are a means of boiling down the essence of a business into a package of financial schedules. These schedules can describe the past performance of the company (called "historical" financials), or its expected future performance (called "projections"). Or they can be used to analyze "what if" scenarios (*i.e.*, what would the business have looked like if a business being acquired had actually been bought a year earlier?). These are referred to as "pro forma" financial statements.

Most businesses use accrual accounting and prepare their financial statements in accordance with Generally Accepted Accounting Principles (GAAP), established by the Financial Accounting Standards Board, an accounting industry standard-setting committee. The principles lay out how transactions and economic activity should be recorded in a company's financial statements. At its heart, GAAP attempts to model the economic reality of a company's day-to-day operations.

For example, if a sale of a company's product is paid for in cash at the time of the sale, this transaction would be simple to account for, as revenue and cash receipts are recorded immediately. However, if that sale is made on terms that require subsequent payment, the accounting becomes more complex. If revenue recognized depended upon actual cash receipts, no sale would have been recorded. This view misstates the economic reality of the transaction. In this case, all of the costs of making the product would likely have been recorded, but none of the revenue. GAAP attempts to remove this anomaly and match expenses with revenues.

Three basic schedules make up "financial statements." These schedules are accompanied by explanatory notes. It is essential not to underestimate the importance of these accompanying notes, as the information they contain usually provides tip-offs about potential issues. The Income Statement lists the revenues and expenses of the firm, with the difference being reported as net income. The Balance Sheet takes a "snapshot" at a given point of the value of assets, liabilities and equity, the latter being the excess of assets over liabilities. The Statement of Cash Flows interprets relationships between the other two. And there is also a statement regarding changes in the equity accounts that we will not dwell on in this text.

For example, increases in liabilities are a source of cash, while increases in assets are uses of cash. If a company is reporting significant profitability while consuming large amounts of cash, that can a "red flag" to the vigilant investment banker. See the Phar-Mor example, discussed below.

The Balance Sheet

We believe the balance sheet is the most important single part of the financial statements, although as we discuss later, the three financial statements should be analyzed together. We have developed this bias directly out of our work as financial restructuring professionals. Indeed, we are inclined to be suspicious of companies that lead their financial presentations with their income statements rather than their balance sheets.

The concept of the balance sheet is straightforward. The accountants total the value of the assets on the one hand and the liabilities on the other. The difference is shareholders' equity – the value to the owners, otherwise known as "book" value. In another day and time, this presentation may have had a tangible link to public equity market valuations. However, the accounting entries do not generally track market values. That is why the market typically trades at several times the "book" value of the companies in the market.

If we all agree that the balance sheet does not translate directly into market values, why do we care about it? Because it tells us about the character of the business. Like the relative importance of fixed assets to current assets (manufacturing plant vs. receivables and inventories, for example). Or how much of the assets are comprised of "intangibles" – which are difficult to value and may have no real value at all. And how much of the liabilities are due in the near-term, in contrast to those that may be payable far down the road. Or whether the liabilities are financial (*i.e.*, indebtedness) rather than operational, such as accounts payable or pension obligations. Or whether the financial liabilities are secured.

In addition, changes over time in the individual accounts within the balance sheet can raise other questions. If certain items – receivables or inventories, for example – are changing dramatically, that can be a sign of normal growth. Or it can be a sign of real problems.

Each of these factors is enormously important in understanding a business.

The Income Statement

The Income Statement is critically important to understanding a company's performance. It is on this statement that we see the profitability – or lack thereof – of a company.

The income statement begins with revenues. Within a given period, revenues are supposed to represent the amount of sales by an enterprise. But that is only the tip of the iceberg. It is fundamentally important to understand the trends in revenue and the components of total revenue.

For example, how much of revenues are actually collected in the form of cash? If such transformation into cash is not happening, then receivables may be increasing – raising questions about the "hardness" of the revenue stream. Is the company being a "bank" for its customers (and if so, is it charging sufficient interest on the debts?), or are the receivables subject to prospective write-downs due to uncollectability (implying that the revenues were overstated in the first place)?

What is the revenue mix? The company may have been bragging about being in certain attractive business areas. But if the revenues associated with such sexy areas are relatively modest in relation to the rest of its business, the braggadocio must be tempered with reality. By reviewing the segment disclosure and the company's Management's Discussion and Analysis (MD&A) of its financial statements, the investment banker can discover the facts behind revenue composition and detailed trends.

And what is the revenue trend over the last few quarters or years? Is this a growing business or a declining one? How have the revenues changed, segment by segment? Is the company moving into more attractive areas? How has competition affected revenues? Is the revenue trend muddied by acquisitions or divestitures? Or by significant recent capital expenditures efforts (such as the opening of new stores)? In order to have a view as to the actual underlying trends in the business, the investment banker must be able to dissect this data.

The next step in the compilation of the income statement is to deduct costs of doing business from the revenue line. Operating costs include items such as Costs of Goods Sold and Selling, General and Administrative expenses. The investment banker needs to analyze trends in these items, both on an absolute basis and in relation to sales (see "Ratio Analysis" below).

Such cost trend analysis can be informative on a number of levels. Increases in costs in relation to sales can flag signs of impending trouble. Perhaps the sales mix is being skewed toward lower profit items. Or the company is being adversely affected by increased competition or inflation in the costs of raw material inputs. Or, if the trend is paralleled by decreases in sales volumes, perhaps the company's fixed costs cannot be reduced fast enough to offset the sales decline.

The difference between revenues and operating costs is operating profit – sometimes referred to as Earnings Before Interest and Taxes (EBIT). This represents the economic profitability of the enterprise, without taking its capital structure into account.

Frequently, bankers add the amount of depreciation and amortization (D&A) to EBIT to derive Earnings Before Interest, Taxes, Depreciation and Amortization (EBITDA). Advocates of this approach argue that EBITDA is a better measure because it represents operating cash flow before capital expenditures and other such items. In the near-term, this may be so. Over longer time frames, however, we do not believe that capital expenditures are so discretionary – they must be made if a business is to continue to function.

Accordingly, we think that EBIT is a much better long-term measure than EBITDA. Or, if the investment banker thinks historical D&A is not a good proxy for future capital expenditures, then the banker needs to develop an alternative metric – such as EBITDA less estimated capital expenditures.

After determining operating profit, the investment banker needs to account for the company's capital structure. Typically, this entails computing the amount of interest accrued and/or paid on the company's debt, and subtracting it from operating profit. Similarly, any non-operating income from cash and investment balances is added to operating profit. Although this sounds straightforward, and often is, the use of actual interest costs can be a little misleading. Interest costs can vary widely due to such factors as whether they are fixed or floating (floating rates tend to be lower than fixed in most market environments), when the debt was incurred (rates can change materially over time) and the maturity of the debt (longer maturities tend to have higher rates than shorter ones). Accordingly, the investment banker must understand the composition of the debt in order to understand whether the actual interest expense is truly representative of current market conditions, or whether the interest expense will change as debt is refinanced. Again, a review of the Company's debt and long-term obligations footnote is imperative for a complete view of the Company's financial obligations and costs.

Deducting capital structure-related costs from operating profits and accounting for other income yields pre-tax profits.

Tax Expense is then calculated in the income statement. Actual taxes paid can be materially different from the tax expense recorded. Deductions for tax purposes may vary from those for income statement purposes – leading to a different level of pre-tax income between the two presentations. The company may have built-up historical net operating losses that can be offset against current income. Depreciation in tax returns is sometimes accelerated when compared to financial statements. And so forth. Any taxes unpaid, or pre-paid as compared to the Income Statement, are accounted for on the Balance Sheet in the deferred tax accounts. A review of the Company's tax footnote is a first step toward understanding the Company's tax position and any change in tax expense.

Deducting taxes from pre-tax profit yields net income.

And then net income is also stated in terms of earnings per share (EPS). A company with a "simple" capital structure can take net income, divide by the average number of common shares outstanding, and voilà – derive EPS. However, many companies have more complex capital structures that involve convertible securities, options and warrants. Those additional equity-related securities are entitled to share in the earnings available to the common holders. Therefore, in order to present a more complete picture for the holders of equity securities, the income statement must take the dilutive effect of such instruments into account. The techniques involved in such accounting involve increasing the number of underlying shares by some or all of the contingently-issuable shares, while perhaps adding back items such as interest expense on convertible securities.

The Cash Flow Statement

The cash flow statement is essentially a "bridge" between the income statement and the balance sheet. In fact, if you have two of the three statements, you can largely create the third.

The cash flow statement can be cast in one of several ways. Usually, the statement starts with net income, and adds back D&A. It then accounts for changes within the balance sheet, such as increases or decreases in certain balance sheet items. For example, an increase in inventories costs cash – and represents such a use of cash in the cash flow statement. After totaling up all of these items, the investment banker can see how much cash the company actually used or generated from operations during the period. It is here that the astute analyst ferrets out the difference between actual cash and Income Statement earnings. Non-cash items, whether they be gains or losses, are specifically listed as reconciling items. Changes in working capital items such as inventory and accounts receivable are highlighted here. The Income Statement smoothes the timing of cash flows to match revenue and expenses; the cash flow statement charts the actual cash flows from the activity. It then deducts funds used for capital expenditures and acquisitions in the Investing Section.

The amount of funds related to operations and investing will correspond exactly to a mirror-image amount in the financing elements in the cash flow statement. These financing elements include cash, debt and the equity account. If a company uses cash in its operations through losses or otherwise, the money needs to be provided by a combination of a decrease in cash, an increase in debt or an increase in equity (net of dividends).

Ratio Analysis

One of the most important parts of financial statement analysis entails computing and tracking financial ratios over time. These ratios fall into several categories, including balance sheet ratios, income statement ratios, asset efficiency ratios and coverage ratios.

Balance sheet ratios examine the relationships between various asset and liability categories to determine factors such as liquidity and leverage. Typical balance sheet liquidity statistics include the current ratio (the ratio of current assets to current liabilities) and the quick ratio (the ratio of cash and receivables to current liabilities). These measure the ability of a company to meet its near-term obligations. Leverage statistics include the debt-to-equity ratio (the ratio of the amount of debt to the equity account) – both including and excluding intangible assets from the equity account. The leverage statistics attempt to demonstrate the relative degree of indebtedness a company has.

Income statement ratios can "normalize" the income statement as a function of the sales base. Sometimes called "common size" analysis, the investment banker can express the various income statement line items as a percentage of sales. This technique is particularly useful in tracking profitability trends over a period of time. Absolute levels of profitability may be increasing along with sales – a favorable trend. But if the profits as a percentage of sales are falling – then the trend may not be seen to be all that favorable. This would be a "red flag" for the investment banker to look at more closely. Key statistics include gross margin (sales less costs of sales as a percentage of sales), Selling, General and Administrative expenses as a percentage of sales, EBIT margin (EBIT as a percentage of sales), EBITDA margin (EBITDA as a percentage of sales), tax rate (taxes divided by pre-tax income) and net margin (net income as a percentage of sales).

Another important income statement ratio is the growth rate in sales or other line items over time. The investment banker can get a sense of the growth rates inherent in the business – as well as any changes in the growth rate (*i.e.*, is growth speeding up or slowing down?).

Another important set of ratios deals with asset efficiency. Key statistics include asset turnover (last 12 months, known as LTM, sales divided by assets), days receivable (receivables × 365 days per year, divided by LTM sales), inventory turns (LTM cost of goods sold divided by inventories) and days payable (payables × 365 days per year, divided by LTM cost of goods sold).

These efficiency ratios link elements of the income statement to the balance sheet, and they are integral to an analysis of whether the business is remaining healthy. For example, deterioration over time in statistics such as days receivable or inventory turns can foreshadow problems leading to future write-downs. In the extreme case, they can be harbingers of fraud, as in the Phar-Mor case discussed below.

Credit ratios are also used to assess a company's financial health. These look at the relationship between operating profits and the level of indebtedness – measured either by the amount of interest or the amount of borrowings. Typical credit ratios include coverage ratios, such as LTM EBIT-to-interest, LTM EBITDA-to-interest, or Net Debt-to-LTM EBITDA.

But not all financial obligations are set forth neatly into their debt components on the balance sheet. Accordingly, the investment banker must use appropriate judgment in determining which items should be included in the analysis. For example, if a company has a material amount of underfunded pension or retiree health-care obligations (generally set forth on the balance sheet as operating liabilities), the investment banker may choose to consider such amounts as the functional equivalent of debt. Of course, the banker may need to consider whether such items need to be tax-effected (if such payments can be deducted for tax purposes) and whether historical benefit payments should be added back to EBIT in order to have a consistent presentation (in certain cases, this may be appropriate to avoid double-counting). Once again the notes to the financial statements will inform the investment banker as to the facts of the situation.

Similarly, a company may have a material amount of "disguised" indebtedness off-balance sheet. The most common example of this is operating leases for real estate, such as stores and office locations. One way to account for this is to "capitalize" these obligations by multiplying the LTM rental expense by an appropriate multiple. In order to avoid double-counting the effect of the additional leverage, the investment banker would need to add the LTM rental expense back to EBIT and EBITDA. Another way of measuring this off-balance sheet leverage is to add a portion of lease expense (for example, one-third) to both the interest expense and the operating profit. This allows the investment banker to compute the ratio of modified operating profit to modified interest expense (referred to as "fixed charges") to determine the "fixed charge coverage" ratio.

In short, ratio analysis is one of the most important pieces of overall financial statistical analysis. Just as a doctor can monitor a patient's vital signs, the investment banker can use ratio analysis to monitor and assess a company's financial health.

Pro Forma Analysis

When a company consummates a major transaction, such as an acquisition or divestiture, the historical financial statements may no longer be a reliable proxy for the company's future performance. Typically, in connection with material transactions, the company will file statements with the SEC that allow a careful reader to see what the pro forma company would look like for the immediately preceding periods.

However, in order to get a longer trend line, it may be necessary for the investment banker to restate historical financials from prior periods in order to present them as if the transaction had occurred several years before. Of course, the historical information may not be available if the acquired company was not public or if the divested business was not large enough to merit a separate segment analysis in the seller's SEC filings. Unfortunately, the fewer historical pro forma data points, the less comfort financial statement analysis can give the investment banker.

Benchmarking

Another important financial statement analysis tool is "benchmarking" the company against its comparables. This entails evaluating the company's ratios against the other companies to determine relative strengths and weaknesses.

This comparable approach can provide a number of insights. If a company has higher growth rates or higher profitability margins, it may deserve a higher multiple than its peers. And the converse would also be true.

Inferior asset utilization statistics could indicate room for improvement and potentially enhanced value. Or it could signal the potential for future write-downs. In any case, it is a "red flag" that the investment banker should investigate.

If a company has much greater leverage than its competitors, that could signal trouble ahead. Such a company may need to direct much of its cash flows into debt service. On the other hand, well-capitalized, aggressive competitors would have more financial flexibility and could try to seize market share from the highly leveraged company.

Five Common Pitfalls in Financial Statement Analysis

Pitfall #1 – Concentrating Too Much on One Statement

We cannot stress enough that financial statements are part of an integrated whole. The analyst cannot simply pick one statement and make reasonable conclusions regarding value or solvency. Yet, too often, this is exactly what happens, and the focus is usually on the income statement.

By myopically focusing on the income statement and ignoring what is going on in the balance sheet and the cash flow statement, the investment banker runs the risk of missing some extremely important facts. A far better approach is for the banker to analyze the relationships among different sets of data from various financial statements (see "Ratio Analysis," above).

The investment banker who neglects the relationships and focuses only on the income statement runs the risk of missing information and producing materially misleading valuation judgments. In the worst case, the banker can miss telltale signs of fraud.

GORDIAN KNOTS/Phar-Mor

Phar-Mor was a rapidly growing discount retailer whose revenues ultimately exceeded $1 billion annually. It achieved profitability, and became a darling of the investment community, which threw bucketfuls of cash at it. It looked great on paper – at least on the income statement. The problem is, Phar-Mor was also one of the largest frauds in corporate history.

The Company's management understood that Wall Street rewarded high revenue and profit growth. And management's business plan gave Phar-Mor the opportunity to achieve such objectives (at least on the revenue side). By discounting even deeper, Phar-Mor could basically manufacture sales. But only by incurring huge cash losses. If you are selling at such a loss, you are not going to "make it up on volume."

Phar-Mor's fraud plan was pretty simple. First, it created fictional inventory accounts. By keeping inventory levels artificially pumped up, Phar-Mor was able to report accounting profits instead of the massive losses actually being incurred. The next trick was to figure out how to finance its massive need for cash to fund these losses. Phar-Mor's solution was to fuel its growth through hundreds of millions of dollars of debt and equity financing. Investors were lured into Phar-Mor's web by its great-looking income statement. And when some investors questioned how Phar-Mor could actually achieve such profitable growth, management concocted a cover story – that its costs were far lower than they actually were, claiming that Phar-Mor was such a major force in the market that its "power buying" allowed it to obtain products at price levels much lower than its competitors were able to negotiate.

We have seen this type of fraud numerous times – particularly in retailing and wholesaling operations. Phar-Mor's accountants missed it, but we believe many clues were available that could have tipped off investors to the potential problems.

In situations like this, the fraudulent increases in profitability had to be booked somewhere. At Phar-Mor, they were booked to the inventory accounts. How could the investment community have figured this out?

An alert investment banker could have examined the ratios of inventory-to-sales or cost-of-goods-sold-to-inventory (inventory turns). Had that analysis been performed (see "Ratio Analysis," above) during the period of Phar-Mor's fraud, the analyst would have determined that there were very clear trends that Phar-Mor had needed to use an ever-larger inventory to support each dollar of sales.

Such an observation does not necessarily mean that fraud is under way. But it certainly indicates that there may be problems attributable to any number of sources. And such problems would not have been noticeable if the investment banker were focused solely on the income statement.

After the discovery of the fraud, we were called in, and we were able to demonstrate that outside investors should have been able to determine that something was very wrong at Phar-Mor.

GORDIAN KNOTS/MiniScribe Corporation

A $600 million disk-drive manufacturer, MiniScribe had funded its rapid growth over several years with bank and public debt. The management was replaced in an attempt to correct the company's operating difficulties, and the new management uncovered fraudulent activities. The company had even shipped bricks in lieu of disk drives and recorded them as revenue. MiniScribe began to experience a cash crisis and was forced to file for bankruptcy. It announced that because of its desperate cash situation, it would be sold quickly.

Maxtor Corporation, a major disk-drive manufacturer, engaged Gordian Group to advise it in acquiring MiniScribe. Gordian Group assisted Maxtor in assessing MiniScribe's business values, structuring a bid and negotiating with creditors. As part of the assignment, Gordian

> Group was required to re-create financial data, because the historical financial statements were rife with fraud. Without this, valuation views would be extremely difficult to derive. Gordian Group's efforts in this regard enabled it to develop the best views of valuation among the competing bidders, and these were a linchpin of Maxtor's successful credit bid strategy, and the assets were acquired by our client.
>
> A substantial portion of MiniScribe's assets were in Hong Kong and Singapore, outside of the U.S. bankruptcy court's jurisdiction. Gordian Group worked with Maxtor and the bank to devise a mechanism for foreclosure of the offshore assets and their subsequent sale to Maxtor.

Much more common than fraud is a disconnect between income and cash flow. A myopic focus on net income can lead to the wrong answer. For example, if a company will need to upgrade its physical plant in a big way because of environmental regulations – just to maintain its market position – the effect of the capital expenditures needs to be deducted from the value of the business.

Similarly, if depreciation or amortization expense is inadequate to deal with the annual decreases in the value of a company's assets, the valuation techniques relying on the income statement can overstate the company's values. This can occur when a company has acquired contracts that produce an income stream over time – alarm-monitoring contracts, advertising contracts, and so on – and those contracts can be terminated by the customer at will. In such cases, the annual cancellation rate (referred to as "attrition") can be high. When that cancellation rate exceeds the reported amortization rate, the profits can be materially overstated.

As we said above, the financial statements are of one piece – no one part can be understood in isolation. The investment banker must fully appreciate the interplay among the various schedules and the notes. Without such a full understanding, the investment banker is courting disaster.

Pitfall #2 – Not Taking Into Account Whether Income Is Recurring or Non-Recurring

One tenet of valuation and financial statement analysis is that we should focus on items that are likely to recur – and give much less weight to events that are unlikely to recur. For example, if a company incurs a one-time charge related to an oddball lawsuit, that charge should be added back to the accounting earnings in order to get a better picture of the company's steady state. Were we to perform a credit analysis or a valuation analysis of the company, without adding back the unusual expense, we would develop an overly pessimistic view.

This requires the investment banker to comb through the company's financial statements and related disclosures. The investment banker must make a series of judgments regarding which items are recurring, and those which are not. And these non-recurring items can be both positive (*e.g.*, unusual gains and extraordinary gains) and negative (one-time charges or write-offs).

In a related vein, the investment banker needs to isolate charges (some of which may be recurring) to reflect their cash and non-cash components. Non-cash components (such as fixed asset or intangible write-downs) may need to be reflected in the financial statements. However, they may have little bearing on the ongoing cash flow picture of the company. And at the end of the day, it is prospective cash flows that drive credit analysis and valuation.

When a company takes definitive steps to exit a line of business, the accountants frequently carry the non-core assets as "discontinued operations." On the one hand, the accountants have made life easier by splitting the company into its continuing vs. other businesses. However, unless the discontinued business has already been sold – without any further contingencies – then the investment banker needs to look closely at the discontinued operations to make sure that the valuation and liability assumptions embodied in the discontinued operations accounting are indeed realistic.

Pitfall #3 – Not Adjusting for the Consistent Inconsistencies among Financial Statements

It would be great if Moses had come down from the Mount with tablets that mandated all financial statements to be more or less consistent from one company to another. However, someone forgot to tell Moses.

For most businesses, financial statement reports are supposed to be produced in accordance with GAAP. This is great in theory, but GAAP allows a great deal of subjective determination. As a result, two companies in the same industry may prepare their financial statements in completely different ways.

For example, GAAP permits inventories to be valued in different ways. One way is to value them on a first-in-first-out (FIFO) basis. That means that a unit of inventory used in the last reporting period may have been purchased months (if not years) before. In inflationary periods, this means that profit for the most recent period may be overstated because old, lower-cost inventory is being charged to expense, rather than the new, higher-cost units. Another means of valuing inventory is on a last-in-first-out (LIFO") basis. This means that the most recent inventory purchases would be charged to expense in the most recent period – thereby giving a more contemporaneous picture of profit. However, problems can occur with LIFO if sales dramatically exceed production. In such case, it is possible that the financial statements can pick up really old units of inventory, thereby creating a large unusual gain in the most recent period.

Both FIFO and LIFO are accepted inventory accounting methods. Yet they can produce dramatically different financial statement results. And this is but one example of differing treatments that can result from disparate accounting methodologies. What's an investment banker to do?

As noted above, the first step is to eliminate any "non-recurring" gains or losses. In the LIFO/FIFO example, we would likely eliminate the LIFO gain created by sales of old, low-cost inventory. From there the analyst needs to determine if raw material prices and other inventory costs components have been changing in the recent past. If so, LIFO and FIFO may be adjusted to ensure comparability with competitors in benchmarking exercises and the like. That may not make the two sets of financial statements completely "apples-to-apples," but it clearly helps.

Vlasic Foods – A Financial Statement Analysis Case Study

In 1998, Campbell Soup spun off Vlasic Foods, a group of underperforming businesses, to its stockholders in a leveraged transaction. At first, Vlasic was a high-flying stock, with an equity market capitalization of more than $1 billion. Yet, less than three years later, Vlasic was in bankruptcy and the creditors were severely impaired. The Vlasic estate sued Campbell, alleging that the transaction was a fraudulent conveyance.

What happened to cause this decline? We were engaged by the Vlasic estate to find out. As it turned out, financial statement analysis provided the roadmap.

In connection with the spinoff, Campbell filed carve-out financial statements of Vlasic with the SEC. These financials showed that Vlasic enjoyed stable operating profit, year after year, of $90 million to $115 million. Investors were told that shortly after the spinoff, Vlasic would incur some unusual expenses in connection with revitalizing the business. But the investors believed that based on LTM performance the base level of profitability was $130 million because of the pro formas filed with the SEC.

However, the pro formas were fraudulent, the Vlasic estate argued. For years, Campbell management had aggressively grown reported earnings by a number of mechanisms, including the use of "loading." Loading (sometimes called "channel stuffing") involves the sale of goods to customers in advance of their current needs. Typically, Campbell would incentivize retailers (its customers) to take such goods by offering a discount. This would have the effect of bolstering immediate sales and profits at the expense of future periods. Ultimately, the piper would have to be paid.

And if Campbell was aggressive in pumping the earnings of its core units, it was doubly so with Vlasic in the periods leading up to the spinoff. After all, future periods' problems would rest with Vlasic's management, not Campbell's.

We were able to identify the loading that went on in Vlasic's financials, and quantify the impact on sales, profits and cash flow. In essence, this was a temporary boost to Vlasic, and was non-recurring. So we backed out about $20 million of LTM operating profit.

Similarly, there were a lot of one-time gains in Vlasic's financials. Items such as gains on sales of assets, gains from insurance settlements and LIFO gains added up to another $25 million in the LTM period. So we deducted these as well.

Moreover, Vlasic was going to need to spend additional monies on corporate overhead. When a company is spun off as a public entity, frequently these redundant costs will cause pro forma expenses to exceed the costs that had been historically allocated by the parent. We were able to determine that this figure was another $17 million in the LTM period, and deducted it. And so on.

After adjusting for these non-recurring gains, we determined that LTM operating profit would be $57 million – not the $130 million reported to the SEC.

Plaintiffs argued that Campbell had succeeded in temporarily pulling the wool over the market's eyes. Campbell argued that Vlasic's ultimate failure was not Campbell's fault – in other words, Campbell said that Vlasic was a healthy company at the date of the spin.

Unfortunately, the court agreed with Campbell's arguments. The court was persuaded by the fact that the stock market had given high values to Vlasic – until Vlasic tanked. Ultimately, this decision boiled down to expectations of growth. For a period of time, the stock market thought Vlasic had good growth prospects. We did not, and neither did the buyers for Vlasic's businesses in the merger market after it went bankrupt.

Pitfall #4 – Failing to Adjust for Differences in Presentation Format

The format of financial statements can vary widely, depending upon their intended use. Statements used in connection with periodic financial reporting may look materially different than schedules prepared internally by management to analyze historical trends or to develop projections.

The most voluminous presentation may be that associated with a company's annual audit. These audited historical financial statements generally include income statements for two or three years, two years of balance sheets, two years of cash flow statements and an analysis of changes in equity capitalization over recent years. They also typically contain a set of notes that accompany the numbers in order to better explain the dynamics of what is going on.

The audited statements will be accompanied by an opinion from the company's auditors discussing any problems they may have encountered in connection with their review. For example, the accountants could express a concern that the company's losses are so great that there is doubt as to whether it can continue in business (known as a "going concern" opinion). To the extent that such an opinion highlights these problems, this should be a "red flag" for the financial analyst.

Companies (whether public or private) generally prepare historical interim financial statement reports on a basis consistent with that of the annual audits. These interim presentations will generally contain the same basic schedules as the audit, although much of the information may be in more summarized form. In the U.S., these interim reports are typically prepared quarterly. Frequently, these will compare year-to-date results with the comparable periods in the previous fiscal year. Interim statements also will likely contain notes to the financials, although with far less detail than the notes to the audited statements.

For the foregoing financial statements prepared for financial reporting purposes, there is a reasonable degree of uniformity among companies, reflecting accounting and SEC regulations. However, statements prepared for other investor purposes may be materially different from company to company. No formal rules govern this kind of presentation, and the variances may reflect long-standing customs within a particular finance group or the creativity of a 23-year-old with a spreadsheet.

Whatever the reason, the investment banker needs to be able to understand the financial presentation and to be able to make sense of it all.

A key tool in the understanding of the financial statements and their underlying trends is the MD&A section of a company's public filings. In this disclosure, the company is expected to set forth its analysis of trends and give breakdowns of key items, such as unusual or non-recurring expenses and gains. Some companies do a lot better job in this regard than others. But in any case, it is a good place to start to pick up information that sheds light on the numbers themselves.

Finally, we acknowledge that we have limited this primer to a discussion of U.S. companies. Foreign firms are subject to different sets of accounting rules and disclosure requirements (not to mention the possibility of a language other than English) that can render a comparison to U.S. companies completely unreliable. If such a comparison is critical, it is incumbent on the investment banker to become familiar enough with international accounting presentations in order to develop a meaningful analysis.

Pitfall #5 – Failing to Review the Notes to Financial Statements and the MD&A

Financial statements do not stand alone. Companies prepare accompanying notes that explain accounting policies and underlying details to amounts presented on the financials' face. Without reading the notes, the investment banker will miss many items that are of interest and will potentially change the investment banker's view.

The same can be said of the MD&A. Financial performance changes over time and the MD&A explains the changes presented in financials and provides a foundation for their understanding. Without reviewing the MD&A, an investment banker can be at a loss for much of what is happening in the business. All too often, financial analysts take the number in the financial statements at face value and, too often, they miss factors that should be reflected in their analysis and views.

GLOSSARY

Accepting Creditor Class. For a class of creditors to accept a Plan under Chapter 11, in excess of two-thirds of the dollar amount and half of the number of claimants voting must approve. The measurement is of those actually voting, so a plurality of actual claims may be able to accept on behalf of the class. In an accepting class, non-voting and rejecting holders are bound by the vote of the accepting holders.

Accepting Interest Holders Class. For a class of interest holders to accept a Plan under Chapter 11, in excess of half of the shares in each such class must approve. In an accepting class, non-voting and rejecting holders are bound by the vote of the accepting holders.

Adequate Protection. If a bankrupt debtor has secured debt, it must be able to demonstrate that the secured creditors' collateral value will not deteriorate past the position where their par recovery is jeopardized (or if the expected recovery is already below par, that it will not get worse). See "Cash Collateral". If the creditors' underlying collateral is being impaired, the debtor must provide additional collateral as "adequate protection." If no such additional collateral is available, the debtor must change its operations and avoid the use of the creditors' collateral – or basically hand the company over to the secured creditors. In practice, this hand-off is typically achieved through a "going concern" sale of the company's assets, although a conversion to a Chapter 7 liquidation is certainly possible.

Administrative Priority. A claim incurred after a company has filed for Chapter 11. It must be paid before any recoveries can be had by pre-petition unsecured claims holders.

Agent. A person acting on behalf of one or more of the principals involved. Typically, an agent will be an investment banker or an attorney representing the debtor or one of its creditor constituencies.

Allocation. The portion of overall recoveries received by an individual claim or interest holder, or class of such holders.

Allowed Claim. A claim that has both (i) been timely filed (see "Bar Date") and (ii) been agreed-to in amount by the debtor and the creditor. If the amount of such claim has not been agreed to, it is referred to as "disputed." See "Disputed Claim."

Asset Divestiture. Disposition or sale of an asset by a company. A company will often divest an asset that is not performing well, not vital to the company's core business, worth more to a potential buyer or as a separate entity than as part of the company, or in order to raise funds for continuing operations.

Asymmetry. The concept that in a negotiation or conflict between unequal forces, the weaker can create a dynamic that offsets the disparity of forces – by choosing the terrain, the timing of the conflict and its duration. As the weaker side may have little to lose and a lot to gain, and the other side could lose a lot and perhaps gain little, the use of asymmetry can allow a given constituency to obtain significant negotiating advantages over other parties.

Auction. Generally, the sale of assets of a bankrupt company in a court-orchestrated process. See "Section 363 Sale". May also refer to the "controlled auction" process (in or out of bankruptcy), in which a company or its assets may be marketed to a defined group of potential buyers.

Automatic Stay. When a company seeks bankruptcy protection, the law automatically provides a stay against secured creditors seeking to foreclose on assets or otherwise enforce their liens. Such a stay is integral to the debtor's rehabilitation process and may be lifted only through a judicial process, after the creditor has shown it would otherwise suffer irreparable damage.

Avoidance. The bankruptcy court has the ability to set aside, or "avoid," certain transactions. For example, if a transaction of questionable merit involving insiders had been consummated just prior to the company's filing for bankruptcy, the court might avoid the transaction and force rescission. See "Preferences."

Bankruptcy Abuse Prevention and Consumer Protection Act (BAPCPA). In 2005, the Bankruptcy Code was substantially modified, primarily to strengthen creditors' rights against consumers. However, certain changes were made that had the effect of diminishing corporate debtors' powers as well. Principal among these corporate changes was the effective shortening of the debtor's exclusivity period.

Bankruptcy Code. The Code is a body of laws (as modified by court interpretations) that governs bankruptcy proceedings for businesses, individuals and government entities. For most corporations, the relevant sections are Chapter 11 (governing reorganizations) and Chapter 7 (governing liquidations). The Code is subject to review and amendment by Congress.

Bankruptcy Remote Vehicle. Secured creditors are frequently frustrated in their attempts to collect on amounts due and owing from a bankrupt debtor. See "Automatic Stay." In response, attorneys and investment bankers have devised structures that seek to circumvent the bankruptcy laws. In a common example, the company would sell receivables to a newly formed subsidiary, which would then borrow money secured by the receivables. The proceeds derived from the borrowing would then be upstreamed to the parent. Were the parent to seek bankruptcy protection at a later date, the secured creditors lending to the newly-formed subsidiary would expect that their legal rights against the receivables would be unaffected by the parent's bankruptcy – hence, "bankruptcy remote." However, we note that judges have held that the subsidiary was not "bankruptcy remote" and "forced" the secured creditors to continue to lend.

Bar Date. For purposes of asserting claims in connection with a bankruptcy, creditors must file a proof of claim before a deadline set by the court – the "bar date." Any claims asserted after the bar date are automatically disqualified.

Basis Point. In the bond market, typically the smallest measure used for quoting yields is a basis point. One basis point is 1/100th of one percentage point.

Best and Final Offer (BAFO). In constructing bidding strategies, it may be appropriate to call for one last bidding round. This can have the effect of causing a potential buyer that really wants the asset to put its best offer forward, without holding anything back in terms of price.

Best and Really Final Offer (BARFO). If the BAFO process falls short of expectations, it may be necessary to go back to the potential buyers once again for a (truly) final round of bidding.

Best Interests Test. In order for a court to confirm a Plan of Reorganization, it must make several findings regarding the prospective viability of the reorganized company and the treatment of the creditors. The "Best Interests Test" seeks to ensure that creditors are not being treated unfairly. To do this the test imposes a yardstick of what such creditor classes would have received in a hypothetical Chapter 7 liquidation. As long as the creditor recoveries in the Chapter 11 plan (based on valuation testimony, in addition to other factors) exceed such hypothetical liquidation recoveries (also based in part on testimony), the test would be met.

Bidder Protection. Sales of assets in bankruptcy – particularly in an auction context – are subject to overbid at the actual auction. This can be discouraging to certain bidders that would otherwise be willing to incur upfront costs involved in reaching a definitive agreement with the bankrupt seller. On the other hand, the bankrupt seller clearly benefits from a "floor" placed under the sale proceeds by having a firm "lead" or "stalking horse" offer on the table. In order to bridge this gap, debtors frequently provide incentives to buyers to act in a stalking horse capacity by giving them various bidder protections, which may involve break-up fees or favorable bidding rules. See "Break-Up Fee" and "Overbid Protection."

Black-Scholes Value. Reorganizations frequently involve the issuance of various types of securities, including those that provide for contingent payoffs in the event of higher eventual stock prices. See "Options" and "Warrants." One method typically used in valuing such contingent securities is through one of a number of mathematical "black box" models. The best-known of these is named after its creators, Fisher Black and Myron Scholes, and values options and warrants based upon the relationship of (i) the stock price to the "strike" (or exercise) price, (ii) the volatility of the underlying stock price, (iii) the maturity of the warrant and (iv) prevailing interest rates.

Break-Up Fee. In connection with sales of assets in bankruptcy court or otherwise, buyers frequently seek certain advantages to being a "lead" bidder. See "Bidder Protection." One common economic benefit given is a "break-up" fee that is payable to the initial bidder that first enters into a definitive agreement with the seller. Depending upon the size and complexity of the deal, such fee can range from 1% to 5% of the purchase price, and is payable if a buyer other than the lead bidder acquires the assets. Frequently, the amount of the break-up fee can be credited against the purchase price at auction. Such break-up fees are generally in addition to any fees paid by the seller in connection with the buyer's due diligence. See "Work Fees."

Breakeven. The period of time it would require an investor to recoup the dollar amount of the conversion premium from the coupon income on a convertible instrument. Assume a convertible priced at $100 with a 5% coupon and with a conversion feature of 10 shares per bond. With an $8 underlying common price, the total common value of the bond would be

$80. The conversion premium would be $20 ($100 less $80). The annual coupon income would be $5 (5% of $100). The breakeven (assuming no common dividends) would be four years ($20 conversion premium, divided by $5 coupon income per year).

"Burn Rate." The rate at which a company with negative cash flow is using up its available cash. Often expressed as a rate of millions of dollars per month.

Business Plan. One key underpinning of any reorganization is the debtor's business plan. It provides the basis for understanding the "core" business around which the company is to reorganize, as well as the extraneous assets that can be divested to help fund the financial reorganization. It also provides the basis for assessments of both the value and debt capacity of the business, which in turn drive the structure of the financial reorganization and the expected recovery for the company's various constituencies.

Cancellation of Indebtedness ("COD") Income. See Section 382.

Capital Structure. The makeup of the ways in which a company has raised the capital needed to establish and expand its business activities.

Cash Collateral. The use of cash derived from operations is absolutely critical for the survival of a company. Otherwise, collections from receivables cannot be plowed back into purchase of inventories and the conversion into saleable products. If a bankrupt debtor has pre-petition debt secured by its working capital, it must be able to demonstrate that such working capital collateral will not be diminished to the point where it would impair the secured lenders' recovery. See "Adequate Protection." If the debtor can demonstrate that losses will not seriously erode the lenders' position, it will be able to use its cash collateral. Otherwise, it will be at the mercy of the secured lenders.

Cash Flow Bond. Restructuring negotiations frequently balance the demands of senior creditors for cash or more certain consideration vs. the needs of the debtor for liquidity. In certain circumstances, the negotiations can lead to the creation of a debt instrument that repays greater amounts if the reorganized company posts better earnings.

Chapter 7. The liquidation chapter of the Bankruptcy Code. If the debtor is deemed to be unable to reorganize, its assets will be liquidated for the benefit of its creditors. In most cases, this liquidation value will be less than that were the company to be successfully reorganized. See "Going Concern."

Chapter 11. The corporate reorganization chapter of the Bankruptcy Code. Chapter 11 was written by Congress to give companies a reasonable shot at being able to stabilize their operations while keeping creditors at bay. The end result for a "successful" Chapter 11 could be an internal reorganization (in which claimants receive new securities of the reorganized entity) or a sale of all or a part of the business. However, not all companies can be reorganized, and "unsuccessful" Chapter 11 processes can end up in liquidations – either through conversions to Chapter 7 or through what is known as a "Liquidating 11."

Chapter 15. In 2005, the Bankruptcy Code was modified to permit greater flexibility and court powers with respect to cross-border insolvencies. However, Chapter 15 doesnot yet solve the difficulties in dealing with conflicting laws and inability to effect legal solutions in two international jurisdictions simultaneously.

Chapter 22. A term of art for companies that return to Chapter 11 once they fail after being reorganized the first time.

Chapter 33. A failed Chapter 22. Achieving this status in the "Frequent Filers Club" is a rare event.

Chief Restructuring Officer (CRO). In recent years, CROs have become more prevalent, particularly in major cases. They may be court-appointed and can serve to expedite the restructuring, to broker peace among warring constituencies or even to perform a supervisory or investigative role.

Classification. In bankruptcy, claims are grouped according to similarity. These groupings are based upon various factors, such as identity of the obligor (claims of parent companies vs. their subsidiaries may be separately classified), collateral interests, senior vs. subordinated, post-petition vs. pre-petition, claims entitled to certain priorities (such as governmental claims), and so forth. Interests are also grouped in the same manner, with preferred stock and common stock having their own classes.

The theory underlying the classification system is that equal-ranking claims should receive more or less equal treatment. This implies that dissimilar claims should not be placed in the same class (*e.g.*, subordinated debt should not be placed with senior debt). It does not mean that claims that are entitled to receive similar distributions necessarily need to be in the same class.

Classification Establishment. One key consideration in classifying claims is how such classes are expected to vote in connection with the Plan of Reorganization. In fact, a debtor's professionals may expend great effort in "gerrymandering" the classifications in order to produce a voting outcome in which dissident claimholders are outvoted or in which a narrowly-defined impaired class can approve – allowing the plan to be "crammed down" on all other constituencies.

Classification Risk. In order for a Plan of Reorganization to be approved by a bankruptcy court, the court must find that the plan meets various requirements. One such requirement is that the classifications of claims and interests were done appropriately. If the court determines that the debtor's gerrymandering efforts were inappropriate, then the entire plan process must begin anew. This can be particularly vexing for a company that has gone through the trouble of having a "prepack" approved – only to be told it must redo the solicitation process in bankruptcy.

Collateral. Assets that backstop a secured loan. Such assets can include working capital assets (receivables and inventory) or fixed assets.

Common Stock. The most widespread form of equity in the corporate world. Technically, holders of the common stock are the "owners" of the enterprise, after all claims and any senior equity interests (*i.e.*, preferred stock) are paid off. Their shares represent "interests" in the company, and generally entitle them to vote to elect the company's Board of Directors.

Confirmation. In order for a Plan of Reorganization to be consummated, it must first be "confirmed" by the bankruptcy court. Such a confirmation hearing occurs after the voting process has been completed. At confirmation, the court must determine that the classification of claims and interests has been done appropriately, that the voting process met certain technical requirements and that the requisite number of claims (by both dollar amount and number of creditors voting) and interests (by number of shares voting) approved the plan. In addition, the court must find that the plan is "feasible" (*i.e.*, not likely to result in a Chapter 22), that creditors receive more than they would under a hypothetical Chapter 7 liquidation, and that no creditor receives value for more than 100% of its claim.

Conflicts of Interest. The Bankruptcy Code recognizes that the company's former advisors and principals may have their own agendas with respect to the case, such as limiting any liability they may have for the organization's demise. Moreover, the Code recognizes that certain professionals and other participants in the case may have strong relationships with other entities also in the case. These agendas and relationships can lead to situations where an individual or firm has conflicted loyalties to the debtor and its best interests. In order to deal with these "conflicts of interest," the court and the U.S. Trustee oversee a process whereby participants in the case must disclose their conflicts. Based upon these disclosures, the court determines whether a firm may continue to be engaged in the case.

Consensual Chapter 11 Reorganization. Simply, a plan that is approved by the impaired parties subject to the bankruptcy. As is typical with processes involving compromise, a consensual reorganization will generally include various "give-ups" by the respective constituencies. For example, senior creditors may allow subordinated creditors to achieve a recovery, even if the senior creditors are not paid in full. To be sure, the subordinated creditors' percentage recovery is likely to be a lot lower than that of the senior creditors. Similarly, impaired creditors may permit old equity holders to receive consideration. Such compromises are effected to avoid protracted litigation involving valuation and other matters. See "Cram-Down" with respect to an alternative to a consensual plan.

Consent. The approval by an individual or group (typically, creditors) with respect to a change, amendment or waiver in connection with an existing agreement.

Consent Solicitation. In out-of-court restructurings, companies frequently need to obtain approvals for a variety of issues. This could include allowing a company to miss an interest payment with impunity or to change a technical default feature in an instrument. When the company seeks such approvals – particularly in situations entailing publicly-traded instruments it is referred to as a "consent solicitation."

Consideration. The payment given in exchange for an asset, claim or interest. The payment may be in cash, debt, stock or other form of currency.

Conversion Premium. The degree to which the conversion price of a convertible exceeds the current market price of the underlying instrument. Assume that a convertible bond is priced at $100 and that it is convertible into 10 shares of stock currently trading at $8. The underlying common value would be $80, and the conversion premium would be $20. Expressed as a percent, it would be 25% (20 divided by 80).

Convertible. An instrument that has an additional feature of being able to be swapped into another security. Terms of these popular securities vary widely, but most have elements of both fixed income and equity instruments. The basic instrument generally is comprised of either debt or preferred stock with a coupon. In addition, the instrument can be converted (typically at the option of the holder) into another security – generally the common stock of the issuer.

Coupon. The amount of money paid on a fixed-income instrument as interest or preferred dividends. It is generally expressed as an annual rate (*i.e.,* 10%) and may be payable annually, semi-annually, quarterly or otherwise.

Covenants. Obligations that a company promises to perform under an agreement, typically in connection with a debt instrument. Covenants may be affirmative – the company agrees to make scheduled payments, maintain its business and so forth. Or they may be negative – the company agrees that it will not incur additional debt in excess of certain levels.

Cover Bid. The second-highest bid in an auction.

Cram-down. A feature in the Bankruptcy Code that permits a debtor to force consummation of a plan over the objections of one or more dissenting classes. Ideally, all classes of creditors would be expected to vote in favor of a plan before the Court can confirm it. However, the Code allows a plan to be confirmed in the face of class rejections if certain tests are passed. These tests include the approval of the plan by at least one impaired class of creditors, and the prohibition of any payments made to junior creditors unless more senior creditors are paid in full (*i.e.,* strict priority payouts).

Cram-up. A cram-down imposed on a senior class, based upon approval of the plan by junior classes.

Credit Bid. The use of a secured claim in lieu of cash in a Section 363 auction sale. Although it rarely occurs, a Court has the power to limit the face amount of the claim used in the credit bidding process,

Creditor. Any holder of a claim against a debtor, such as a debt instrument, lease, trade payable or tax due. Such claim may be secured or unsecured, contingent or actual, disputed or allowed.

Creditors Committee (a.k.a. Official Unsecured Creditors Committee). Shortly after the filing of Chapter 11, the U.S. Trustee will appoint a committee of unsecured creditors willing to serve. These groups will typically consist of an amalgam of trade claimants, landlords and bondholders. We note that secured creditors are generally not on these committees – even if the value of their collateral is minimal. Sometimes, though rarely, two or more unsecured committees are formed if a significant debtor has multiple subsidiaries with competing and conflicting interests.

Cross-Border. Referring to a transaction involving entities from various countries. In bankruptcy, this complexity can be particularly challenging. The U.S. Bankruptcy Code can only bind constituencies of companies domiciled domestically. When insolvent foreign subsidiaries enter the picture, the game can get messy quickly. U.S. bankruptcy laws are generally much more debtor-friendly than those of other countries – leading to sharp differences in approaches to reorganization for related companies.

Current Yield. The amount of interest paid on a fixed-income instrument in relation to its price. Assume a $100 bond with a coupon of 8%, trading at $80. The dollar amount of the coupon would be $8, and the current yield would be 10% ($8 divided by $80). We note that the current yield in this case is less than the yield to maturity, which would include the additional deferred yield that results from the gain at redemption over today's price ($100 face value at maturity vs. the $80 current price).

Death-Spiral Security. An instrument issued by a company in financial extremis. Typically, such a security will be convertible or exercisable into the underlying common stock of the issuer at a price fixed at issuance. However, if the price of the company's stock subsequently plummets, the conversion or exercise price would be reduced in accordance with a formula tied to the new, lower stock price. In concept, this security could ultimately be convertible or exercisable into virtually all of the company's pro forma equity if the stock price fell enough. Hence, the name "death spiral."

Debt Capacity. The maximum amount of debt that can be issued by a firm or secured by a specific asset.

Debtor. A company, person or other entity that owes money to creditors.

Debtor-in-Possession ("DIP"). The technical legal terminology describing a debtor, upon seeking the protection of Chapter 11. Literally, the debtor and its management are allowed to "remain in possession" of the debtor's operations – unlike a Chapter 7 bankruptcy where authority is fully vested in a court-appointed trustee.

Default. A breach of a covenant, either payment (failure to pay interest or principal) or "technical" (failure to comply with a covenant to maintain certain debt ratios, etc.).

Dequity. A colloquial term for a combination of debt and equity, most frequently a debt-plus-warrant package or a convertible security.

DIP Financing. Senior financing obtained by a bankrupt debtor. The Bankruptcy Code provides incentives for lenders to provide new capital in order for a debtor to have the liquidity to reorganize its affairs. These incentives include "super-priority" status, so that the new loan can be repaid before any other unsecured claim. Depending upon the facts of the case, the DIP financing may even be able to obtain a senior interest in the collateral of the estate – above the collateral interests of the pre-petition bank lenders.

See "Priming." The DIP financing must be approved by the bankruptcy court at a hearing where the competing views of the affected constituencies are weighed.

Disallowed Claim. See "Disputed Claim."

Disclosure Statement. In connection with the solicitation of a Plan of Reorganization, the debtor issues a prospectus-like document, called the Disclosure Statement. It is intended to contain all material information needed for a claimant or interest holder to make an intelligent decision. It must include historical and forecasted financial information, a description of the business, history and prospects, and a summary of the plan. Prior to its dissemination to the company's constituencies, the court must find the disclosure in the document to be "adequate."

Discount Rate. See WACC.

Discounted Cash Flow ("DCF"). A financial technique that allows the analyst to determine the present value of the future (*i.e.*, projected) cash flows. Each future year's cash flow is "brought back" to the present using a discount rate. If next year's cash flow was $10, and the discount rate was 10%, then the DCF model would product a present value of $9.09 **(($10/(1+10%)))**

Disinterested. More or less, the opposite of "conflicted." The court must find professionals (particularly those of the debtor) to be "disinterested" in order for them to be eligible to work on the case.

Disputed Claim. Some claims asserted by the bar date are relatively easy to quantify. For example (absent unusual circumstances), the amount of a note holder claim would be the face amount of the bonds plus accrued and unpaid interest. Conversely, many trade claims are subject to set-offs and other factors. Certain litigation claims may also be hotly contested. If the debtor files an objection to such claims, they are deemed to be disputed. Ultimately, the claim must be "allowed," "disallowed" or "allowed in part and disallowed in part."

Due Diligence. A term that covers the process of discovery into the risks, merits, prices and overall potential of an investment opportunity.

Duration. A measure of the remaining life of a bond, similar to "weighted average life." Duration takes into account both interest and principal payments on the bond.

Dutch Auction. A form of exchange or tender offer in which the company does not set a specific tender price. Instead, the holders submit offers to the company indicating the amount of securities and price at which they would be willing to buy. Based upon such information, the company notifies the holders which securities will be purchased, and at what price.

Earn-Out. In M&A transactions, buyers and sellers frequently disagree over the attainability of projections or of specified future events. In order to bridge this gap in expectations, the parties may develop a contingent payment schedule that is based upon the achievement of certain pre-agreed targets.

Earnest Money. In M&A bidding situations where there is some question as to the financial wherewithal of some of the participants, the selling investment banker may require that qualified bidders advance a portion of the anticipated purchase price in order to be allowed to bid at all. Although such monies may be returned if the erstwhile bidder is "topped", the money serves to establish a certain level of financial credibility for the buyer, as well as to backstop any representations if the successful bidder withdraws inappropriately.

Earnings Per Share. A company's net income, divided by the number of shares outstanding.

EBIT. "Earnings Before Interest and Taxes," a measure of earnings. Because EBIT is stated prior to deductions for interest expense, it is used as a base to derive values for the "enterprise value" of the company.

EBITDA. "Earnings Before Interest, Taxes, Depreciation and Amortization," a measure of earnings, sometimes called "pretax cash flow." EBITDA is sometimes viewed as an estimate for the amount of money (at least in the very short term) a company can afford to plow into debt service. Like EBIT, it is also used as a base to derive values for the "enterprise value" of the company.

Enterprise Value. Sometimes referred to as the financial value of a company, it consists of the aggregate value of the financial debt and equity values, net of excess cash on the balance sheet. It represents the value – independent of capital structure – that would equate to owning all of the financial interests of the company.

Equitable Subordination. A bankruptcy court has the power to examine the behavior of the company's constituencies to determine if their pre-petition actions adversely – and unfairly – affected the estate. For example, if a creditor took steps to advantage itself unfairly over others in the case, the bankruptcy court would have the power to subordinate (therefore, "equitable subordination") its claim to other creditors of the estate.

Equity. The ownership interests in the company, which are junior to the claims of the creditors. See "Common Stock" and "Preferred Stock."

Equity Buyback. When a company purchases its own stock.

Equity Committee. If there is sufficient value in the estate to convince the court that old equity could be "in the money," the Bankruptcy Court has the power to establish an equity committee. This relatively rare situation could occur at times when the capital structure of an otherwise sound enterprise collapses. Such collapse could occur, for example, due to lender unease related to "accounting improprieties" or other such factors.

Equity Value. The value of the equity interests of the company, consisting of the values of the common and preferred securities. The value can be derived from an analysis of the prospective cash flows available to equity after debt service or from a determination of the enterprise value, net of debt. For a distressed company, these different approaches can lead to materially different results. The equity standalone value is virtually always higher than the enterprise value, less debt. This difference is partially attributable to the "option value" of a corporation's old equity – it can be positive, but never negative.

Examiner. From time to time, the Bankruptcy Court is faced with questions regarding inappropriate conduct by officers, directors, lenders or other constituencies in the case. When this arises, the court frequently appoints an examiner with powers sufficient to pursue an investigation.

Exchange Offer. In an out-of-court restructuring, the debtor may offer to swap cash or newly-issued common stock or bonds in exchange for outstanding indebtedness that is creating problems for the company. This "exchange offer" may need to be registered with the SEC (an expensive and time-consuming process) or may be able to be done privately pursuant to various exemptions from the securities laws. Frequently, exchange offers contain minimum tender conditions (*i.e.,* at least 90% must accept), so that non-tendering holders do not adversely warp the economics for everyone else. See "Holdouts." In other cases, a minimum threshold may be 50% or 67%, which represents the minimum percentage of bonds that must consent in order to modify indenture provisions.

Exchangeable. A security that is issued by one company, but that is convertible into the securities of a different company. Typically, this is seen when the issuing company has a historical investment in the stock of another, and is seeking to divest itself of the ownership position.

Exclusivity. Chapter 11 provides that the debtor has the exclusive right to pursue a Plan of Reorganization for a period of months, with an automatic extension period. In practice, courts regularly grant debtors additional extensions for a year or more. The underlying theory is that – particularly for large and complex cases – the debtor needs time to stabilize its operations, explore its alternatives, negotiate with its constituencies and develop a restructuring proposal that maximizes value and accommodates the conflicting goals of multiple groups in the case. From a negotiating perspective, exclusivity gives the debtor a lot of power and leverage. Unless a constituency in the case is successful in revoking exclusivity (possible, although infrequent), no one other than the debtor can promulgate a Plan of Reorganization – key to emerging from the case. Constituencies motivated by the time value of money and with getting on with their lives may be willing to make more concessions to the debtor than they would in the absence of the debtor's exclusivity.

Executory Contracts. Companies have various types of money obligations. One form is debt, in which the creditor has put up the money and basically requires nothing more from the creditor. Another type of liability is a contract (such as a building lease), where the company agrees to pay monies over time (rent) in exchange for continuing to be provided with benefits (in this case, space). This latter type of liability is called an "executory contract" and can include employment agreements, service contracts and supply contracts, in addition to leases. Bankruptcy allows the debtor to reject such executory contracts. This rejection gives rise to an unsecured claim against the debtor, the amount of which ultimately must be approved by the court.

Exit Tender. In connection with an exchange offer or tender offer, a debtor will frequently insist that tendering holders execute a waiver, allowing the company to modify the terms of the instruments being tendered. For example, a bond may have onerous covenants, and in order to change such covenants, the indenture may require that a majority of the bonds approve any modifications. In such case, the exchange offer may contain a minimum condition that 50% of the bonds be tendered – thus permitting the covenant modifications. Once modified (or in certain circumstances where the covenants are modified on a wholesale basis, referred to as "gutted"), the old bonds may not be as onerous to the company and may not be as attractive to the non-tendering bondholders. Such dynamics act as an "incentive" to tender and not to hold out. See "Holdouts."

Fair and Equitable Test. In connection with the "cram-down" provisions of Chapter 11, a company needs to meet the "fair and equitable" test for its Plan of Reorganization to be approved. The test requires that junior creditors receive no consideration unless crammed-down senior creditors are paid in full.

Fairness Opinion. "Fairness" is a financial concept that is applied to a variety of negotiated transactions, including mergers and reorganizations. At its most basic level, fairness addresses the question of whether the consideration received by a given constituency is "enough." This can be answered from the perspective of either "procedural fairness" – was a reasonable market test run? – or from the perspective of "relative fairness" – is the price reasonable in light of other transactions that have taken place? Investment bankers are retained to examine the fairness of a transaction to a specific constituency and to issue an opinion thereon.

Feasibility. In connection with its confirmation of a Plan of Reorganization, a court must find the plan to be "feasible." A feasible plan is one in which the debtor is deemed to have a good prospect of being able to continue in business without having to resort subsequently to bankruptcy.

Financial Advisor. A financial professional engaged by a constituency in the estate to advise with regard to business plans, valuations and negotiations with respect to sale, financing and restructuring transactions.

First Day Papers. A series of motions filed on the first day of the bankruptcy case by the debtor. Key among these would be requests relating to financial liquidity, such as the use of cash collateral and approval of DIP financing. Typical first day papers also include applications for retention of legal and financial professionals.

Fixed-Income Instruments. Assets that pay a fixed dollar amount, such as bonds and preferred stock.

Fixed Rate. An interest rate that does not change during the life of the loan.

Floating Rate. An interest rate that is determined and reset periodically (such as the prime rate), allowing the interest rate to change as market conditions change.

Force Multiplier. In asymmetric negotiations, a means of enhancing and leveraging the dynamics against the opposing side. For example, protracted delays in the restructuring process could be viewed as a force multiplier against a creditor whose success was measured by achieving high IRRs (which would be diminished through the passage of time).

Foreclosure. Steps taken by secured lenders to seize the collateral underlying their loans. Such actions are delayed through bankruptcy due to the "automatic stay" provisions of the Bankruptcy Code. However, if the court subsequently determines that the secured lenders are not receiving "adequate protection" on their loans (*i.e.,* the collateral is declining in value), the court has the authority to lift the automatic stay in favor of the secured lenders.

Fraud. Known misrepresentations designed to gain advantage over various constituencies.

Fraudulent Conveyance. If a company transfers an asset to a third party under circumstances where both (i) the consideration it receives for the asset is subsequently deemed to have been inadequate and (ii) the company was insolvent before the transaction, or the transaction itself rendered the company insolvent, then the transaction would be a "fraudulent conveyance." Under these circumstances, it would be a fraudulent conveyance regardless of whether actual fraud were involved. The remedies for a fraudulent conveyance can be onerous for the third-party involved.

Going Concern. The concept of a company continuing in business. Conversely, if a company is unable to continue as a going concern, it may have to liquidate. In general, a company capable of continuing in business is far more valuable than one in liquidation mode.

Haircut. An economic concession suffered by a creditor in connection with a restructuring. The "haircut" may be effected through a reduction in principal and/or interest owed, a "stretched out" payment schedule or various other mechanisms.

Hard Consideration. In a Plan of Reorganization, constituencies receive their recovery in various forms of consideration. "Hard" forms of consideration include cash and senior debt instruments (compared to "softer" consideration, such as equity securities).

High-Yield Bonds. See "Junk Bonds."

Highest and Best. In considering alternatives (such as choosing bids in a bankruptcy sale), debtors, creditors and the court need to consider a variety of factors. This would be relatively straightforward if all bids were in cash and were fully financed. However, that is rarely the case in the real world. Bids are frequently comprised of a package of consideration, including equity and debt instruments that need to be valued. Some bids may be unconditional, while others may resemble "Swiss cheese," with "holes" in the bids due to financing and other contingencies. Under these circumstances in Bankruptcy Court, the highest nominal bid does not necessarily prevail. Instead, the parties to the case will consider factors such as the need for cash vs. speculative value, and the ability to close quickly vs. needing to satisfy various conditions.

Relative certainty of closure and consideration can be more valuable than nominal amount of consideration. As a result, the winning bid is frequently referred to as "highest and best," rather than just the "highest."

Hockey Stick. A term used to describe projections depicting increasing profits on the heels of years of flat or declining performance. The graph of such trends resembles the shape of a hockey stick.

Holdouts. In out-of-court restructurings, non-consenting creditors cannot be bound by the will of the majority of similarly-situated creditors – as can be done in bankruptcy. In many cases, where consenting creditors agree to significant economic concessions, other creditors have a major incentive to hold out. Not only do they avoid having to take "haircuts," but they will benefit from having a more creditworthy company (courtesy of the concessions made by the other creditors).

Hope Certificates. Contingent securities issued in connection with a restructuring. If the debtor's fortunes improve significantly, or if a series of other good things happen, then the recipients of these securities will have a "hope" of receiving something.

Impaired. If a claim is paid in full in cash or is otherwise reinstated on its original terms, it will generally be deemed to be "unimpaired." Otherwise, the claim will be "impaired" and its holder entitled to vote on its treatment in a Plan of Reorganization.

In-Court. Refers to a reorganization undertaken through the auspices of the Bankruptcy Court.

In the Money. Options and warrants derive much of their value from the relationship between the price of the underlying security (generally common stock) and the strike price of the option. To the extent that the trading price exceeds the strike price (in the case of a call option), the option is said to be "in the money."

Indenture. The contract between a company and the holders of its bonds. The indenture will contain affirmative covenants (promises to pay and so forth) and negative covenants (restrictions on certain activities) that are intended to protect the interests of the bondholders.

Insolvent. A company is insolvent when it is unable to pay its debts as they become due, its assets are worth less than the face amount of its liabilities, or it has an unreasonably small amount of capital with which to conduct its business.

Interest Rate. The periodic cost of a debt instrument.

Internal Rate of Return (IRR). The rate of return that would make the present value of future cash flows plus the final market value of an investment or business opportunity equal the current market price of the investment or opportunity.

Intrinsic Value. If an option or warrant is "in the money," it will have a component of its value stemming from the positive difference between the current trading price of the underlying security and the strike price of the option. This positive difference is referred to as "intrinsic value."

Investment Banker. A financial advisor qualified to do business as a broker-dealer. This qualification distinguishes investment bankers from accountants and other financial professionals. Investment bankers are permitted under U.S. securities laws to issue debt and equity securities on behalf of companies; other such financial professionals are barred from doing so. There is a persuasive case that such other financial professionals are barred from other activities dominated by investment bankers, such as M&A for public companies and most other situations.

Junk Bonds. Technically, straight debt securities that are rated at less than investment-grade status (*e.g.*, less than BBB). Accordingly, junk bonds would receive ratings in the BB, B, CCC, CC and C range. Below that, the bonds would be in default. The rating agencies' definitions of these ratings vary across the junk categories but generally signal that the bond has a significant risk of prospective default. The gradations correspond with what "significant" means in each case.

Kickers. In many cases, investors seek additional return beyond the rate promised through the interest rate on a bond, and negotiate with the issuer for additional securities to provide such return. These instruments, called "kickers," frequently take the form of warrants or other equity securities that give the investor significant upside reward if the company is successful.

Lead Bidder. See "Stalking Horse."

Lender Liability. Claims against pre-petition lenders relating to the lender group's inappropriate and actionable steps that may have led to the company's demise. See "Equitable Subordination."

LIBOR. (London Inter-Bank Offered Rate). A floating rate contained in borrowing arrangements, used increasingly more frequently than the prime rate. Typically, companies borrow at a spread over LIBOR, with weaker credits paying higher spreads. Of note, several major banks have been severely criticized for their attempts to "rig" LIBOR.

Liquidation. Generally refers to a company unable to continue as a going concern, and may be effected through Chapter 7 or Chapter 11 (*i.e.*, a "liquidating Plan of Reorganization"). In practice the liquidation can take a variety of forms, ranging from (i) a cessation of the company's activities and contemporaneous auction of inventories, furniture, equipment, etc. to (ii) a more orderly sale of businesses within a relatively short (one to three months) time frame. In general, the more time available for liquidation, the higher the gross proceeds. Such higher potential values need to be weighed against any "burn rate" the company has – and how to fund such burn rate.

Liquidity of Securities. The ease with which financial assets can be converted to cash without creating a substantial change in price or value. Liquidity is influenced by the amount of float in the security, investor interest and size of the investment being converted to cash. A blue-chip stock like ExxonMobil is liquid because it is actively traded so its share price won't be dramatically affected by a few buy or sell orders. Money-market funds and checking accounts provide instant liquidity because you can write a check on the assets.

LTM. Last Twelve Months. Generally used in the context of the four most recent quarters of operating results.

M&A. Abbreviation for "mergers and acquisitions."

MAC. Acronym for "material adverse change."

MIS. Management Information System. The computing resources that hold and allow access to the information owned by an organization.

Motion. A request by a party to the bankruptcy case for the court to make a ruling.

New Money Plan. Generally refers to a Plan of Reorganization in which Old Equity invests new funds and retains control of the company. Bankruptcy Courts have held that such a new money plan cannot be promulgated in a vacuum. In order for such plan to be confirmed, Old Equity proposal must be shopped to other potential buyers and investors through a market test (at a minimum).

NOLs. See Section 382.

Old Equity. The owner or control party behind the extant equity securities of the company going through a restructuring.

Option. A contract that entitles the owner to buy (call options) or sell (put options) the underlying security from or to a counterparty (which can be the issuer itself) at a certain price on or before a specified date.

Out of Court. Refers to a restructuring undertaken without resort to the Bankruptcy Court.

Out-of-the-Money. An option or warrant, where the trading price of the underlying security is below the strike price (in the case of a call option).

Overbid Protection. In connection with bankruptcy auctions, "stalking horse" bidders frequently demand certain provisions giving them certain advantages over competing bidders. One such feature is "overbid protection" in which (i) any overbids by third parties must be in meaningful, specified increments, and (ii) the "stalking horse" bidder may beat any overbid by matching such bid.

Payment Default. Failure by a company to make a scheduled interest or principal payment.

Perfection. When a company begins to encounter financial difficulty, unsecured creditors often demand that the company grant them collateral in exchange for waivers and other company requests. However, such collateral grants on old loans may not "perfect" for 90 days. If the company were to file for bankruptcy protection within such 90-day period, the collateral grant could be rescinded.

Plan Effective Date. After a plan is confirmed by the Bankruptcy Court, the Court sets a date to implement the restructuring. Such latter date is referred to as the "Plan Effective Date."

Plan of Reorganization. The central documents in a bankruptcy restructuring are the Plan of Reorganization and the related Disclosure Statement. The plan is a legal document that provides for the treatment of each affected constituency.

Pre-Negotiated Plan. A bankruptcy plan for which agreement in principle has been reached with key constituencies prior to going into Chapter 11. Unlike with a pre-pack, the constituencies are not legally bound.

Pre-Pack. See Prepackaged Plan.

Prepackaged Plan (or Pre-Pack). A bankruptcy plan for which the requisite votes have been obtained prior to going into Chapter 11. Generally, the prepackaged plan is conducted in parallel with an out-of-court exchange offer. If the exchange offer fails to achieve specified minimums, then the parallel bankruptcy plan is implemented.

Pre-Petition. Referring to events or the status that existed pre-bankruptcy.

Preferences. If (i) a creditor received a pre-petition payment from a then-insolvent company and (ii) the payment was more than what such creditor would receive in a hypothetical Chapter 7 liquidation, then the pre-petition payment may be considered to be a "preference." Companies are presumed to be insolvent for the 90 days preceding the bankruptcy filing – except in the case of insiders, where the presumptive period is extended to one year. The bankrupt estate is entitled to pursue preference claims against pre-petition creditors or interest holders.

Preferred Stock. A form of equity senior to common stock.

Present Value. See "Discounted Cash Flow."

Prime Rate. A floating rate common in bank borrowings, representing the "base rate" for the financial institutions involved.

Priming. In connection with DIP financings, the new lenders must establish their claims on collateral relative to those of the pre-petition secured lenders. Naturally, each DIP and pre-petition group would prefer to have its own facilities receive a first lien in the collateral. If the collateral base is barely able to support the loans of the pre-petition group, then such pre-petition group will likely retain its first position. However, if there is sufficient collateral "cushion," the debtor may argue that the pre-petition lenders will remain adequately protected even if the new DIP loan were to come on top – or to "prime" the pre-petition lenders. The Bankruptcy Court would settle this priming fight.

Price/Earnings (P/E) Ratio. A valuation multiple for an equity security representing the relation between the share price and earnings per share.

Proof of Claim. Each pre-petition creditor must file a proof of claim with the court prior to the bar date. Failure to do so will result in the creditor being unable to have a valid claim and to receive a recovery.

Release. Refers to a release from litigation claims, frequently granted pursuant to the Plan of Reorganization to various entities involved in the case.

Reorganizable. Referring to a company that can be restructured as a going concern vs. being a candidate for liquidation.

Reorganization. Restructuring of a company, either through a Plan of Reorganization or through an out-of-court plan.

Re-trade. When a buyer of assets takes advantage of the vulnerability of a distressed seller to insist on new terms, at the last minute, for a deal already agreed to.

Rights Offering. Issuance to shareholders (or another such established group of creditors or interest holders) that allows them to purchase additional shares, usually at a discount to market price. Holdings of shareholders that do not exercise rights are usually diluted by the offering. Rights are often transferable, allowing the holder to sell them on the open market to others that may wish to exercise them.

Sealed Bid. A tactic used in auctions, whereby each bidder submits its "best and final" offer – rather than allowing rounds of bidding to continue. If a buyer really "must have" the auctioned asset, the sealed bid may provide the highest value.

Section 341 Hearing. An organization meeting early in a bankruptcy case involving unsecured creditors, the U.S. Trustee and the company.

Section 363 Sale. A bankruptcy auction sale. In bankruptcy, debtors can sell assets two ways – through a plan and through the exemptions provided pursuant to Section 363. Sales are allowed pursuant to Section 363 if certain criteria are met – such as if the asset's value is sinking fast or the company simply will not be able to afford the cash burn through consummation of a plan, and needs to effect going concern asset sales sooner rather than later.

Section 382. A Tax Code provision relating to cancellation of indebtedness (COD) income. When a company discharges pre-petition debt at a discount (a common event), the haircut is recognized as taxable gain. In many situations, a company will have incurred net operating losses, or "NOLs," over a period of years. Such NOLs can be used to offset the gains from discharge of indebtedness. However, Section 382 sharply limits the use of such NOLs to shelter COD income if there has been a "change of control" of the company's equity. This highly technical issue frequently drives the structure of restructurings and may indeed cause a company to use Chapter 11 to implement a restructuring – rather than stay outside of bankruptcy.

Secured. Refers to indebtedness backed by a security interest in collateral.

Secured Debt. Debt that has first claim on specified assets in the event of default.

Secured Lender. A lender who holds secured debt and has first claim on specified assets in the event of a default.

Securitization. A financing facility that is backstopped by a pool of assets, such as receivables. Such financings are generally established through a separate subsidiary that owns the assets, and borrows against them. This structure can permit the organization to borrow more cheaply than it could on the parent's own balance sheet.

Security. A financial instrument, such as indebtedness, common stock, preferred stock or warrants.

Senior Obligation. A claim that is not subordinated to another liability. However, senior obligations may come behind secured obligations to the extent of the value of the collateral underlying the secured debt.

Small Company Premium. As part of the WACC determination, the required discount rate may be increased by a number of "adders." One of these is the so-called "small company premium," which is based upon decades of empirical observations that small company stocks enjoy higher annual returns than do larger ones.

Soft Consideration. In connection with a reorganization, certain constituencies receive cash or debt instruments (see "Hard Consideration"). Other constituencies (typically more junior ones) may receive more speculative consideration, such as equity securities or notes that pay out if certain operating performance targets are hit.

Solicitation. The process of contacting claims and interest holders, and seeking their consent, by tender or vote – either in bankruptcy or out-of-court.

Solvency Opinion. Solvency is the mirror image of insolvency (see "Insolvent"). If a third party enters into a transaction with a company on the verge of insolvency, such third party can encounter significant risk that the transaction can be undone – or worse. (See "Fraudulent Conveyance.") In order to shield itself against subsequent arguments that the company was insolvent at the time of a transaction, well-advised third parties frequently demand a solvency opinion in connection with such transaction. Such solvency opinion is generally provided by an investment banker, and can form a significant due diligence defense for the third party.

Stalking Horse. In connection with a bankruptcy auction sale, debtors generally find it beneficial to have a "stalking horse," or "lead bidder," that provides a minimum price that the company will receive for its asset in the sale. By entering into such agreement, the stalking horse will forgo its opportunity to pick up the asset at an even lower price – if interest at the auction is disappointingly low. Accordingly, the lead bidder will need to have incentives to enter into a minimum price agreement with the seller. Advantages such lead bidders frequently obtain include overbid protection, break-up fees and the ability to negotiate a definitive purchase agreement with which it is comfortable.

Status Quo Approach. In effect, this strategy plays for time, in the hopes that market forces or operational initiatives can adequately address the capital-structure challenges that have arisen because of the mismatch between leverage and operational performance. In this approach, the company monitors the situation, perhaps trying to improve liquidity internally, perhaps without seeking new financing.

Straight Debt. Debt without a conversion feature or other equity-like features.

Stretch-Out. A restructuring centered on delaying the payment dates for interest and principal on a company's existing indebtedness. Such a program can be effective in dealing with a situation where a company has encountered a temporary "bump in the road," but is expected to be able to return to profitability over time.

Strict Priority. An approach to allocation of reorganization proceeds, in which the senior-most creditors receive 100% of their claim in full before the next class receives anything. Such value "cascade" continues until the reorganization value is exhausted.

Strike Price. The price at which an option or warrant is exercisable into the underlying security. If the trading price of the underlying security exceeds the strike price at maturity, it generally makes sense for the option holder to exercise the option.

Structural Subordination. A senior obligation at the "parent" level can be effectively subordinated to the recovery of a claim at a subsidiary if the parent's only legal claim on the subsidiary is its equity ownership.

Subordinated Obligation. A debt instrument that is expressly subordinated by contract to senior debt. In a restructuring, if the senior debt is unable to obtain a full recovery, the subordinated debt must recycle proceeds it would have received in the restructuring to the senior lenders.

Swap. A contract between a company and a counterparty that seeks to offload risk in exchange for a fee or other consideration. In an interest rate swap, for example, the company contracts with a lender to pay to the lender a fixed interest rate on a notional principal amount, and receive a floating rate. When combined with a floating rate borrowing, the company would effectively have a fixed rate obligation.

Technical Default. A default under a loan agreement related to a breach of a financial covenant or other such promise. This is distinct from a payment default, where the company actually fails to make a payment.

10-K. An audited report of a corporation's year-end financial results and operations that is required by and filed annually with the SEC. The report contains detailed information related to the company's business, financial condition and legal liabilities.

10-Q. An unaudited financial report required by and submitted on a quarterly basis to the SEC by any public companies whose securities are listed with the SEC. The report contains financial and other relevant information.

Tender Offer. A narrow form of exchange offer in which the consideration is cash (see "Exchange Offer.").

Third-Party Lenders. Lenders willing to provide additional financing to a company.

363 Motion. A powerful tool for the financial advisor in restructuring a bankrupt company. Section 363 of the Bankruptcy Code allows companies in Chapter 11 to sell all or a significant portion of their assets in a bankruptcy auction sale. The court is able to give buyers assurances regarding clean title.

Trade Creditor. A supplier or vendor who has provided goods or raw materials to a company and has not yet collected on its bills. Generally, trade creditors are concerned about maximizing their recovery and maintaining their customer's viability as a going concern.

Trustee. A court-appointed supervisor of the estate. Trustees are typical in Chapter 7 cases but are relatively rare in Chapter 11 cases. In our experience, trustees have been appointed in situations involving massive fraud.

Ugly Duckling. A business whose superficial characteristics make it quite unattractive – but which can become very valuable (become a swan) under certain circumstances.

Unsecured Obligation. A claim against the company that is not backstopped by any collateral interest.

U.S. Trustee. A federal officer who works in conjunction with the bankruptcy court. The U.S. Trustee's charge includes the appointment of the members of the Official Unsecured Creditors Committee and supervision of fee applications submitted by professionals.

WACC. Weighted Average Cost of Capital. A company's cost for its mix of debt and equity. Typically, the WACC rate will be used to discount a company's future cash flows back to the present value.

Wallpaper. Worthless securities that can be more effectively used for wallpapering one's bathroom.

Warrants. Longer-term options that are typically issued by the company itself, rather than a counterparty. (See "Options.")

Weighted Average Life (WAL). A measure of a bond's maturity. It takes into account principal payments made over time, so that a bond making interim principal payments will have a WAL shorter than the actual maturity.

Whack-Up. A term of art describing the process of allocating the finite pie of restructuring value among the various constituencies.

When-Issued. After a Plan of Reorganization has been confirmed, but before the new securities are issued on the Plan Effective Date, such securities may be traded on a "when-issued" basis. The trades would be settled once the securities were actually issued and available.

Winnowing. The process of eliminating certain potential buyers that have expressed interest in specific assets or properties that may be for sale, in order to maximize the efficiency of the sale process and to eliminate the merely curious and those who seek competitive advantage in obtaining inside information about a rival's assets.

Work Fees. Prospective lenders exploring extending new money to distressed companies need to perform significant due diligence activities, including assessment of collateral values and business plans by third parties. Such prospective lenders frequently request that the company pay "work fees" to offset such costs – even before the lenders have committed to lend any funds.

Work-Out. Another term for a restructuring.

Yield-to-Call. The rate of return on a debt instrument from the present to the date of the first time the company has the opportunity to call the bond, based upon a combination of both interest income and the gain or loss resulting from the difference between the current price and the call price.

Yield-to-Maturity. The rate of return on a debt instrument from the present to maturity, based upon a combination of both interest income and the gain or loss resulting from the difference between the current price and the payoff at maturity.

Yield-to-Worst. The lowest of (i) the current yield, (ii) the yield-to-maturity and (iii) the yield-to-call.

Zone of Insolvency. A financial state of affairs in which the company has deteriorated to the point where creditors may be adversely affected. The company may not be actually insolvent yet, but would be close.

INDEX

Page numbers in *italics* refer to glossary terms

H

I

M

N

CPSIA information can be obtained
at www.ICGtesting.com
Printed in the USA
BVHW042114040422
633381BV00006B/10/J

9 781587 983047